What People are Saying about
Jason

"His story is not only personally mo...
management ...."
— Stewart Glendinning
(CEO, Molson Coors International)

"As the first blind person to run from California to New York, Jason has quite the story to tell, and he does so eloquently and passionately...."
— Jim Browning
(COO, Goodwill Industries)

"Jason motivated me and the audience to reach deep within ourselves to 'go the extra mile' and to improve our lives and the lives of others."
— Mark Lucas
(CEO, US Association of Blind Athletes)

"Jason Romero has one of the most remarkable stories you will ever hear. Running across the United States in 60 consecutive days is only the starting point."
— Dr. Michael Kragt, Ph.D.
(Psychologist & Executive Director)

RUNNING INTO
THE DARK

a blind man's record-setting run across America

JASON ROMERO

For my children Sierra, Sage, and Sofia
You are my world!
I love you with all that I am.

Copyright © 2017 by Jason Romero
ISBN: 978-1-941528-52-5 hardcover
ISBN: 978-1-941528-53-2 trade paperback

I'm Possible Books, an imprint of
Parker Hayden Media
5740 N. Carefree Circle, Suite 120-1
Colorado Springs, CO 80917

All rights reserved. No part of this book may be reproduced in any form or by any
electronic or mechanical means, including information storage and retrieval systems,
without permission in writing from the author, except by a reviewer, who may quote
brief passages in a review.

Art credits:
Cover design: Copyright © 2017 Mike Jones Graphic Design
Cover graphics: Copyright © 2017 Gretchen Pilcher (www.pilcherphotography.com)
Back cover photo: Copyright © 2017 Carly Gerhart

Sometimes ordinary people do extraordinary things.

The Last Day

With every ending there is a new beginning.
— Unknown

It was 2:00 a.m. on May 23, 2016, and all I heard was my alarm screaming at me. The song *Shut Up and Dance* by Walk the Moon was once again blaring in my ear. I was in a foreign place: a small motel room with two beds, and the usual desk, lamps, and TV. But where was I? I was confused for the first couple of minutes of waking. Was I in California, Texas, Missouri, Illinois, Pennsylvania? What state was I waking up in? This question had wracked my mind for the last two months. Not knowing where I was waking up had become normal, and wasn't cause for anxiety or discontent. I wasn't in any of those states. I was at a Comfort Inn somewhere in west New Jersey and my sixty-nine-year-old mom was in the bed beside me.

My mom was already dressed and ready. She had showered the night before, dressed for the following day, and slept in her clothes. She wanted to be as efficient as possible as she knew today was going to be a very long day. A very important day. She flipped on the light and said, "Jay, are you ready?" I rolled my body to look at her. My entire body was too tight and sore to turn just my head. Rolling my entire pain-ridden body toward her was a better option than just turning my neck, which caused horrible pain and sometimes triggered a morning headache. I smiled at my mom and said, "Let's do this."

She threw off the covers and rose from her bed like doves being released from a cage. She seemed to be everywhere in the room. After a quick bathroom stop to wash her face, do her hair, and become "presentable," she dug in the motel mini fridge, getting me food and drink, which consisted of fruit, some pastries, and a yogurt. She went in and out of the room to get ice and prepared my morning ice bath for my feet: a motel trash can with about four inches of water and the rest ice. She set the can at the side of my bed. There were no words uttered between us. There didn't need to be. We had done this dance for the last sixty consecutive mornings. As I saw her whirring around and began to more fully wake, I realized she wasn't moving as fast as I had originally thought. She, too, was exhausted, in pain, and not feeling good.

I had yet to even sit up in bed. I couldn't move my legs. They were locked into a semi-bent position as I lay on my side. They felt like rigor mortis had set in. I knew that this was no good, and I had to get moving. I took a deep breath, and with all the might I could muster, I pushed my legs to straighten them out. They locked into the straightened position and immediately cramped up. Then, both feet followed suit and cramped up. I screamed, and then slowly took deep calming breaths. I had learned that this technique could help me ride out the morning cramps, and get my lower body back to functioning. I rolled side to side a couple of times, trying to see how my back was going to react this morning. It seemed to be doing okay—just some soreness, but no significant strains or cramping.

It was finally time, I had to sit up and put my swollen feet into a morning ice bath. My mom looked at my agony and groaning, and shot me a smile. Her smile wasn't because she was amused by my agony. I'm sure that smile was a capstone smile—a sense of pride, compassion, and relief that our torture would soon be coming to an end.

My right foot went into the trash can filled with ice. *"Ahhhhh!"* It was startling, but also refreshing. My foot was pounding. I could feel the foot pulse with every heartbeat. The foot seemed to be stretching the skin, muscles, ligaments, and tendons. Before going into the ice bath, the foot felt as if it was going to explode at any instant. My right foot was suffering from severe plantar fasciitis, a very painful and somewhat common running injury. It felt like I was being stabbed by a knife in the bottom of my foot every time I put pressure on it.

I had also developed a strange popping in the arch of my foot every time I stepped on it. It was disturbing and concerning, but the pain just stayed steady and didn't continue to increase—I could tolerate it. I had neuromas—swollen bundles of nerves—in each foot which had developed between the second and third toes. Every time I stepped and the toes squeezed together, horrible pain shot through my entire body. So the game was to keep the toes separated as much as possible, and to ignore the pain as much as possible. Icing and ibuprofen helped keep the pain at bay. After seven minutes in the ice bath, my right foot was numb and feeling good. It was now time for my left foot to get the shocking joy of the morning wake-up call. My left foot wasn't as beat up as my right foot. It only felt like a hammer had been pounding on it for the last sixty days. Nothing was broken, but the entire appendage was crying for mercy. Somehow, it just dangled from my ankle and slowly slipped below the ice to a position where it could no longer be seen.

As I let my feet ice, I gobbled down all the food my mom had set in front of me. During this time, I grabbed my phone and texted some friends that were in nearby rooms in the same motel. They had collectively travelled thousands of miles to be with me on this particular day. One friend, Greg, was a college roommate who had flown in from Austin, Texas, and was now a high-ranking executive at a commercial real estate firm. Another friend, Jay, was also a college roommate and a high-ranking muckety-muck with significant responsibilities who had driven twelve hours one-way with his family of five to be with me on this day. Another friend, Camilo, was a business owner who had taken time off and given up an opportunity to run a race in the Florida Keys, so he could help me on this day.

I sent them messages like "IT'S ON!" "TIME TO ROLL!" "ONWARD TO CITY HALL!" As I typed these messages I felt adrenaline begin to course through my veins. I felt life invigorate my beaten body. I felt myself come to life again. My left foot was done, and it was now time to try to stand. As I sat on the edge of my bed, I leaned forward, hoping the momentum alone would force my torso to be directly above my legs; then, only my legs needed to straighten out and I would be upright . . . standing! The first attempt failed. As I rocked back, then went forward, my legs weren't able to straighten and lift my body, so I ended up rocking back onto the bed into a sitting position. I wouldn't be denied. I told myself, *I must get up!* With all my strength, I rocked forward again, and timed the exertion of my legs at just the correct moment so I rose into a standing position when my torso was above my legs. I wobbled a few times with arms outstretched trying to steady myself and not collapse onto the bed. Once I was steady, I knew I had to try to walk. I needed to get to the bathroom for a wake-up shower and morning duties. I flung my left foot forward without bending a knee. Then I flung my right foot forward. Then, left, then right. I'm sure I looked like Frankenstein as I slowly moved to the bathroom. My mom didn't even bat an eye at this morose excuse of humanity that looked like it should be in a hospital room instead of a motel room.

Soon, I was in a *hot, hot* shower. I knew the heat could help the stiffness in my legs, and I tried to move my legs like I was walking in place. The pain in my feet was back, but it wasn't as bad as when I first woke. After a quick rinse, I was out, toweled off, and primping. I fixed my hair, and put deodorant and cologne on. I brushed my teeth and gargled with fluoride mouthwash. Then, I put on my running shorts. These were my favorite pair of running shorts—red shorts made by Race Ready. The inner liner looked like a shotgun had blasted holes through it; they were over seven years old and had been sewn up many times. The liner was useless when it came to providing support, but the sentimentality of these shorts provided all of the mental support that I needed at that moment. They had gotten me through some of the toughest runs of my life in Death Valley in July, in the Rocky Mountains at two miles above sea level, and in the depths of the Grand Canyon. They surely would be able to take me one more day, for what would be the culmination of the longest run of my life.

I could hear my friends knocking on the door while I was locked in the bathroom finishing my morning routine. They yelled, "Twenty minutes!" That was the amount of time remaining until I had to start running. The start time was 3:00 a.m. I heard them asking my mom what needed to be taken to the van. We had suitcases with clothes and first-aid equipment. We also had a bag of moist, sweat-drenched running clothes that reeked of dirt, human excrement, blood, Mountain Dew, frappuccinos, and coffee. We had coolers with ice, food, and drinks. We had bags with foam rollers, therapy sticks, ultrasound units, electrical stimulation (e-stim) units, air leg compression sleeves, and a compressor. We had a portable battery that we recharged nightly so we could have an extra power supply in my brother's twelve-year-old minivan. All of this equipment had to be repacked, organized, and reloaded so we could start moving.

My job was simple—eat, get dressed, and run. But, how could I run? Just forty minutes previously, I could barely roll over to look at my mom. I had twenty minutes to search within my soul and find the hope that I needed to again take that first step of the day toward my goal—the finish line. I played music: *Thunderstruck* by AC/DC, *Right Now* by Van Halen, *Lunatic Fringe* by Red Rider, and my theme song for this expedition—*I Lived* by One Republic.

I looked into the mirror, at my body. I could make out that I was very thin. My arms had withered and my torso was trim. I had six-pack abs—not because of doing crunches. My body had been slowly consuming itself for the past sixty days because I hadn't been feeding it enough calories. I was down over fifteen pounds and had almost no body fat on my frame. My cheeks were drawn and veins were visible on my arms, torso, and legs. Who was this person I was looking at in the mirror? I didn't recognize him. Was this the same person who had lived in this body for 46 years, or was this some other entity that had possessed my body?

"Fifteen minutes!" someone shouted. My buddies were hooting and hollering. It was like we were back in college in San Diego, about to throw a big bash. Only, it wasn't San Diego. We were over three thousand miles away from San Diego, somewhere in New Jersey, and we were heading east.

I came out of the bathroom. We all smiled at each other. No words. We hugged, and I was again moving. My legs and feet were stiff and sore, but they were working. Mom was doing her best to load things onto a luggage dolly; however, it was apparent that she was as exhausted, if not more so, than I was. I asked my friends to help my mom. For two months, Mom had loaded and unloaded luggage, coolers, ice, and supplies for me—this was in addition to all the other duties she was performing. I was constantly amazed to look at this woman who was five feet tall, and barely tipped the scale at a hundred pounds. From her, I was born. She raised me. She was the strongest person I had ever met, and the only person who would —and could—have done what I needed for the past sixty days.

Within minutes, the van was loaded. I had been guzzling water. I had a coffee in my hand. We had gotten coffee the night before and heated it up in the morning. We knew no gas stations or coffee shops would be open at 3:00 a.m. I had grown to need coffee in the morning to get me moving. It was like a magic elixir.

I was dressed in sweat pants over my favorite red shorts, a T-shirt I had made for the run, my favorite Pearl Izumi coat, a PrincetonTec headlamp, and a highly reflective LED lightvest. As I exited the automatic sliding glass doors of the motel, I stepped into a dark, cold, humid New Jersey morning. I stood outside the doors with Jay and Greg, waiting for Mom to pull up in the van. She wasn't driving, and was in the passenger seat. Camilo was driving the van for her so she could rest. Greg pulled up behind the van in a truck he had rented. The plan was to put me between the truck and the van so they could protect me from being run over by cars. Jay walked me through the dark motel parking lot. We had about a hundred yards to navigate, curbs, bushes, trees, and cars. He had to get me to the place where the motel parking lot intersected the street.

The day before, I had stopped running at that exact point. That point marked the end of the previous day's sixty-mile run. Today, it marked the beginning point of a seventy-plus-mile run, and my sixtieth consecutive day of running. Sixty days earlier, I had started running on the other side of America, in Los Angeles, California. I had run almost three thousand miles across America from the Pacific Ocean. I wouldn't stop today's run until I was on the steps of City Hall in Manhattan, New York—my finish line.

As I stood in silence on the road, I lowered my head, closed my eyes, and said a prayer, then I raised my head, looked deep into the darkness, and started running.

PART I

Makings Of A Man

1

Early Years

Relationships shape who we become.

I remember sitting in the corner of a couch in our living room when I was two years old. My brother, who was three, was snuggled up against me. The couch seemed vast, as if it could go on forever. And we were squeezed together, trying to fit on one half of a cushion. We stared nervously at the other side of the room, across a glass-top coffee table at a television that wasn't turned on. The house smelled lived-in, not dirty and not reeking of Pine-Sol—a pleasant, reassuring smell.

That moment, however, was anything but reassuring. People were arguing, and yelling. I turned my head to the right and saw my mom and dad sitting at the four-person table where we ate breakfast, lunch, and dinner. There was no food on the table. They were facing each other, with their mouths moving and sounds spilling out. I couldn't understand what they were saying. One spoke with a finger pointed, then the other responded, cutting the other person off.

Oh no! What was going to happen?

More yelling and loud voices. Finally, my dad stood up, pushing the chair he was sitting in backward with the force of his vertical momentum. He stood over my mom, yelling. She didn't flinch and stared him in the eye. He turned, walking past my brother and me, not acknowledging us at all. He yelled, "I'm leaving!" My mom asked, "Where are you going?" He said, "To my mom's." The door and screen door opened, then the screen door slammed shut.

I didn't know how to feel. Confused. Sad. Scared. Numb.

This is the first memory I have in my life. My parents breaking up, and my mom leading our family fearlessly into the unknown.

My brother and I lived with Mom full-time and saw my dad every other weekend. She kept the house we were living in, and she somehow managed to pay for it on a secretary's salary. I remember her working many jobs and us going to different babysitters all the time. I remember her pushing a lawnmower in the hot sun, cutting our grass on the weekends. I remember staying up late with her on the weekends, laying on top of her, watching movies, until the TV station shut off for the night and static consumed my visual and auditory senses. My mom slept and slept after long days of work. She was always working, it seemed.

We had cousins who lived across the street—they were my godparents, and I called them aunt and uncle. They had two children—Frankie and Judy—who used to babysit us. Frankie was an amazing musician. He could play drums and keyboard, and was an amazing singer. Judy was a braniac, brilliant and extremely intelligent. There was also something special about my cousins Frankie and Judy—they were both congenitally blind. This was my first encounter with people who were blind. I really didn't even notice a difference with one exception—when Judy babysat us and gave me cereal, she let the milk run over her finger. I remember thinking it was gross. I didn't understand that Judy was measuring how much milk was in the bowl, and taking care not to let the milk overflow the bowl. That is the only difference I remember about my cousins and their blindness. Each of them were incredibly independent and talented in their own ways. They used canes at times, and at other times got around without canes, by memorization or by using their bubbly and jovial personalities. They were inspirations to me as I grew older.

I never looked forward to the time spent with my dad. I always wanted a father figure in my life, but this man never fulfilled those desires. He came and went—running away when things got tough, just like when I was two. Anger and disappointment were the prevailing feelings I had about him. At best, this man was a friend.

The good news was, I had a lot of uncles, aunts, and cousins on my dad's side who I came to know and love. I had many uncles who were surrogate father figures for many things. I had uncles who were fierce competitors and athletes. None went to college, though a few went into the military. The brothers and sisters were tight, and whenever you dropped into somebody's home, you were never an imposition. People stopped what they were doing and took out food, then we all ate and talked to each other. I always felt wanted by my dad's family, but I never felt wanted by him.

Our house was in a rougher part of town. It wasn't where doctors and lawyers lived. We lived where blue-collar people lived. Our neighbors were good people, but, like with any lower socioeconomic situation, there were struggles. My mom saw that kids were getting pregnant and doing drugs in the local junior high. She wanted to get us out of that side of town, and give us a better life. She didn't want us to grow up thinking that the behaviors we experienced were normal. She had to save every penny she had in order to move to a better part of town.

By the time I was in second grade, Mom moved us to a nice part of town. The neighbors were pretty much all married with kids, and most everybody seemed to have a college education. The houses and yards were well kept, and our house had three bedrooms. That meant my brother and I would each get our own room! I loved our new house.

Those elementary school years seemed to fly by. I remember feeling like I had to prove myself. I found myself getting into fist fights when we first moved into our new neighborhood. There weren't a lot of people with brown skin (Latin) living in the neighborhood. I was called names and teased, despite being a straight-A student. I stood up to bullies. What they did wasn't fair or right, and I wouldn't let them be mean to me or somebody I cared about. Inevitably, my choice to not accept this bullying behavior landed me on the bike path after school with a bunch of kids surrounding me, and yet another bully squaring off. I was a smaller kid, but I never lost a fight. It seemed like I was having to fight week after week. Soon, however, there were no more bullies to fight. And I learned some important things about bullies—you have to stand up to them, sometimes you have to fight them, and most of the time you have to beat them in order for them to leave you alone. I didn't like to fight, but when I was backed into a corner with no other options, I did what I had to do.

Even after having to fight, feeling different, struggling with not fitting in, everything was perfect when I got home. My mom, my brother, and I were my first team. Our family unit helped each other, struggled alongside each other, and celebrated with each other. I had a safe place in my home where I knew I was loved, accepted, and would be cared for.

2

Diagnosis

Sometimes life can change in an instant
and you may not see it coming.

I t was a beautiful Colorado day with a clear, blue sky. I was thirteen, and in middle school in Denver. It was like any other day in junior high. I walked to school on the bike path for about a mile. I'd meet up with friends, and we walked together, joking and laughing all the way to school. Once at school, we went to our classes and soaked up information and new concepts like sponges soaking up spilled water on a table.

On this particular day, we had our annual hearing and vision screening in the nurse's office. Our class lined up and walked through the halls toward the main office, where the nurse's office was located. We were constantly told by our teacher to quiet down and use our hallway voices. The fact is, we had thirty boys and girls just starting to go through hormonal changes, so there was no quieting us down. We lined the hallway outside the office, waiting for our turn to go in and get tested. We whispered our jokes to each other, and, once in a while, somebody couldn't control the volume of their laughter and an eruption of sound filled the hallway. Soon, it was my turn to get tested. I entered the small office and sat in a chair. I put on headphones and was handed a clicker. The nurse instructed me to press the clicker whenever I heard a sound. Sometimes the sounds were high-pitched, sometimes low-pitched. Sometimes the sounds came from only one side, and sometimes the sound was on both sides of the headphones. After the hearing test, I gave back the headphones and the nurse told me to look at the eye chart on the far wall. There was nothing special about this eye chart, and she did the usual examination. She asked me to read the chart with one eye, then the other eye. Then, she had me read the chart with both eyes.

After I finished the testing, I got back in line with the members of my class who had already been tested. We joked and wrestled as the remaining class members were tested. When everybody was done, our class straightened up and prepared to go back to class. As we were being dismissed by the nurse, she asked to see me individually. My classmates jaunted off down the hallway, laughing and making faces at me because I was left behind. I went to the nurse and asked what she needed. The nurse looked at me and said, "You can't see." I was puzzled by her statement. I was looking directly at her face, eyes, hair, etc. I said, "Of course I can see. I'm looking at your face and I read the eye chart." The nurse said, "You were supposed to read five lines more on the eye chart." Now I was really confused. I remember looking at the eye chart. I couldn't even tell there was print, let alone letters, five lines lower than where I had stopped reading. The nurse said I needed to go see an eye doctor, and that I probably needed to get glasses. That night, I shared my experience with my mom and we made an appointment to see an eye doctor to get glasses.

A couple of weeks later, I was at the eye appointment getting my eyes dilated and again struggling to read an eye chart. Soon, it was the part of the eye appointment where you look through a machine at an eye chart and they put different lenses in front of your eye until you can see 20/20. They kept trying lens after lens, but my eyesight didn't seem to get any better. The lenses didn't seem to make any difference with my visual acuity. They only served to blur my eyesight more with the lenses than without the lenses. The eye doctor seemed confused by this outcome. He moved the machine aside, and asked to look into my dilated eye. When he did, there was a long, silent pause. He sat back, turned to Mom and me, and said, "Your lenses are fine; there appears to be something wrong with your retina." I was even more confused. First, I didn't know what a retina was, and second, I thought I could see just fine. I was in school making straight-A's. I played sports and I had friends. My mom, brother, and I had moved to a good part of town and things were good. My mom was even engaged to be married to a lawyer, Fred Epstein.

The eye doctor recommended that we make an appointment with a retina specialist. We followed instructions and made the appointment. A couple of weeks later, I found my eyes again being poked and prodded. The tests were different this time. My eyes were dilated, kept open, and lights were flashed into them. I pushed a button when I saw a flash of light in my peripheral field. Finally, the retina specialist looked into my dilated eye, saying "Hmmm" and "Ohh." At the end of all the testing, my mom and I sat in a dark room with the doctor. He busily flipped through paper notes and test results. It was deafeningly silent. My mom said nothing and seemed to be just as uncomfortable with the situation as I was. The retina specialist looked up from his chart and said four words that would forever change the trajectory of my life: "Jason, you're going blind."

My mom and I said nothing, failing to process what the retina specialist had just said. He continued to explain that I had a genetic disease called Retinitis Pigmentosa (RP). The retina is located in the back of the eye and is attached to the optic nerve. The retina has light sensors called rods and cones. He explained that RP slowly causes its victim to go blind as the retina deteriorates. The retina dies from the outside in, causing the person to have narrowing tunnel vision, until there is no light perception at all. He explained that there was no cure or treatment for the disease. Next, he asked me what I wanted to do with my life. I told him confidently, "I am going to be a doctor or a lawyer."

Nobody in my family had gone to college, and my mom had brainwashed my brother and me, convincing us we would both go to college and graduate school. In response to my statement he said, "Forget about that. You will be blind with no light perception by the time you're thirty. Most blind people don't work. And I have five minutes before my next appointment, if you have any questions."

Neither my mom nor I had any questions at the time. We left the office, walked down the hall to the elevators, and exited the building in silence. As soon as we got out of the building, something very unexpected happened. My mom burst into tears, crying uncontrollably. I didn't know what to do. I had never seen my mom cry before. She was the strongest person I knew. She had raised two kids alone, and had overcome so much with a work ethic that was second to none. This time, there was nothing she could do to stop her child from going blind, being scared, hurting, and having a life of challenge.

My head and heart were immediately filled with fear of what might happen in the future. Would I be able to finish school? How quickly would my sight deteriorate? Would I need to learn Braille? Would I be able to work and live alone? Would I use a cane or a dog? What would people think of me? Why did I have to be different? Why did this have to happen to me? Would it be dark when I could no longer see? Was this doctor totally wrong? Could a cure be discovered? Would I be able to drive? Why me? Why now?

I don't remember much about school after that. I think I immediately flipped on my teenage-testosterone switch and went into ignore-adult mode. I literally just ignored what that retina specialist told me, and chose to go on with life. A psychologist might call it denial, and it probably was; however, that is how I coped with the situation for decades to come.

I was given an IQ test to see if I needed to have a specialized education plan to learn in school. It turned out, I scored off the charts at a genius level. They offered me large-print books to make it easier to read. I accepted the large-print books, but soon realized that I didn't like feeling different and bringing them to class. For one regular-sized math book, I had six large-print books that were 18 inches x 24 inches each. Each letter was about a half inch in height, and the lines were double-spaced. Sure, it was easier to see, but I felt like it made me really different . . . and what teenager wants to feel different? Hence, I left the large-print books in my locker, and took the regular-sized book to class—the book that I had trouble reading because the print was too small for me to see.

By the time I was in high school, my mom had remarried a wonderful man, Fred Epstein. I was blessed to witness this relationship first-hand, and finally learned what true love looked like. He was so good to me, my mom, and my brother. Fred was an attorney, and very well-respected in town. When Fred and my mom married, we moved into a new home. Because my brother and I were teenagers, I saw this as a very smart move. It wasn't us moving in with him, or him moving in with us. We all moved in together.

Our new home was nice. Everybody had their own room, with extra rooms to spare. Our yard was big, and beautiful. It was right across the street from a park. I remember some really wonderful times with Fred. Fred paid for my brother and me to go to Mass Eye and Ear to have our eyes evaluated and tested by the leading RP researcher. He took us on vacations and, eventually, paid for our education at private universities. More important than financially supporting us, Fred spent time with us. He came to our athletic events and school activities. He loved to shop for deals, and he loved to sit and watch the sunrise in the silence of morning.

Fred also had four children—Lori, Steve, Eileen, and Becky, who were ten to fifteen years older than my brother and me. I always liked spending time with my stepsiblings. Although they were older and we had different upbringings, I felt like we were in it together, and I liked having stepsiblings who were older and had gone to college and graduate school. They were role models, and I was able to understand that going to college was not beyond my reach.

My stepfather, Fred, used to wear reading glasses and suggested that I should try some. We went to Walgreens and tried on reading glasses. They actually worked. They magnified the text of my books just enough so I could make out the print. I started wearing half-glass readers at the age of fourteen. I was teased and made fun of because I had to use the glasses. I was smart, so it just kinda went along with being a nerd. However, I was also a decent athlete, so it didn't quite make sense to people who were teasing me. And it didn't make sense to me either. I could read the text for a while with the readers until my eyes became too strained, and then I just couldn't see anymore. So I learned that I had limited time to use my eyes for intense reading in classrooms and textbooks.

I did what I could to get along and keep up with schoolwork. As the topics became more and more complicated, I was required to spend more and more time in my books. The teachers simply couldn't teach all the concepts during the course of the class. I moved to the front row of all my classes, so I could try to see the chalkboard and what was written on it. I couldn't see it from the front row. My mom bought me a monocular—like binoculars, but it had only one tube to look through and was more discreet. I was unable to read the chalkboard with the monocular, take notes, and pay attention in class all at the same time to learn the material. I had to find another way to keep up in school.

Again, the answer came from my stepfather. He had magnifying glasses lying around the house. One day, I tried to read a textbook while using a magnifying glass and my reading glasses. Voila! I could read for at least double the time before my eyes were too strained to see the text. The other thing I learned was that I could see better when there was a lot of light. My mom bought me a few lamps to put on my desk in my room. I discovered that I was able to see indefinitely when I read textbooks with tons of lamp light, a magnifying glass, and my reading glasses.

Once I made this discovery, school was back on track. I faked being a regular kid and learning in class. I just listened to what the teacher said, and, if called on, I came up with a clever comment that was on point. Meanwhile, I really wasn't learning much in class, because I couldn't see what was going on. I did the best I could, but it wasn't enough. After the school day, athletics, and socializing were done, I retreated back to my desk in my room with lamps and studied deep into the night, learning from my textbooks. It was different, took more time, and I had to discover it with the help of my family, but, in the end it worked just fine.

This was where I began learning about adapting when you confront adverse conditions. My mom has been my greatest role model for work ethic, and I learned that work ethic is the great equalizer in life. Some may have gifts and talent, but the ability to endure, persevere, and work relentlessly can level any playing field.

3

Ted Epstein

Sometimes, even when you see it, it's hard to believe it.

Fred had siblings, and one of them was also an attorney—my Uncle Ted. Ted was a few years younger than Fred. He was a very kind man, in the truest sense of the word. He was soft-spoken, and always seemed to have a smile on his face. His personality was calm, almost Zen-like. Ted practiced law for a few decades, then one day, he decided to start running and pursue his passion for art. He created art and logged miles. His running morphed into a passion for endurance, whether it be on foot, on a bike, or in the water. He moved at a slow pace, but he never stopped moving.

One weekend in particular, I remember Fred suggesting that we should all go up to Boulder, Colorado to see Uncle Ted compete in a race. As I was a city boy, I always enjoyed trips up to Boulder—the land of the hippies. It was also home of the University of Colorado, which had a field house with an indoor track. That was where Uncle Ted's race was taking place. On the way up to Boulder, I imagined that we were going to the Senior Olympics. I thought I'd see a bunch of "blue-hairs" hobbling down a track trying to finish the hundred-meter limp. I really didn't know what to expect, but thought our purpose was just to go out and show support for a family member. After all, Uncle Ted was a lawyer turned artist, and now he was running a race. He was in transition in the truest sense of the word. We'd probably cheer a little, go out to lunch afterward, and then head home—no big deal and just another weekend at the Epstein-Romero house.

What I was about to experience wasn't at all what I expected, and it would forever change my life.

As we walked to the CU Field House, it didn't look like there were any people there. The parking lot was just about empty, and you couldn't hear anything from the outside. I was told there was a one-eighth-mile indoor track inside the field house. I assumed that was where we'd watch the senior Olympics. No lights were on, and the only light was coming from the windows which were a couple stories from the main level. It was empty. No bleachers were pulled out, and nobody was there.

Then I realized . . . there *was* somebody there. As I struggled to look at the dimly lit track area, I saw something moving. It looked like a person. As we walked closer, I realized it was a person—a man. He was hunched over, and was shuffling around the track, barely faster than a person could walk. That man was my Uncle Ted. He looked horrible—like death. When he saw us, he looked at us, waved, smiled as best he could, and kept right on shuffling. I asked my mom and Fred what was going on. They explained that Uncle Ted was running around this track to see how far he could run in six days. It was his sixth day. A tent inside the track was used for him to sleep. He ran eight hours at a time, slept one; then ran another eight hours, and slept one, and so on.

He looked morose. His face was contorted, barely recognizable except for his smile. He usually stood a little over six feet tall, with erect posture. This person looked about my height—five feet, eight inches; hunched over and limping. He couldn't talk. We said, "Hi!" and he tried to talk to us, but words wouldn't come out. It sounded like a wheeze. I got on the track with my Uncle Ted and shuffled a few laps with him. I was simply awestruck at what he was doing. He was an ordinary person who didn't seem to possess any exceptional athletic abilities. However, he was obviously exceptional in some way that I had totally missed. And he was doing something that was extraordinary. His feet had swollen, and he had humongous shoes— five sizes larger than his normal shoe. I was told later in life that Frank Shorter, US Olympic Gold Medalist in the marathon, visited my Uncle Ted during his six-day race. Uncle Ted gave Frank one of his shoes as Frank had never seen a shoe so big. Whether that is fact or fiction, I don't know, but I like the story.

We stayed at that field house as long as my family could tolerate watching Uncle Ted go around and around the track. I could have watched and trotted with him forever. The others, however, were getting bored watching this spectacle, and we eventually left.

That experience stained me. I wanted *that*. I saw something *amazing* first-hand. I knew at that moment that all things are possible, even things you think are impossible.

I had the desire to push myself physically. I immediately wanted to run a marathon. I also remember watching ABC's *Wild World of Sports* when Mark Allen and Dave Scott were squaring off, going toe-to-toe at the Ironman Triathlon World Championships.

How did people do these things? How could *I* do these things?

I remember once in a while, Fred fold me of some crazy adventure that Uncle Ted was on. At one point, Uncle Ted was training to go to Antarctica and climb a mountain. So, he went to a meat locker in Brighton, Colorado and spent his days running, climbing ladders, and walking in a large freezer. Apparently, he was trying to acclimatize. When stories were told about Uncle Ted, others laughed and said, "He's crazy." I was amazed, intrigued, and I thought to myself, *How amazing!*

Once, Uncle Ted decided to run a hundred miles around some mining town, high in the Rocky Mountains in Colorado. That turned out to be one of the first runnings of the Leadville 100 Trail Race. As I've adventured and gone through life, I learned a lot more about Uncle Ted. He was extremely well respected by the best of the best ultra-endurance athletes. Marshall Ulrich told me a story about how he and Uncle Ted were supposed to be teammates on the very first Eco-Challenge. They were training at the Denver

Athletic Club. Marsh said they were in a stairwell, and Uncle Ted had dumbbells in his hands and was going up and down the stairs, seemingly forever. He told Marsh to come and do the stairs with him, and Marsh obliged. At one point, Uncle Ted said, "Your shoe is untied." Before Marsh could stop to retie his shoe, Uncle Ted was on his knees, had put down his dumbbells, and was retying Marsh's shoe. He picked up his dumbbells, stood up, looked Marsh in the eye and said, "Everybody deserves to be treated like that." Then, he turned and started climbing up the stairs again, dumbbells in each hand.

Uncle Ted suffered from Alzheimer's later in his life, and passed in May of 2016. His life was a constant reminder and inspiration to me that a pursuit of a passion will make you rich in kindness and love. It is important to me to share just how great my Uncle Ted is, and below is a list of just some of his accomplishments and awards:

- First person to complete the Grand Slam of Triathlons, completing a double, triple, quadruple, and quintuple Ironman Triathlon in one year. Uncle Ted did this in six months, and had a surgery to repair a herniated disc during that six-month time period.
- Climbed Mt. Kilimanjaro in Africa, and Mt. Vinson in Antarctica.
- Ran 480 miles across Siberia, getting lost from the expedition for a couple of days, then he rejoined, finished, and won the race.
- Completed a Deca (ten) Ironman triathlon, swimming 24 miles, biking 1,112, and running 262, nonstop.
- Swam around Manhattan Island.
- Swam across the Bering Strait from Russia to Alaska.
- Swam halfway around Hong Kong Island.
- Inductee to the Colorado Sports Hall of Fame, US Senior Athletes Hall of Fame, and East High Athletic Hall of Fame.
- Completed three, six-day races.
- Ran the Pikes Peak Marathon a bunch of times.

- Biked halfway across America, until he crashed his bike.
- Carried the Olympic Torch in 2002.

Uncle Ted and I aren't related by blood, but we were connected by vision, sweat, and the satisfaction of discovering areas of ourselves that we never knew existed. Knowing him, and how he lived life, gave me the courage to have epic dreams.

Rest in Peace

Ted Epstein, Jr.
July 23, 1935 - May 7, 2016

4

Teenage Years

Feeling awkward.

I t was a Friday night, and I was at All-City Stadium. My high-school football team, the Thomas Jefferson Spartans, were playing a rival school. The bleachers were filled with students who were cheering, laughing, flirting with one another, and doing what high-school kids do. The night was perfect for a football game. It was fall in Colorado, and that meant cool night air and cloudless skies filled with stars (I've never been able to see stars, but you get the point).

I was on the field all suited up in my uniform. My energy was at an all-time high. It was my first night game, and I was playing under the lights at All-City Stadium. I had dreamt about this moment since I first started playing football. Would I make a critical tackle? Or, maybe I could cause a turnover, and maybe pick up a fumbled ball and run it into the end zone for a touchdown. I didn't know what could happen, but this night was filled with possibilities, and I was going to play my heart out.

We won the coin toss and chose to receive the kick-off in the second half of the game. That meant we needed to start the game by kicking off the ball to our opponents. I was on the kick-off team as well as playing right guard on offense and inside linebacker on defense. I was small at 145 pounds, but I was fearless and would do what was asked of me, most of the time sacrificing my body to a much larger lineman or running back. Our kick-off team ran out onto the field, after we did our team cheer.

We rushed onto the field like a pack of wild animals. I was lined up on the right side of the field. Our kicker had said he was going to kick the ball to the right side of the field. This was going to be my moment. The ball was coming to my side of the field, and I was going to run as fast as I could and tackle the opponents in a collision of epic proportions. My adrenaline was racing. My breathing was accelerated. I was already sweating from the excitement. The whistle blew, and the screaming fans became a deafening roar.

Our kicker ran toward the ball, and I heard his foot strike the ball with a loud *thud!* I saw the ball go sailing off into the air, and it disappeared into the darkness of the night sky. I sprinted as fast as I could in a straight line, knowing that soon there would be a wall of opponents I needed to collide with and get past in order to tackle the ball carrier. I was running at top speed in a straight line down the field to where the ball was supposed to have been kicked. Something was wrong. There were no opponents to collide with. In fact, none of my teammates were around me. I was all alone on the right side of the field. All of the players from both teams were on the other side of the field, colliding and crashing into one another. The referee blew the whistle as the ball carrier had apparently been tackled.

I was confused, and as I trotted off the field to the sidelines, I heard the coach yelling at me, "Romero! What were you thinking?" I told the coach that I ran to where the ball was supposed to be kicked, so I could tackle the ball carrier. The coach yelled at me, "Kenny messed up the kick, and it went to the left side of the field! You need to keep your eye on the ball and go where it goes!" I told the coach I was watching the ball, but as soon as the ball was kicked, I couldn't see it anymore in the darkness. I had no idea where the ball was once it was kicked. The coach knew about my eye condition, and the night blindness that came along with my disease. He'd seen me leave my car at school after practice and walk home, whenever practice ran late and it got too dark for me to drive. He yelled at me, "Get off the field! You're done playing night games!"

I had many times in my life where my dreams of being normal were dashed because of my eye disease. When these times of being different occurred, it was extremely difficult. I was a teenage boy with all of the insecurities of a boy going through puberty. I felt like I was good at a lot of things, but I wanted to be *great*! I never felt great at anything. It was like I was always second best. Whether it was academics, sports, socializing, etc. For some reason, I could never be satisfied with myself or what I did in life. Many times I blamed my eyes when I felt this way.

I remember lying on my bed as a teenager and crying into my pillow. I screamed at the top of my lungs, angry, scared, and sad that my eyesight would be taken from me. Looking back, I realize it wasn't so much about my eyesight—it was about a crippling and paralyzing fear of the unknown. I wasn't prepared to go blind and live in a cage of darkness. I didn't want to lose sight of trees, flowers, football games, and the faces of my family and friends. I didn't want to be special. If I was only second best as a teenager, what would I be as an adult who couldn't see?

I screamed. I raged. I punched. Basically, I was acting like a three-year-old having a temper tantrum. I didn't know how to cope with this situation, or the fear and anxiety that accompanied my prognosis of ultimate darkness. The coping mechanism that I eventually settled in on was denial. I just didn't accept that I was going blind. I continued on with my life and just moved forward, despite this lurking nemesis that was coming to rob me of my sense of sight.

And, even though I was living every day and trying to ignore my poor eyesight, I was constantly reminded of this enemy. It creeped into all areas of my life, including social situations. Whenever there was a school dance, I always tried to muster up the courage to ask a girl to the dance. If I liked a girl, I did the usual teenage things like becoming nervous and giddy around the girl before I asked her to a dance. I remember one time I was going to ask a cheerleader to a dance—her name was Carol. She was nice, pretty, and we were friends. The dance was coming with the days ticking away. I had done my homework and knew that nobody had asked Carol to the dance yet. I was scared of asking and being rejected. But I was even more scared of her accepting. If she accepted, I had to figure out how we would get to the dance. I could drive during the day, but my license was restricted to daylight driving only. At nighttime, I couldn't see much. I wasn't even thinking about being in a dark gymnasium and trying to not bump into people while we were dancing. Carol didn't know the details about my eyes, the symptoms, or my insecurities.

I finally mustered up the courage to ask Carol to the dance. I picked my time, and found a time of day when it would just be her and me. If she turned me down, I didn't want it to be in front of a large crowd. I hoped she'd say yes, because I thought she was very nice and it would be fun to go to a dance with a person like Carol. I started the conversation casually, and I felt like I was going to throw up because I was so nervous. After making silly conversation for a bit, I got to the topic of the dance and asked if she was going. She said that nobody had asked her yet. Then, I felt my hands sweating, and my legs started shaking. I took a deep breath, and asked her if she wanted to go with me to the dance. Carol smiled. I didn't know if that smile was going to precede a comment that would let me down easy, or if she would agree go to the dance with me. It seemed like there was an eternal pause before she spoke.

When I did hear Carol speak, these words came from her mouth, "Sure, Jason. I'd love to go to the dance with you." I was doing backflips inside. We were both smiling ear to ear. I wanted to scream, *"Yes!"* I'd spent so many days carefully planning for this moment. So much research to read the signals and see if maybe she would go to the dance with me. And finally, it would happen.

Oh, there was that tiny detail about how we were going to go to the dance. I was, and have never been, great with timing. I figured I'd let Carol know that I couldn't drive at night and ask if she could drive to the dance. I hated this part. I felt less than human.

As we looked into each other's eyes, smiling ear to ear, I

continued speaking and told her that my eyes weren't the greatest. She didn't seem to mind at all, and her beautiful smile continued radiating. Then, I explained with a saddened voice that I didn't drive at night, and her smile lessened. Then, in an embarrassed voice, I asked Carol if she could drive us to the dance, because I wasn't allowed to drive at night due to my eyes. Carol's face was expressionless as she tried to process my words, and it felt like our balloon of excitement and giddiness had just deflated to a lifeless shell of nothingness. We ended up going to the dance, but the experience was awkward. I felt like a burden on Carol, and I think she picked up on that, making her experience awkward as well.

I would never be the guy who drove to a girl's house, picked her up, and took her on a date at night. This was very hard for me.

RP had won again, and I had let it steal my happiness and confidence. I danced many times with RP throughout my teenage years. Sometimes, it led and sometimes I sat it on the sidelines and boogied by myself. It was always there waiting, watching, and knowing that we were inextricably intertwined. And I knew we would be forced to waltz, even though I didn't want to. I was tormented by a feeling that in the end, RP would lead the last dance when my sight would be stolen from me.

5

College Entrance Exam

Testing my confidence.

Somehow, I made it through high school, and did pretty well. I was in the top ten in my class, had a 4.57 GPA due to taking advanced courses, lettered in three sports, and was the captain of the team in two sports. It was time to move on to the next chapter of my life and be part of the first generation in my family to graduate from a university. First, however, I needed to take the college entrance exams—the SAT and the ACT. These standardized tests were given in large dimly lit lecture halls with proctors who ensured that exam takers didn't cheat, talk, or distract other testers, and adhered to time limits and rules of the test. The test needed to be administered under controlled conditions, in order to ensure that the thousands upon thousands of results were comparable.

My older brother had taken the test the year before. He told me about the testing and lighting conditions for the test. I felt very anxious and asked a lot of questions. It had taken me years to perfect my strategy to learn in a school setting. I had come to accept that I was unable to keep up with school-based learning, and that most of my learning needed to come from self-study at my desk, with lamps and magnifiers late at night. I was okay with that. However, I had been told that college admissions offices evaluated these SAT and ACT test scores on par with my GPA. I worked for years to earn my GPA, and the SAT and ACT would take just three hours, but carry the same weight as my GPA. This was an important test, and it was important that I score well.

After speaking with my brother, I was worried about the testing environment. Would it be light enough for me to read the test? If it wasn't as brightly lit as my lamp-lit desk learning environment, I knew my eyes would fatigue, and eventually my eyes wouldn't function well enough to read, even with magnifiers. Based on past experience, I knew better than to attempt to read in dimly lit environments.

My attempts to read in dim environments looked like this—my class was given the entire period to read a few chapters of a book. The lighting was okay, but not super-bright like I needed in order to be able to read, digest, and process text without struggling to see it. Usually, I needed a magnifier as well, but I carried those with me wherever I went. I tried to be normal like everybody else, and I tried to read the text. I would be okay for a while, depending on text size and the lighting conditions. After five to thirty minutes, the text seemed to get smaller. Then, it became fuzzy and blurry. I moved my head closer to the text in an attempt to increase the size of the font. This behavior, however, gave away the fact that I couldn't see, and I hated that. At times, I had my face 1 to 2 inches away from the text. I looked out of place, and people said out loud, "Are you blind, or what?" I never answered, but I felt very bad and ashamed inside when people said these things to me.

After having this experience on many occasions, I learned to just fake as though I was reading. I read whatever I could, then, when my eyes gave out, I just flipped the pages as if I was reading. It was all an act, to try to fit in. I knew that I was just buying myself more time catching up that night at my well-lit desk. However, I didn't mind working hard and long hours into the night, in order to be accepted as being normal by my peers during the day.

The SAT and ACT were different animals, however. I wouldn't

be able to fake reading them, and retreat to my desk that night to finish. I had to finish the test during the testing period. Whatever I didn't finish would be marked as incorrect. This would have a significant negative effect on my score, and hinder my chances of getting into a good university and receiving scholarships. I didn't know what to do. I was stuck and frustrated.

The strategy I had settled on was to just go into the test, work as fast as I could before my eyes gave out, and guess on all the questions that I couldn't read because of my eye fatigue. I was hoping to be right on all the questions I could read, to offset all the wrong answers I was sure to get on the questions I couldn't. I had heard from somebody that on multiple choice tests, *b* was the most common correct answer. I planned to use that as a strategy when I was guessing blindly. It upset me that I wouldn't be able to do as well as I could because of my eyes.

It was just like when I was pulled out of nighttime football games. My failing eyesight was the nemesis, and it felt like it was winning and I was losing. Why did I work so hard in high school to get straight-A's, only to be put in this harrowing situation with these standardized tests? I was competing against fully sighted people to score well on a test to gain admission to universities and receive scholarship offers. However, at best, my eyesight would last for a third of the allotted time for the test. I would have to guess at two-thirds of the answers. How was I going to do it?

I talked it over with my mom. She didn't know what to do either. We settled on a strategy to just do the best I could, and that would have to be good enough. We both knew that I wasn't going to do as good as I could. Implicit in our strategy was the thought that I would do as good as my eyesight would permit me to do. We were both settling on a lower standard for me and my performance because of my failing eyesight. My mother had never taken these tests, as she hadn't gone to a university. She had taken some college-level courses, but as a single mom raising two children and working multiple jobs, there was just no time to earn a degree from a university. I knew I would fail miserably, unless I happened to get real lucky on my guessing. I was resigned to let the chips fall where they may.

As the test got closer and closer, Mom kept talking about my problem with others. She ended up discussing the situation with a person who taught students how to take the college entrance exams. As it turned out, people with special needs are allowed to request special accommodations for the SAT and ACT. All you had to do was fill out a request form, and submit medical documentation proving the condition and substantiating your special accommodations.

All I needed was to be able to have a lot of lamps and magnifiers, and I thought I would be fine. I hated asking for help and accommodations, but I knew taking a test blind was certain failure. A part of me felt humiliated and ashamed for needing these accommodations. I wanted to be treated just like everybody else. However, I wasn't like everybody else. I needed to park my foolish pride on the sidelines for this one.

Mom and I filled out the request form, and gathered all the documentation justifying my eye condition and request for accommodations. As it turned out, the visual acuity of my left eye was 20/200 (legally blind) and my right eye was 20/80 at that point in my life. It was uncorrectable with glasses. Because my retina was deteriorating, less light was detected; hence, dimly lit environments were very difficult for me to function in. Sometime after we submitted the request we received a letter from the testing organization. They had accepted our request, and approved my accommodations to use additional lamps and magnifiers. They also added to my requested accommodations. They would give me a large-print test, and I wouldn't be tested with the general population. I would be tested in a separate room.

I wasn't sure how I felt about these additional accommodations. I was concerned about the large-print test. In my experience, if the print was too large, it was difficult to move quickly through the test as you would be flipping back and forth from page to page. There is a big difference between reading and understanding text that has twelve to fifteen words per line versus text that has three to four words per line. I asked the testers to give me a regular-print test in addition to the large-print test, and they agreed.

For their second accommodation to test me in a separate room, I was insulted. Did I have leprosy? Why couldn't I be in the same room as everybody else? Why was I so different? I asked to be tested in the same room as my peers. The request was denied with an explanation that my accommodations weren't suited to a general testing environment. I felt bad and ashamed. This eye disease had again won, and made me feel less than human. I was smart and a hard worker. But in the end, all my intelligence, strong work ethic, and complaining wouldn't change the testers' decision to have me sit in a separate room with my lamps and magnifiers.

As I look back at this situation, I can understand the reason why I was tested in a separate room. There are strict rules to avoid cheating and to ensure consistency of results on these tests. Almost every student who took the test was challenged by the content of the questions, the time constraints, and the stress of how much importance the test had on college admissions. If the testing organization sat me in a room of nervous teenagers, and I had a desk with all kinds of lamps and magnifiers, they would inevitably get questions about whether it was fair for me to have those accommodations. People might not have scored as well as they would have liked, and they would remember this student with all this special equipment. The student would have looked normal, not using a cane and doing everything by himself. He would have even read the test by himself and obviously could see.

The complaints would have been justified from what the other testers perceived as reality. Only with a long explanation to each one that I had a deteriorating retinal eye disease, which couldn't be cured and glasses didn't help, would these complaints be put at ease. And some would never accept the explanation. Some people would feel that if they didn't do well on the test, their score should be nullified or improved just because another person received different treatment, special accommodations, and possibly did well on the test. The testers were probably right to make me take the test in a separate room; however, that didn't change how I felt.

This was but another lesson that I needed to hide my eye condition if I wanted to be treated as normal by the general population. I had to fake being able to see so that I wouldn't be treated different. Why did I feel like I had to fake it? What was so shameful about being born with a disease that I didn't ask for? After all, I would rather play night football games, not make girls feel weird for driving on dates, and not make standardized testing organizations choose between making me feel like I'm quarantined or risk an upheaval of complaints from fellow testers. Again, I felt beaten by RP and I was down, but I wasn't yet out.

6

College Daze

Laughter is powerful medicine.

As it turned out, I did okay on the SAT and ACT tests. Things were looking up for me. I had beach and bikinis on the brain and my heart was set on Southern California. I applied to universities on the Pacific coast from Santa Barbara to San Diego. I was accepted to all universities I applied to, and was offered scholarships of varying amounts. All I had to do was pick which school to attend. I ended up at the University of San Diego, a small private Jesuit University. When I arrived, I saw nuns and priests walking around, and the girls' and boys' dorms were separate. It was a beautiful campus—all white and pristine, up on a hill.

Despite the nuns and the priests, this university offered the experiences of any other post-secondary school. I learned about studying hard, pulling all-nighters, chasing girls, catching them and not knowing what to do, drinking too much, and throwing wild parties where a friend jumped off of the roof of our rented house, naked, with toilet paper on fire between his butt cheeks, eventually landing in our swimming pool.

I learned a lot academically. USD is a fine university, and challenged me intellectually. However, I learned more about myself and different social situations where my deteriorating eyesight presented challenges.

I had never gone to bars before, so I didn't know what to expect. I learned they are very dark. Also, for some reason, college parties are usually really dark. Didn't these people know that I couldn't see in the dark? I had a big problem. I wanted to meet people, go to parties and bars with friends, and do the normal things that college kids do. However, I couldn't see. And, I didn't bother to go into long explanations with people about this blinding eye disease that I had. I simply said, "I have bad eyes." Most people took that to mean that I just needed to wear some glasses and I'd be able to see fine.

I didn't want to be different.

When I first started going to bars, we went to "quarter drink night." You could get any drink for a quarter. That bar was pitch-black, I remember. I really liked quarter drink night because everybody got so drunk, they couldn't tell I was unable to see anything. In fact, the people at the bar were probably stumbling more and bumping into more things than I was. I also learned to sit at a table and stay in one place. If I was moving in a dark environment, I was more likely to trip and spill my drink on somebody, or bump into somebody else and cause them to spill their drink. I also learned to "look" at voices. I couldn't see faces, but I could hear voices. If I looked at where a voice was coming from, I assumed I was also looking at the person's face. I didn't want people to know I couldn't see. I learned to become a really good listener in the dark. I let other people speak the majority of the time, because then I could face their voice and hopefully, seem normal. It seemed like my sense of hearing was heightened. Maybe it was because my eyes were bad and my hearing compensated for weak eyesight. Maybe it was because I was actually focusing and paying close attention to words and sounds because that was all I had in dark environments. Whatever it was, I was doing everything I could to hide the fact that I was going blind.

I ran into another problem, however. On occasion, I met a really interesting girl, but I couldn't see what she looked like. From the conversation, I could find out that we went to the same school, and her name, where she lived, etc. However, if we were walking by each other on the street the next day, I'd have no idea that was the girl I met the night before. This conundrum plagued me for my entire life, and not just in my relationships with women.

I had to figure out a way to know who these people were the next day. I learned that if I asked good, unique, and deep questions, I could learn details about who they really were. Sometimes I learned that they had childhood injuries and had a scar, or a limp, or some other unique characteristic that I could use to identify them when it was light. I also used my olfactory senses and learned to identify girls by their perfume. I even made a game of it. In dark noisy parties or bars, usually you have to lean into a person to hear what they are saying because it is so loud. Women usually put perfume on their neckline. As I leaned in toward their voice, I sniffed their perfume. At first, I asked what perfume they were wearing. I eventually memorized perfumes, and was easily able to guess what perfumes girls wore. This was another tool in my arsenal to be able to identify who these people were, when we met again in daylight.

My college roommates were pretty jealous of my ability to identify perfumes on different women because I always got a smile, or some sort of attention. My roommates were infuriated, in a good way. They didn't think it was fair that my sense of smell was so good, and that my cheesy act of noticing a detail about a girl brought me into her good graces.

My roommates were some of the only people I really told about my deteriorating eyesight. I had to tell them. They were sure to figure out I couldn't see. There was no way I could live with them, and not have them figure out I was night blind, legally blind in one eye and going blind in the other eye. They did what any good college-age guy friends did—they tormented me.

One particular example of this loving torment stands out in my mind. I was an honors student in college, and still was unable to learn and keep up in class due to my eyesight. I couldn't see notes on the whiteboard, and wasn't able to copy what the professor had written. So I used my usual coping strategy of learning from books at the end of the day. I had "my place" in the library. Almost every night, I was in the library studying and learning from my books until the library closed. I had to catch up on everything I missed in class, and I tried to get ahead when the subjects weren't too complicated. I was living a few blocks off campus at the time with my roommates. There was a walking path from the back of the library to some steep stairs that had switchbacks for about a hundred yards. Then, you had to cross a four-lane road, and then descend six blocks into an older neighborhood with next to no streetlights. That was my walk home every night in my senior year of college. I had memorized this path. I walked it many times in the day to know how many steps to the stairs, and how many stairs there were, where the potholes were located in the streets, and how many steps I had to take when I was walking down pitch-black streets. As you can imagine, after a full night of studying, and a half-hour walk home, I was ready to go straight to bed.

The house I lived in my senior year of college had two levels. I lived in the lower level, and my three other roommates lived in the upper level. On one particular night when I came home from a long night of studying, I noticed that our outside light was off. Usually, the guys left the light on for me so I could tell which house was ours. I remember I had to feel the fence with my hands to see if it was the correct house. I also turned around and walked to the corner, counting my steps to ensure I had walked the correct distance to get to my house. I opened the gate and walked down some steps to the front door. It was totally dark and I was scared I was going to fall. But I had the path to the front door memorized fairly well as I'd entered and exited hundreds of times in the light, so I took baby steps just to be sure I didn't fall. I finally got to the front door and had to find the right key. It took a while for me to fumble to get the right key right side up so it would open the door. I unlocked the door in the black void and reached inside for the light switch to turn on the entryway light. I was looking forward to being able to see something again. It had been about an hour since I left the library, and it was almost pitch-black for that entire time. I flipped the switch, but the light didn't come on. My heart sank. I wouldn't be getting light anytime soon. The power must have gone out, as it did sometimes in the neighborhood. It was then that I remembered some neighbors had lights on in their houses. The power had to be on in the neighborhood, it must have been a problem with our breaker box. *Oh, well,* I thought. *We'll just have to fix it in the morning.*

I stepped into the blackness of the hallway, turned, closed the door, and felt for the deadbolt to lock the door behind me. After locking the door, I turned 180°. I knew there was a staircase of about twenty stairs directly in front of me, and about twenty feet to the top of the stairs. I figured I could touch the wall and follow that, then slowly baby step until I got to the top of the stairs. I'd hold the railing to get down the stairs, then enter my room and go to bed in the darkness. I was tired, but had a plan to get through the situation. Now all I had to do was execute it.

I touched the wall and started walking forward toward the stairs. *"Ouch!"* I yelled when my shin hit something hard. Something was obstructing the hallway. Was I in the right house? I began doubting my navigation and became scared that I was in somebody else's house. Uh oh. Do they have a gun? Is this the beginning of a really bad situation? Then I remembered that my key had opened the door and I had retraced the number of steps from the corner to our front gate two times. I was in the right house. But this thing that I hit with my shin was new.

I reached down. It was a glass table. As I felt it more, trying to get information about what it was, I came to realize it was the table that should have been in our living room around the corner. "What is this table doing in the hallway?" I said to myself in a quiet voice, trying not to wake my roommates. I pushed it aside and kept moving forward. I tripped on something and fell down. "What was that?" I said. It felt like the couch that was supposed to be in the next room, a good twenty feet away from where I had fallen. I felt for more light switches and turned all on that I could find. No lights came on. I was lost in my own house in the dark. I was disoriented and getting really nervous. I didn't know what to do.

It was at that point that I heard something that sounded like giggling. Then, it got a little louder, and it sounded like multiple people. *Hold on*, I thought. That sounded like my knucklehead roommates.

I was confused. It was past midnight on a weeknight and those lazy guys were surely asleep. The sounds became louder and the giggling turned to laughter. It was them! What were they laughing at? Then I had a bright light shined at me—it was like having a police officer shine his flashlight directly into your eyes. The guys started coming toward me and laughing hysterically. I was beginning to put two and two together. They had moved the furniture into the hallway. As I finished that thought, lights came on in the house, and I saw three guys who were some of my best friends. It turned out, they had decided to play a prank on me. They unscrewed all the light bulbs in the house and moved the furniture in the house. Then, they waited to watch me come home and fumble around in the blackness.

As I look back, these guys were either really cruel, or we were like brothers who all took turns being the butt of the joke. These guys taught me to laugh at my deteriorating eyesight. As all the lights went on, I saw the glass table and couch obstructing the hallway, but, that wasn't all. There were bar stools, dressers, and a bookshelf directly in front of me. The guys were nice enough to put a STOP sign at the top of the stairwell, so if I made it that far, I wouldn't fall down the stairs. Actually, the sign wouldn't really matter in the pitch-black as I couldn't see it anyway. The stairwell was filled with chairs, clothes, books, and any other tripping obstacle they could find. To a bunch of college guys, this was the epitome of "a good one." They got me. I think we ended up celebrating by having some beers and reminiscing about the times I'd gotten them. I was thankful for this experience. This time, with the help of some nutty friends, I was able to put RP down for the count, and learn to accept my frailties a little bit more.

7

A Glimpse

Running to live or living to run?

My college years were some of the best years of my life. I had even fallen in love in my final year of college. I had earned a business degree with honors and wanted to pursue a career in business. However, I was living in a world of lawyers. My stepfather was an attorney, and my brother had just gone to law school. In order to get into a top-level business school, you needed to work for at least two years. I decided to take the Law School Admissions Test, and did very well. I was waitlisted at Ivy League law schools, but had full-ride scholarship offers to the next tier of law schools. I was taught that more education would provide more opportunities, and so I made the decision to go to law school. The girl I had fallen in love with was moving to San Francisco to take a corporate job. I was moving to Colorado to go to law school. I told her that as soon as I was done with law school, I would come for her.

My law school years were unremarkable. Time seemed to just flow by. It seemed like a never-ending stream of questions, without any real true answer. We always needed to attend to every detail, and to take care to use precise vernacular like "and" or "or", which could be the difference between winning and losing. The nightly reading load for law school ranged between fifty and two hundred pages per night. Sometimes I had no idea how I got all the work done. I lived in the library, and read incessantly. Somehow, I was able to get through and graduate.

During my law-school years, something incredible happened to me. I remember going to a restaurant one day and flipping through a local Denver paper, *Westword*. This weekly publication told about all the happenings going on in Denver. In it, I saw an ad for the Denver International Marathon. It was going to be run in a couple months. I was in law school at CU Boulder, the same place I had seen Uncle Ted hobbling around an indoor track almost a decade earlier. A spark was ignited. I was going to do it.

I was a casual runner during law school. I ran a few times a week along the Boulder Creek Path, maybe four miles at a time. I wasn't really training for anything, and I wasn't all that healthy. I just knew that when I ran, I always felt better. Boulder was also such a beautiful place at the base of the Rocky Mountain Front Range.

As soon as I saw that ad, I signed up for the marathon. The next thing I had to do was figure out how I was going to train. I didn't know anybody who ran marathons. Uncle Ted was off on an adventure somewhere and couldn't be reached. I decided I just had to run, and run, and run some more. I soon noticed that the runners on the path looked different than me. They seemed to have snazzy running shoes, short shorts, and tank tops. I wasn't into the short shorts or the tank tops, but I did think that my walk-around shoes weren't that well suited for running. So I went to a local shoe store. As I sat there, I looked at a wall full of running shoes. A shoe salesman came out and asked if he could help me. I explained that I was going to run a marathon in a couple of months and I needed shoes to train in. He had me take off my shoe so he could size my foot. As I stepped onto the contraption, the salesman made a sound of concern: "Ahheeemmmmmm." In response, I said, "What?"

He went on to tell me I had flat feet. He told me how people with flat feet weren't accepted into the military because their feet prevented them from being able to run enough to make it through basic training. Was he trying to tell me my dream of running a marathon was impossible? I asked for the best shoe for my feet. He explained that because I had flat feet, I overpronated, which meant my ankle collapsed medially (internally) when I ran. I needed a shoe to keep my ankle in a neutral position so I wouldn't get injured.

I remember looking at the shoe salesman, who was a little on the chubby side, and thinking I was taking a lot of advice from a guy who didn't look like he ran. I stood up, walked toward the shoe wall, and examined my options. A bright blue shoe with a white sole caught my eye. It had a piece of carbon fiber on the arch to provide support. The shoe was extremely light and the upper was made of mesh. When I tried it on, it fit like a sock and was extremely light. I liked how it felt, but, more importantly, I liked how it looked. The salesman ended up telling me the shoe would be great for my training as it was a racing flat. This was a new term to me. I figured that if I trained in a racing flat, I'd probably be faster for my marathon. I took the salesman at his word and didn't understand that racing flats lacked support for my feet and cushioning for long distance running on asphalt and concrete.

I ran every day after my classes ended, and before it became dark and was time for me to retreat to the library for countless hours of reading. I ran for thirty minutes to an hour, five to six days a week. I felt like I was getting in okay shape. I had no idea what I was doing. I didn't know anybody else who was training for the marathon. All the people I knew thought I was crazy. I didn't know how far I was running either—this was well before the days of GPS watches. Sometimes, I drove as close as I could to the bike paths to try to measure out the distance on my car's odometer. With about four weeks to go until the marathon, I thought I should try a run longer than an hour.

When I drove from law school in Boulder to my mom's house in Denver, I noticed that the distance was twenty to twenty-five miles, depending on the route. On one weekend when I was staying in Denver with my mom, I asked her to drive me to Boulder so I could run back to her house. She obliged me. The plan was that I should get to her place in two, three, four, or maybe five hours. I really didn't know how long it would take, since I'd never run that far before. I took some quarters with me in case I needed to call her from a pay phone. My plan was to run along the highway in the break-down lane, since I knew how to get to her house on the highway.

I had my cool-looking racing flats, and I just started running. I remember it was about 10:00 a.m. when I started. There was no tree cover or shade on the highway, and it was very exposed. I felt pretty good about halfway from Boulder to Denver at about noon. The sun had come out and the clouds had burned off. It was another sunny, blue-sky Colorado day. It was getting warm, near 80°. I was getting thirsty, but I didn't have anything to drink. It hadn't occurred to me to carry a water bottle. Then I started to get hungry. It hadn't occurred to me to bring food either, and I only had fifty cents for a telephone call—not enough for water or food. So, I just kept running. My feet began to hurt, right where that carbon fiber arch support dug into my foot. As it turned out, the pressure from my flat foot snapped the carbon fiber arch support in half. Maybe my flat feet weren't suited for these high performance racing flats. Or, maybe these racing flats weren't suited for long miles on asphalt. Could that salesman have been wrong? Another hour passed, and it seemed like Denver was still an eternity away. My mouth was as dry as cotton. My skin was burnt red and sensitive to the touch. My stomach was making noises like I needed to put something into it soon, or else.

I just kept running. I didn't know where a pay phone was to call Mom for help to pick me up. I also wasn't okay with quitting. I just had to suffer and chalk this one up to experience. Finally, I rounded a corner and could see my mom's house. I stopped running and walked the final steps to her house. She opened the door before I could ring the doorbell and greeted me with a big smile. I smiled back. Neither one of us could believe I had made it. However, that didn't stop us from doing the same exercise a couple more times before the big race.

It was finally race day. Mom took me to the start area in down-town Denver where there was an inflatable "Start" line overhead.

The sun had yet to rise, and it was still dark except for a few strategically placed streetlights. There were a lot of runners at this race. Many of them looked very thin. I felt a little on the thicker side when standing at the start line. I didn't know what to expect, but I did remember walking into the CU Field House and seeing Uncle Ted going around that track—barely moving— three hundred plus miles into a six-day race. He was my inspiration to run that day.

The gun went off. I tried to always keep my breathing steady and easy. If my breathing sped up, I slowed down. After about a mile, I saw a bunch of people crowding around a table. I couldn't figure out what was going on. As I passed the table, I saw people throwing cups. I discovered that they gave out water and Gatorade along the course. I guzzled a drink every aid station, about every mile. The time flew by and before I knew it, I was closing in on the finish line. I got a sudden rush of adrenaline knowing that I was about to finish my first marathon. As I turned the final corner, I heard a friend yell my college nickname, "*Chip!*" It was my friend Nick from college. He was running on the side of the street with a huge smile, keeping pace as I crossed the finish line in three hours, fourteen minutes, and forty-two seconds. I didn't know if that was a good or bad time compared to others, but it was the best I could do that day. I did know I had a *great time* running the race, and that was all that mattered at that moment. I had done something that I thought was impossible just ten years prior.

8

Swinging for the Fences

If you're not all in, you're all out.

After three grueling years, I finally graduated from law school. Two weeks after finishing law school, I moved back to San Diego to take the California Bar and to fulfill the promise I had made to the first woman I had ever loved. I didn't tell anybody that I was moving back to find her, but my research told me that she had moved back to San Diego. As it turned out, she lived only a couple of blocks away from the apartment I had rented. What a coincidence! The fairy tale was going to come true. Fate must have been at work; otherwise, how could it be that we were within walking distance of one another? We met for breakfast and were right back to old times. Then, she slowly told me the story of the past couple of years of her life, and her ups and downs. The end of that story ended with her smiling from ear to ear, and she handed me an invitation. She told me that she was engaged and getting married in a couple of months.

My insides sank and I shriveled up into a giant ball of nothingness. I was numb, heartbroken, and empty. I did go to her wedding. I imagined speaking up when the pastor asked if anybody objected to the wedding. I dreamed that she would turn to me, remember our love, and we would embrace the beginning of an eternal life together. That dream was snuffed out when I heard her say, "I do." I had swung for the fences and come up short. I did, however, manage to muster up the strength to dance with her in her wedding dress. She was beautiful. I did celebrate the occasion with her family and friends, who I knew well.

Although I was heartbroken for years and my inner hopeless romantic may never recover, it taught me a very, very valuable lesson. If you really want something or someone, you must risk it all and go all in. I knew this lesson intellectually, but I was scared to put it into practice at many times in my life.

A couple of weeks after the wedding, I moved back to Colorado. I didn't tell anybody about why I was coming back, only that I had decided to move back home. Consistent with all of my successes and failures in my life, my mom was there. She drove out to California to help me pack up, break my lease, and move back home.

I went on to be a lawyer in Colorado, defending companies when they got sued. I defended mining companies in Leadville when it became a Superfund site, and small employers when they were sued for wrongful discharge. The practice of law was interesting. I realized that people usually disliked lawyers until they needed one. I was a hired gun. When somebody needed an advocate to fight on their behalf, they hired me. I liked being able to help people solve problems that they were unable to solve on their own. I didn't like constantly being in the middle of a conflict, however. Even worse was when the attorney on the other side was unscrupulous or cared more about his or her pocketbook than resolving the conflict. Ninety percent of all cases settle. Many of these cases settle right before trial. I noticed that the bigger the conflict, the richer the lawyers became. The longer I practiced law, the more miserable I became. I felt a constant pressure to bill more hours, to make the firm more money. I billed clients forty hours a week, and that took fifty to sixty working hours per week to accomplish. The pressure to bill was intense. Add to that unscrupulous and unreasonable opposing attorneys, and I soon realized that practicing this type of law was just not for me.

During my years as an attorney, a long-time friendship with Kathy developed into a romance, then marriage, and we were about to have our first child. I knew that I had to make a change in my life. I was miserable as an attorney. If I was miserable working, I knew I wouldn't be the father I had committed to be. The pending birth of my first child was the catalyst for me to again swing for the fences and go after a dream I had conceived almost a decade earlier. I was going to pursue a career in business, follow my dream to be happy, and most importantly, be a good father.

In my research, I discovered that GE was world-renowned for training and developing some of the best business leaders on this planet. Further research led me to discover that GE had a business headquartered in Boulder, Colorado. I was living in Denver at the time, a forty-five-minute car commute from Boulder. They had an opening for an attorney position. I applied and was offered the position. My job was to read and edit piles and piles of paper contracts. I always had a stack of contracts at least two inches high, and sometimes as high as twelve inches. The work and reading was neverending. I read all day and all night. I tried using my lamp and magnifier trick, but the reading was just too much. Most days, my eyes gave out after eight hours of reading. I had to suck it up if I was going to make it, and I did suck it up.

In the Colorado winter, it gets light at about 7:00 a.m. and dark at about 4:30 p.m. I had to be at work in Boulder from at least 8:00 a.m. to 5:00 p.m. I hadn't told my boss or any coworker that I couldn't drive after dark, was legally blind in one eye, close in the other eye, and heading toward total darkness. I was afraid they wouldn't hire me or give me a chance. When six months of winter arrived, I started taking the bus to and from Boulder to work. I had to leave my house at 5:30 a.m. in the dark and walk to a bus stop. I boarded one bus, then transferred to another bus that took me to Boulder. When I arrived in Boulder, I had a short walk to the office. The evening commute was usually longer because of traffic, and I arrived home between 8:30 and 9:00 p.m. in the winter months.

It was a hard schedule to keep, but we made it work. I read contracts on the bus rides, and soon I was ahead on the contracts. It took six months of consistently working thirteen- to fifteen-hour days, but I was able to do it. After being with the company for eight months, I asked a VP to help me navigate into a business career and away from the law. I explained my dream of working in business, and I was also vulnerable and shared my eye condition with my boss. As it turned out, she had just battled cancer and was dealing with overcoming adversity in her own life. She gave me a chance and told me, "If you're as good as you think you are, the world will be your oyster. If you're not, we'll fire you."

That was good enough for me, and it began a decade-long career with GE. I spent four years at the Boulder business, rotating through different functions including Risk, Financial Services, and Marketing. Because I was performing well and viewed by the company as "high potential," I was offered another opportunity. I received a call one day from the GE headquarters in Connecticut asking me to move to Puerto Rico to be a Site Leader. As it turned out, it was a coveted expatriate assignment with lots of benefits and a compensation package beyond anything I'd ever imagined. Six weeks later, my wife, two children, and I stepped off of a plane, and we had moved to Puerto Rico.

The new job required me to have a new boss, and I was the first "gringo" with GE experience working at this operations site. I had to use all of my people skills—and develop some new ones—in order to be accepted. A few weeks after I arrived, my CEO visited and told me that either I had to turn the site around, or I was going to shut it down in twelve months. I was again at bat, and needed to swing for the fences. I didn't come all the way to Puerto Rico to put people out of work and dismantle a business. Quite the opposite—I wanted to enrich people's lives, create jobs, and leave a legacy that would long survive my tenure on the island.

My CEO also asked about my eyes. Somehow, she had gotten word that something was going on with my eyesight. I told her everything. She was so kind. She asked what I needed. I told her I couldn't drive at night and might need to take a cab to evening events. She said not to worry, and the company would pay for them. She asked what else I needed, and I said I might need a larger computer monitor or laptop with a bigger screen. She said, "Done! What else?" I said I didn't need anything else at the time. She smiled, and told me to do a good job.

In the next eighteen months, the Puerto Rican team and I turned the site around and made it into a Spanish Speaking Center of Excellence for that division of GE. After three years as a Site Leader, I was promoted to be the General Manager of GE Capital in Puerto Rico, a $400 million business. I spent another three glorious years in Puerto Rico working for GE. In total, I spent six years on the island, which were filled with hard work, long hours, and life lessons that have humbled me, inspired me, and left me in awe.

During my working years at GE, my eyesight continued to deteriorate. I had many things that I needed to learn to work through. Among them was learning to lead a large group of employees who I couldn't see. Part of the team I led was a call center with well over a hundred employees. I always tried to be a personable leader. I worked hard to learn names and glean information about people's lives and families. I wanted to know what was going on in my employees' lives. I believe that if you are human and compassionate to another human being when they are vulnerable, it is possible to change a life. I always enjoyed "walking the floor" and joking and laughing with the team.

My eyesight caused me problems, however. I wasn't able to see people's faces without getting uncomfortably close to them. It wasn't appropriate for me, as the leader, to be standing a foot away from an employee so I could see their face. At times, that caused me problems. I was always very friendly with everybody, mostly because I liked people. However, I also knew there were times when I encountered a co-worker outside of the office, and they saw me but I wasn't able to recognize them. I had countless occasions in my life where people smiled at me or waved to me, and I didn't see them and failed to respond. People thought I was being rude or aloof or intentionally ignoring them. I still faked the fact that I was legally blind at this point—and by faking it, I was offending people. I was scared that people might think differently of me, pity me, or discriminate against me if they found out I couldn't see.

It broke my heart when I crossed paths with employees and their families on the weekends, and I didn't recognize them. We might have had a deep and meaningful conversation on Friday, then I saw them and their family on Saturday at the shopping mall, and I treated them like I did any other person—just waving and saying hi. I couldn't see their face without being a foot away from them. I now know that my shame in hiding my deteriorating eyesight ended up hurting a lot of people's feelings, and I live with that fact daily. I learned to apologize quickly, as a result of these experiences. In fact, I grew to apologize freely for my mistakes, and perhaps this was a blessing of this difficult situation.

It seemed the less I saw, the more I relied on my listening and analytical skills. My jobs for GE required that I master numbers and financial statements. After all, I was working for a Fortune 10 public company that was known for delivering top- and bottom-line results at a consistent 10 percent year over year increase. I had to memorize and stay on top of my numbers at all times. In meeting after meeting, printed spreadsheets of numbers—financial results, key performance indicators, and daily metrics—were pulled out and discussed. The numbers were so small that I couldn't read them, even with a magnifier. I spent hours upon hours studying and memorizing numbers on my computer at the office and at home, so I was able to make decisions and participate in meetings where numbers were being evaluated. I was also trying to learn Spanish as a second language at the same time.

I was always drawn to a challenge. Most of the time, I was able to compensate for my failing eyesight with intelligence, quick wit, and a burning determination to succeed. In my working career, I noticed that the more consistent and better I performed, the more I was promoted to positions of increasing responsibility. The higher-ranking positions I attained were more strategic in nature. These positions required a person to think, have broad business experience, and be relentless in creativity and determination to attain results. There was less of a demand on tactical work that required eyesight, and more of a demand on my ability to use intellect, develop people, see opportunity instead of obstacles, capitalize on those opportunities, and lead teams to do the same. I think GE was a perfect fit for me at that time in my life—the company thrived on people who could see a vision and make it a reality while hitting revenue and income targets. The better you performed, the more flexibility you were given to achieve your results.

My personal life was also providing its fair share of challenges. Just a few months after arriving in Puerto Rico, one of my children, Sage, received a diagnosis that meant he was going to be different. Sage was two and a half at the time. His diagnosis was a stark reminder of my diagnosis of RP. Sage had gone through a battery of tests and evaluations which ended with my wife and me sitting in an office with a Pediatric Neurologist. The doctor said, "Sage, stack this block." Sage went running the other way and looked out the window. The doctor added, "Sage has autism." I remembered watching a movie with Dustin Hoffman and Tom Cruise called *Rainman*. I immediately dismissed my visions of Sage being a football star, and switched to Sage and I driving to Las Vegas to have a boys' weekend of playing cards, and winning a fortune . . . because the movie seemed to tell me that people with autism had amazing card-counting capabilities. When you get lemons, make lemonade . . . right?

"What does that mean?" we asked the doctor. He responded in a monotone voice, "Sage will have an IQ of about fifty, he will not be able to live alone, and I'd like you to read this book." The book was about how to take a child with autism to the dentist. Then he dismissed us from the office. We stepped outside and Kathy blew apart into tears. It was a replay of my diagnosis with RP. A doctor found something wrong, there was no cure. Then, he told us the future was hopeless.

Sometimes I think I was born with RP because God knew that my son would eventually be born with autism. He knew that I wouldn't give up on my life, and that would help me to guide my son to not give up on his life. How better could I have been prepared to guide a child who will live with struggle, than for me to have had my own struggle and work through it?

Consistent with most parents who receive an autism diagnosis, we researched everything, and tried a lot of things. We discovered there were a lot of well-meaning therapists and doctors out there, but nobody knew how to best treat autism. We had people tell us to give Sage daily injections of Vitamin B-12 and he would be cured. Others told us that if Sage took a regimen of twenty vitamins and supplements on a daily basis, he would "wake up" after a week or so and suddenly step out of the fog of autism. Then, there were the folks who insisted we put Sage into a hyperbaric chamber three times a day to cure his autism. And, there were numerous types of therapists from music, to art, to dance, to horse, to sound, etc. We settled on occupational therapy, speech therapy, and Relationship Development Intervention (RDI). The latter therapy was autism-specific, and was aimed at helping children with autism continue through the developmental life cycle, despite missing some stages and stalling out at different stages. Kathy and I became Sage's daily therapists. With long hours, we were trained how to work with Sage. We videotaped ourselves, then uploaded the videos to be analyzed in Houston, Texas. Then, we received feedback and coaching on how we could improve, and help Sage improve. It was a lot of work, extremely expensive, and worth every second and penny. We were fortunate to have people to guide us through this process, and help us maintain hope.

We had many nights and experiences where our hope was deci-mated. We just worked so hard and Sage worked so hard, and it still seemed like autism was winning. It was so heartbreaking when I lost hope. However, Sage always made a comeback from a downturn, and he again gave us hope and strength for a bright future. He was, and is, my biggest inspiration in life.

At the time, there were no therapeutic schools for children with autism in Puerto Rico, so Kathy and I partnered with Sage's occu-pational and speech therapists to start such a school. We had a meeting one evening on the outdoor patio at our home. My role was to help them develop an operating budget. This included developing a business model forecasting expenses and revenues, and deciding on the legal structure for the entity. Kathy was getting her master's degree in Public Administration and Nonprofit Management, and had significant experience organizing and executing fundraisers. She was also very involved in The Newcomers Club, a club for expatriate families who had recently moved to the island for work purposes. This group was fairly wealthy, and always had children's toys, books, and furniture to donate. The building for the school needed some sprucing up, and we all cleaned and painted. Our family ended up donating a big wooden jungle gym. The occupational and speech therapists were busy working toward certifications in RDI, and developing curriculum to become accredited as a school. I felt like I had to do something more to help support Sage's school. I'd given time, money, and a business plan, but that wasn't enough.

And, that was the inspiration for me to run the second marathon in my life, fourteen years after my first marathon.

9

Marathon #2

What happens in Vegas, stays in Vegas.

I knew that my college buddies, and most of my other friends, would contribute to a good cause, if they knew I would suffer. So, I told friends, family, and people I worked with that I was going to run a marathon to raise money for Sage's school. Well, my college roomies came through and coughed up some cash, as well as a host of other folks. I chose the Las Vegas Rock 'n' Roll Marathon in December of 2007. It was close to Colorado, so maybe I could cross paths with family, it was a fun city, and it was supposed to be a flat course. I also had a business trip in LA the week before, and I could stop over in Vegas and run the marathon on the way back to Puerto Rico. Everything seemed to be in order, except for one thing. I hadn't run in fourteen years.

In Puerto Rico, we lived on the same street for five years. We got to be good friends with everybody on the street. There were Puerto Ricans, Mexicans, Danes, and Americans. I was particularly good friends with a couple of guys on the street. We used to wash cars, sail boats, and have *Viernes* social (Friday happy hour) together. These two guys also walked together at a nearby track. I figured I had to start getting in shape for the marathon in three months. After all, I had been in Puerto Rico for three and a half years, and had been eating fried foods, drinking too many rum and cokes (pure sugar), and smoking cigars. I had put on twenty pounds in that time span, and I had a gut and an extra chin as evidence of all the starchy and fried food I was eating.

Holding Sofia in the Caribbean in 2006

I met the guys at the track one day after work, and I saw them briskly walking and chatting up a storm. I walked over and joined them. As we walked the straightaway, I tried to crack some jokes and join the conversation. Then, I realized how fast we were walking. I was getting winded, and I thought it best to stop talking if I wanted to keep walking with the guys. We came off the first curve and I was no longer talking, and focused on swinging my arms to help propel me forward. We finished the second straightaway, and I was sweating and not feeling good. By the time we finished the second curve and made it around the track one time, I was done. My friends kept walking and I made some lame excuse about having to go back to my house to do something. The guys said "bye," and I made my way back to my car where I sat in disbelief.

How could I be in such bad shape? I thought. I used to play football, wrestle, run track. Heck, I even ran a marathon, albeit fourteen years ago. This was my wake-up call. I was signed up for a marathon in three months. I didn't know how I was going to do it. I had to start training, serious training.

My serious training didn't start with instant high-mileage runs or high-intensity speed workouts. I just had to figure out how to not have a heart attack and consistently move my body. I kept going out to the track to do jog/walk sessions. They ranged in length from thirty to forty-five minutes. I tried to do them every other day consistently. It was hard, and my whole body hurt. I had met a friend, Jeff Sommer, who led another GE company on the island and he told me he ran four to five miles on Saturdays and Sundays. He lived by the beach, and I lived a few miles inland. He had invited me to run previously, but I had denied the invitation. I feared I couldn't handle that much mileage. With the marathon looming, I decided that I needed to accept my friend's invitation and join him for weekend runs. After all, if I couldn't handle four to five miles on Saturday and Sunday, how on earth would I be able to handle a marathon of 26.2 miles that was just three short months away?

I vividly remember the first time I went to Jeff's house for our first beach run. It was about 9:00 a.m. on a Saturday, after a raucous *Viernes* social with my neighbors the night before. I'm sure I still smelt of rum and coke from the prior night's festivities. It was heating up at about 80° and the humidity for that time of year was ninety percent. Jeff answered the door, smiling as he always did. Jeff is a kind person, very understanding. His smile always made me feel welcome, and his moderate voice always calmed me. Jeff had his shoes at the door and laced up. Before I knew it, we were off running. The first couple of blocks were an easy pace, and I remember thinking that it was going to be a good experience. That quickly changed when I suddenly tripped over a speed bump. In Puerto Rico, there are a lot of mini speed bumps in neighborhoods which prevent drivers from going too fast. These mini speed bumps are affectionately called *muertos*, or dead ones (aka road kill). I hadn't told Jeff about my eye condition, but realized that this conversation would soon be required. When I tripped again on the next *muerto* just one block away, Jeff laughed a little bit, and asked if I was still experiencing the effects of the prior night's libations at *Viernes* social. I opened up to him reluctantly and told him about my eye condition. He was really understanding, and every time we approached a speed bump from that time forward, he always warned me of the impending "dead ones."

As we approached mile one of the run, we snaked through beach neighborhoods, once in a while catching a glimpse of the sparkling and magnificent Caribbean Sea. Jeff is a great talker, but doesn't dominate the conversation. I was content letting him take the lead in talking as much as possible. I was dying just trying to keep shuffling. The heat and humidity, coupled with my hangover, was making me want to vomit. Jeff's shirt was drenched by mile two, then I noticed that my entire body was wet with perspiration and humidity. I didn't even understand or pay attention to what Jeff was saying. I was barely able to keep shuffling. I was really out of shape, and trying to get back into shape after more than a decade of neglecting my physical health was going to be hard work. Soon, we were at mile three, and I was unable to talk because I was breathing so hard. I think Jeff noticed I was hurting because he slowed his shuffle and stopped asking questions that required an answer. Rather, he told a story that I could just listen to.

At just under four miles, I had had enough. I told Jeff I had to stop and walk. I was a mess. Jeff, in his usual compassionate and kind style, didn't miss a beat and just walked at my pace. He kept talking as we walked, and I walked with my head hanging. I felt like a complete failure. How had I let myself get to this point? I couldn't even jog a few miles at a slow pace? How on earth was I going to run a marathon in three months? I thought about postponing my marathon run, but my son's school needed the money now. And, I knew that no matter what suffering I went through, my son and the other children who would attend the school suffered much more than I could ever imagine. So I decided to just train and do the best I could.

I ran every day as much as I could, then I walked as much as I could handle. Although I wasn't racking up a lot of miles, I was consistent. I learned later on in life and racing that consistency of effort toward a goal is my secret weapon to achieving success. Regardless of how bad I felt, how deflated my ego became, or how hopeless I felt, I just refused to quit. That philosophy in and of itself enabled me to accomplish many things in my professional and personal life.

As the marathon approached, I found that I was able to run with Jeff on weekends, and I became stronger. I slowed my drinking, fried food intake, and cigar smoking to near nonexistence. My weekly mileage had increased to thirty or forty miles per week. I thought it was possible I might actually be able to finish the marathon. And, as usual with Murphy's Law—what can go wrong, usually does go wrong—I had a big setback with two weeks to go before the marathon. There was an outbreak of dengue fever in Puerto Rico. Dengue is carried by mosquitoes, and causes its victims to be sapped of energy, bleed internally, and, in the worst cases, can cause death. I had become infected with dengue somehow, and I felt horrible. I couldn't work, had chills, and felt like I had a horrible flu. I went to *Clinica Las Americas*, our local urgent care, and they confirmed I had dengue. I was told the marathon was out of the question, and it would be at least a month until I was back to a hundred percent.

I had a business trip in LA right before the marathon and I planned to stop in Vegas to run the marathon and celebrate my mom's sixtieth birthday with her, then return to Puerto Rico. I told Mom that I had contracted dengue, and we both agreed to meet in Vegas as planned and just see how I felt on race morning. The next two weeks were torture. The strand of dengue I was infected with didn't require hospitalization, and I wasn't at risk of dying; however, I did feel like I wanted to die at times. By the time I flew to LA, finished the meeting, and met Mom in Vegas, I was exhausted. Mom and I talked over the situation, and decided since we were in Vegas and the marathon was going on, I might as well give it a try and see what happened. A lot of people had pledged money to see me suffer, so I was sure not to disappoint. I became excited the night before the marathon and dreamed that somehow I would be miraculously cured. Maybe I would even run fast enough to qualify for the Boston Marathon—every marathoner's dream. I always had this same dream as I was going into some big challenge. My dream was always that I would overcome whatever adversity I was facing.

On the morning of the marathon, I remember the gun sounding and I started running in the dark with fifteen thousand other runners down the Las Vegas Strip from the Mandalay Bay Hotel. There were so many lights on the strip, it seemed like daylight. One of my college roommates, John Gordon, agreed to come out and help me run until the sun came out. Ironically, this was the same guy who conspired to unscrew all the lights and move the furniture on me in college. The adrenaline from being around that many people at the race start, and the excitement of being in Las Vegas had neutralized the effects of the dengue. After running six miles of the course, the sun had risen high in the sky, and I was off the strip and in the neighborhoods. It was boring, there were no people cheering, it looked like any other city, and the residual effects of dengue fever started sapping my energy. I slowed down and walked quite a bit at aid stations. My deterioration was slow and steady until mile twenty—The Wall.

The Wall is where your body runs out of glycogen and has to switch over to burning fat as a fuel source. I didn't know about taking in nutrition while running, and I had depleted my body of glycogen. I felt my body revolting and cramping. First, my left calf cramped. Next, my right quadricep and hamstring cramped. Then I vomited. I was in serious trouble. I didn't know where I was at in Las Vegas, and I figured the only way to get back to my mom was to keep following the course. For the final six miles, my body felt like it was dying. I cramped, then stretched, then hobbled, then cramped, then lay down, then got back up somehow. When I wanted to quit, I thought about my son and the school, and I kept moving forward. Somehow, I was able to reach the finish line in a pitiful state.

I saw Mom smiling. I felt horrible, but I had gotten across that finish line. I hobbled over to an area that had a fence and lay down. As soon as I was on the ground, everything cramped up.

One limb after the other just kept cramping, and I was overwhelmed with pain. I didn't know what to do. I was convinced that the marathon distance could kill a person. I remember thinking that the body is just not made to run this distance—it's too far for a human. Then I remembered Uncle Ted. I remembered seeing his corpse-like shape shuffling around that track, having run over twelve back-to-back marathons in six days. How come he could do it at age fifty, and I was flat on my back dying after only one marathon at age thirty-four? Maybe it was the dengue? Maybe it was my lack of training? Maybe it was my mindset? Or, maybe it was all of the above, and several more things I hadn't figured out yet?

For the next week, I could barely move. Going up and down stairs was next to impossible. I was happy to have raised money for my son's school, but I swore I'd never run a marathon again. I had kids to raise and responsibilities to take care of. It wasn't prudent to risk my life pursuing silly running goals. What kind of insanity was this?

I was having a fight with the little devil of doubt we all have. It is that part of our mind that stops us from taking risks. That part of us that talks us off the ledge and prevents us from leaping to pursue our dreams. It is that voice that realists rely on, and idealists combat on a regular basis. I was beaten down physically and emotionally, and was vulnerable to doubt. I had first met this doubt character when I was fourteen, and an eye doctor told me to give up on my dreams of becoming a doctor or lawyer. I was strong then and able to ward it off. After the marathon in Las Vegas, however, I was battered, beaten, and every word *doubt* whispered to me I absorbed like a sponge absorbs water. My head was filled with negativity, hopelessness, and shame. I recognized this feeling from before in my life. These were the feelings I had when I had failed. *Doubt* attacked when I was vulnerable and weak.

Two weeks after the marathon was over, I was back in Puerto Rico and able to walk with just a limp. No longer was I moving like a robot. I was also feeling stronger mentally. Part of me was proud to have just finished the marathon. Another part of me felt elated that I had supported my son and a school that would help many other children in need of therapeutic services.

At the deepest level, however, I felt like I had unfinished business with the marathon. I had yet to do my best. Throughout my life, I was plagued with a feeling that I was second best, or not good enough. I always had something to prove, until I knew I had given everything I had, and held nothing back. I needed to be vulnerable, raw, stripped of pretense, and fulfill my mission with focused intensity. Strangely, I couldn't pinpoint what drove this desire to achieve. Was it because I never had the satisfaction of having my father's approval? Was it because I felt like damaged goods because I had been born with an eye disease that made me less capable in some people's minds? Was it because I was insecure on many levels because I am human? Or, was there some other reason that drove my desire to need to either give absolutely everything I had, or consider myself a failure?

I wanted to be in that top 1 percent of marathoners—one who could qualify for the Boston Marathon—and I knew I had yet to give my best performance at the marathon distance. I picked a marathon four months after the Las Vegas Marathon, and created a rigorous training plan with daily workouts on a spreadsheet. Four months later, I qualified for the Boston Marathon, beating the qualifying time by ten minutes.

Then, I discovered there were triathlons in Puerto Rico. In triathlons, the competitors were able to swim, bike, and run in one event. I went to Koishma, the one and only triathlon-specific store in Puerto Rico. I asked the owner, Javier Bosque, about triathlons. He explained everything to me. I asked when the next one was, and he told me there was one in four days on the other side of the island in Rincon, a famous surf hangout.

The devil of doubt popped up and started making excuses for me immediately. I explained to Javier that I wasn't the greatest swimmer. Javier retorted that I could doggie paddle it. Then, I told him that all I had was a mountain bike. He told me I could use that bike, or one of his bikes if I wanted. I told him I didn't have a place to stay, and he told me I could stay with him or camp out on the beach. I had no more excuses, and I also realized that Javier Bosque had dealt with *doubt* in the past in his store and life. This man knew how to go beyond conventional thinking, and his mission was to help people learn this lesson via the sport of triathlon. I went home that night and told Kathy that I wanted to do a triathlon. She was supportive. I told her it was in four days on the other side of the island. She was hesitant, but open to it as we didn't have any plans and it would be a chance for us to see another area of the island.

Before I knew it, four days at work had passed, and I was at the start line of the Rincon Sprint Triathlon, looking at the beautiful Caribbean Sea. Somebody said there were buoys in the water, and the swim course was a triangular shape. As I looked out, I couldn't see any buoys. Either they were really far away, or my eyes weren't good enough to see them. I asked some people at the start line if they saw the buoys, and they looked at me in disbelief. They pointed out to the ocean and said, *"Claro"* (sure, in Spanish). I had a big problem that I hadn't anticipated. I was about to start swimming in an ocean, away from land, toward a buoy that I couldn't see, and neither racers nor the race director knew about my eye condition. What would happen if I couldn't keep up with the other swimmers and I was doggie paddling by myself? *Doubt* reappeared at that start line, yelling into my ear to quit before I even tried.

Bang! The gun sounded, and everybody ran toward the water from the beach we were standing on. I ran too, somehow being consumed by this swarm of humanity. I saw people diving headfirst into the water and flailing their arms as they swam out to sea. I figured I should do the same. It felt like I was in a washing machine being hit by arms and kicked in the face by other swimmers' feet. I tried to swim, but felt like I wasn't moving anywhere. Soon, the washing machine had calmed down and I was feeling better about that. Almost all the other swimmers had left me in the proverbial dust. I couldn't see much as I lifted my head out of the water. Why couldn't I see? Was it foggy? Were my eyes going out right in the middle of this race as I was floating in the ocean? I rubbed my goggles from the outside. Nothing changed. I started hyperventilating with panic. Then I ripped the goggles from my head. I could see all of a sudden. *How was this possible?* I thought. I remembered seeing other people spitting into their goggles before the race and rubbing it on the lenses. I thought it was gross, but maybe they knew something I didn't, so I spit in my goggles and rubbed it around. The fog inside my goggles was gone. As it turns out, spit is a great defogger of swim goggles.

I tried to control my breathing as I floated in the ocean and daydreamed of sharks and manta rays swimming all around me. As I looked out to sea, I saw endless water, but I also saw an orange buoy in the not-so-far distance. This was turning out okay. Then, I turned 180° to see how far from shore I had swum. When I looked back at the land, I realized I was far from shore—very far from shore. I had never done an open-water swim. I couldn't touch the ground, and I suddenly remembered hearing about how rip currents could take swimmers long distances out into the ocean to their demise. I was back to hyperventilating and panicking. Then, I looked around and realized I was all alone. All the other swimmers were gone, and I was by myself. I had a tight-fitting compression triathlon top that was squeezing the air and life out of me. I ripped it off in one panicked movement. It helped, and I could breathe better. I knew I had to swim toward that buoy and turn left. That was the direction the other swimmers went. I couldn't see any other buoys, but I hoped I could swim long enough to bump into another buoy like I had with the first one. I had to doggie paddle as I was having a difficult time controlling my breathing. Was I going to fail, again?

Soon, I saw the second buoy. All I had to do was get to it, then turn toward shore. I couldn't tell for sure where on shore I was supposed to go; however, I could see a large dark mass against the backdrop of light-colored sand. I figured the dark mass was people who had gathered to cheer on their athletes as they exited the water. As it turned out, my powers of deduction were correct. I finally finished the swim and got out of the water in last place, only wearing my tiny triathlon shorts which were a couple of inches longer than a Speedo.

My kids ran to me with sunscreen, but I was too worried about how far behind I was. I jumped right on my mountain bike and started pedaling hard. After about fifteen minutes, I saw another biker, then another and another. I was no longer in last place. I also noticed that I was the only biker on a mountain bike. Most racers had road bikes, or what I knew as ten speeds or skinny-tire bikes. Some racers had these weird bikes with handlebars sticking directly out in front and they were in a strange biking position with their head down and back flat. I later learned that these bikes were called time-trial bikes and the biking position was very aerodynamic, enabling them to reduce wind resistance and move at very fast speeds.

I kept hitting potholes with my bike as I was going too fast for my eyes to observe the ground. It seemed like, as soon as I visually perceived a pothole, I was on top of it. By the end of the bike ride, I was exhausted and drained, but had managed to catch some people. I put my bike in the rack at the transition area and started running. I noticed something curious as I ran. I was passing people. People were walking and I was running, really running. I caught and passed many competitors. I felt alive and fresh as soon as I started running. By the time I reached the finish line, I had caught half the competitors. I hugged my family, and we all celebrated the finish.

As I lay in bed that night, I didn't care about having a panic attack during the swim, or being out of place riding a mountain bike, or the sunburn on my back that forced me to try to sleep face-down. All I could think about was the fact that, four days earlier, I was standing in Javier's triathlon shop in San Juan making excuses about why I couldn't participate in this race. And now, because I didn't let *doubt* have my ear, I had finished my first triathlon and had a medal to prove it. I was just an average Joe, with average athletic ability, and one year ago, I was terribly out of shape. I wondered what else I was capable of doing.

That night in Rincon, before I drifted off to sleep, I remembered seeing that Ironman race on television where Dave Scott and Mark Allen raced shoulder to shoulder in Kona, Hawaii. I never thought I was capable of an Ironman triathlon—a 2.4 mile swim, a 112 mile bike ride, and a full 26.2 mile marathon. *I'm just a human,* I thought. Then I remembered my conversation with Javier, where he took away and neutralized all my excuses. I thought about Uncle Ted who must have had this same experience many times when thinking about tackling his next big goal. That night, I decided to take on an Ironman triathlon as my next goal. And, four months later, I completed that goal.

As I continued working and pursuing these athletic goals, I noticed that I was getting stronger physically and mentally. I performed better at work and with my kids. However, my marriage was strained, and felt like it was falling apart. We found ourselves in deafening silence many times, with no words to say to one another. Over our ten years of marriage, we had grown apart. There was a lot of stress in relation to Sage's autism diagnosis, treatment, and what the future might hold for him. In addition, we had another child, Sofia, while we were in Puerto Rico. During the entire pregnancy and first two years of Sofia's life, Kathy was extremely fearful that Sofia might have autism.

I wasn't good at understanding this fear, and wasn't as supportive as I could have been. I approached the possibility of having another child with autism from the same perspective that I had approached life and my own diagnosis—if Sofia had a challenge, we would just have to overcome the challenge and help her have a successful life to be the best she can be. In hindsight, I wish that I had been more supportive and knew then what I know now about myself. I don't know if that alone would have kept the marriage together, but I do think I could have been more supportive to the mother of the three greatest gifts I have ever been given in life —Sierra, Sage, and Sofia (my children).

After six wonderful years in Puerto Rico, my work assignments were coming to an end. The company had asked me to consider other assignments in different parts of the mainland US; however, Kathy and I planned to divorce when we left Puerto Rico. Since we were both from Colorado, we decided it would make more sense for us to move back to Colorado to go through our family transition, since we both had family in the state.

10

Transition

To feel is to be human.

W hen we came back to Colorado, Kathy and I moved into two different residences. As we went through our divorce, I was hit hard and reminded of a promise I had made to myself. As I grew up without a dad, I had promised myself I'd never get divorced. I had failed in this promise to Kathy, my children, and myself.

As I returned to Colorado, the book *Born to Run* was just gaining popularity. The book was a true story about the author's experience of becoming an ultra-runner, a runner who runs distances in excess of 26.2 miles. Along the way, he developed a theory that the current shoe industry is causing more damage than good to runners, he took part in a crazy race deep in the Copper Canyons of Mexico that pitted the world's greatest running people against some of the best American ultra-runners, and he breathed life into a character named Caballo Blanco who was the genesis for this entire tale, because he happened to be at the Leadville 100 Trail Race one year.

I remembered that Uncle Ted had run the Leadville 100 Trail

Race during its inaugural years, when it was just a bunch of crazy people trying to see if they could survive running a hundred miles at high altitude. Leadville, Colorado is a tiny mining town in Colorado at ten thousand feet above sea level. It is known as the highest town in the United States. During the mining days, it was a very rich, hustling and bustling little town. After the mines closed down, the town became very poor and rundown. In an effort to bring tourism and money back to the town, a couple of ex-miners invented the Leadville 100 Trail Run. They were trying to create a race with a "holy shit!" appeal factor—a race that would be the most difficult thing around. Something for extremists. Something my Uncle Ted would want to do.

As I read *Born to Run*, reflected on Uncle Ted, and went through a painful divorce, I decided that it was my time to try the hundred-mile run. I was also running as a means of dealing with a lot of emotional pain at this point in my life. During the year I got divorced, I turned forty. On January first of that year, I decided to run forty miles—my own personal "Resolution Run." It would also be the longest distance I had ever attempted to run. On that morning, I wrote the following letter to my children, and gave each one of them a signed copy. This run signaled a beginning of something wonderful, as I was going through a tragic ending of something that should have been equally as wonderful.

January 1, 2010

Sierra, Sage & Sofia,

Good morning and HAPPY NEW YEAR!!!

Today is the first day of a new year, a new decade, and a new beginning. Every day gifts you a new opportunity to enjoy the most precious gift we all share—LIFE. My deepest desire is that each of you learn to live every day, every minute, every second to the fullest.

Don't hold on to things that happened yesterday—they are already gone and you cannot change the past. Likewise, don't worry about what may happen tomorrow, it hasn't occurred and you are only wasting precious time in your life if you choose to spend it worrying. Live life for today, this minute, this second. Appreciate each other, the flowers, the snow, the warmth of the sun on your skin, the chill of the winter wind across your bare face, the sound of an unseen animal moving through the brush, the scent of cows on the way into Greeley. :)

Most of all, remember to sing, dance, laugh, love and LIVE.

I run today, to LIVE.

See you tonight and have a wonderful trip with Mom to Greeley and Ault. Please tell everybody "Hola!" for me. I am with all of you in spirit!!!

XO,

Pops

I had bought a GPS watch that measured the distance for me. I wasn't in a hurry to cover the distance. I just wanted to see if I could run forty miles, one for each year of life I had lived. I wanted to go beyond anything I had attempted before. I leapt, and again trusted that the net would appear. My plan was simple. Just run around Denver until my watch signaled forty miles. I didn't have a route planned, and figured I'd be able to stop into convenience stores for food and drink if I got hungry or thirsty. Those people in the book *Born to Run* were able to do it, so I figured I could do this.

I took off trotting, and the day was beautiful with a clear, blue Colorado sky. The temperature was perfect for running, a brisk 50°. I ran and ran and ran. After about four hours, I had covered a marathon's distance and was entering uncharted territory. I remember when I got to thirty miles, I was pooped. I was forced to walk, and didn't have any energy. There was a 7-Eleven on the corner, and I bought a Mountain Dew and Snickers bar. Before I knew it, I had energy and felt like running again, so I did. I had some people honk at me and yell my name, and I waved back. I couldn't see who was honking and yelling at me. I later learned that they were long-time friends who just happened to be on the same street as I was running. The last ten miles turned into a walk and jog routine. I ran until I needed to walk. Then, I walked until I felt like I could run. This was to be my dance—and it would become a very familiar dance I returned to in future runs of extreme distances.

Before it became dark for the day, I was at forty miles and just a few blocks from my house. I was ready to swing for the fences again and register for the Leadville Trail 100. When I logged into the race website, I saw the Leadville Trail 100 Run race registration page, but I also saw something called an "epic challenge." I read further and learned that this epic challenge was called "Leadman." The Leadman Challenge was a series of five events that took place over the summer in Leadville. The events included the Trail Marathon in June, a fifty-mile trail run or mountain bike race in July, the hundred-mile mountain bike race and 10K run in August, and concluded with the hundred-mile trail run the weekend immediately after the hundred-mile mountain bike race. I said to myself, *Go big or go home*, and I registered for Leadman, not having a clue of what I had just gotten myself into. Heavy training and spending time alone in the mountains was the perfect medicine for the low point I was going through as my divorce trudged on.

I had major life changes as I became a single parent. Previously, I was the breadwinner with a wife who stayed at home and cared for the kids. Now, if I was going to be the father I had committed to being, I had to learn how to do all things and become two parents for fifty percent of the time.

As the divorce ran its course, I spent days on end in the mountains of Colorado. I had a driver's license, although my driving was restricted to daytime only. I discovered Pikes Peak fairly early in my Leadville training. Pikes Peak is a mountain whose peak is over 14,000 feet above sea level. In Colorado, many people set a personal goal to climb all "fourteeners" in the state, numbering fifty-eight total. Pikes Peak has the longest trail to the top at thirteen miles, and the most elevation gain from the bottom to the top of the trail at just about 8,000 feet. The Pikes Peak Marathon is run every year, and considered the most difficult marathon in the nation because of the trail and elevation gain.

I figured this would be the perfect training ground for my upcoming races in Leadville. I had to teach myself how to run in the mountains, and navigate trails with limited eyesight. In addition, the altitude training would force my body to adapt and create more blood cells in order for my body to oxygenate itself. I quickly learned that mountain running was going to be a big challenge for me. My eyes can discern contrast very well—dark on light, or light on dark; however, when the trail was dry and the sun was at my back, it was virtually impossible for me to see a root or rock or obstacle in the trail. I tripped, fell and twisted ankles all the time. Sometimes I was so frustrated, I just walked and stopped running altogether. After thirty minutes of walking, I usually started running again because I was frustrated with going so slow.

The other major problem I discovered were the shadows cast on the trail by the canopy of leaves. On sunny days, of which there are on average three hundred every year in Colorado, I was constantly moving between dark and light environments. It takes my eyes a long time to adjust to each environment. For example, when I enter a dark restaurant, it is virtually black for me. After about ten minutes, I start to see some things around the lights. I can see the lights, but have great difficulty making out what the lights are illuminating. I am unable to see faces, so I "look" at voices when talking with somebody so I don't seem socially awkward.

This inability for my eyes to quickly adjust between dark and light environments caused me a lot of problems when running trails. Within a one-mile segment of trail on Pikes Peak, you could move in and out of these two lighted environments no less than twenty times. If I stopped and waited for my eyes to adjust every time the environment changed, It would take twenty-four hours just to get up the mountain, never mind the hardest part—getting back down. In Colorado, the rule on fourteeners is that you must reach the summit by noon. If you're not at the summit, you should turn around and start going back down the mountain. I heard many stories of storms coming over the top of mountains in the afternoon, and lightning and hailstorms stranding hikers and runners on mountains. It isn't uncommon to hear a rescue helicopter on Pikes Peak when a bad afternoon storm rolls in.

On one of my first ascents of Pikes Peak, I made the mistake of assuming the weather would hold, and I was slow going up the mountain. I had taken my time letting my eyes adjust to the dark and light environments. I was way past the turnaround time at 2:00 p.m. when I summited the great mountain. As soon as I reached the top, I could see to the other side and it was dark with fierce black clouds. I filled my water bottle at the gift shop at the top and started sprinting back down the mountain. The first three miles descending from the summit are fully exposed, as it is above the tree line. At that altitude, trees don't grow and there is only small groundcover sprinkled between rocks and dirt.

Within five minutes of running as fast as I could downhill, I was overtaken by the storm. There was a mixture of hail, snow, and 40 mph wind gusts. Before I could get one mile down the mountain, I was in white-out conditions. All I was wearing was a short-sleeve tech shirt and shorts with a pack that had a water bladder and some food. I was in trouble. I was unable to make out the path and was lost. I considered trying to find a big rock to hunker down behind and let the storm pass; however, my body was wet and chilled at this point. I would surely get hypothermia if I stopped moving. I considered turning around and going back to the top of the mountain, only one mile away. I could seek shelter in the gift shop and surely somebody would drive me down the mountain when the storm passed. I had a problem, however. I couldn't see one foot in front of me. My eyes were blinded by all the white. I couldn't see anything except white. I decided that descending was the better option. I thought that if I could get to the tree line, some two miles away, I would have protection from the worst parts of the storm and not be as much at risk of a lightning strike.

I screamed, *"Help, help! Anybody!"* I heard nothing in response. I started going down the mountain, feeling the trail and rocks with my hands. I inched my foot forward, then slowly slid the next foot to catch up. I didn't take a foot off the ground for fear I would step incorrectly and cause a fall or ankle twist. I had no phone reception, and no way to call for help. I was moving very slow, at about one mile per hour. I still believed that as long as I could get to the tree line, I would be able to get down the mountain, or at least hunker down and survive the storm. I wondered if I would be in this predicament if I didn't have my eye condition. I knew I would have ascended faster, and I would have been farther ahead of the storm. I also thought that good eyes would have enabled me to see a bit more so I could discern the trail. Regardless of what could have been, I wasn't in that situation. I scrambled to find a way back down the mountain safely and make it back to my kids. I screamed again in panic, as the storm became fiercer and marble-sized hail pelted my naked skin. *"Help, help!"*

A black shape was off in the distance. It seemed to be moving, but I couldn't be sure. Everything was white except for this fleeting black object that was often invisible due to the snow and hail. I kept screaming. After some time, the black object seemed to be getting closer and closer. It was a person. I felt some comfort, but then I felt some anxiety. I was freezing, having been in a snow storm at 13,000 feet for over an hour at this point. My skin was wet and cold, although adrenaline was keeping me from sinking into a cold, whimpering heap. The person came closer, and I explained that I was legally blind and couldn't see. He was a day hiker from Chicago, and was turning around as the storm came over the top. He had heard me during my first bout of screaming, and thought I might be in trouble, so he headed toward me.

It was obvious at this point that my eyes were deficient for these conditions. This man from Chicago could navigate the trail in these conditions, but I was helpless due to insufficient eyesight. I held his shoulder, arm, and hand, trying to navigate the trail through the storm. When the snow and hail let up, we trotted as best we could, until the next blast of snow came and we were forced to slow to a snail's pace. After about an hour of this dance, we had reached the tree line. Although it was still snowing and gusting, the storm was much less intense at 11,000 feet in tree cover than it was at 13,000 feet being fully exposed.

This stranger probably saved my life, and I had overextended myself and not fully understood that I had limits due to failing eyesight. I told him that he needed to head down, and he agreed. He said he was hiking and had plenty of water, food, and protective clothing. I knew I had to run in order to get to my car and make the hour and a half drive home before darkness closed in on me. I sprinted down the mountain, still fueled by adrenaline and distancing myself from thoughts of vulnerability and what could have happened. That day, I learned an important lesson about remaining calm in the midst of a storm. If I could maintain calm internally, I would be able to use my intellect, ingenuity, and creativity to overcome whatever conditions were taking place externally. This was true in running, and in life. I had plenty of opportunity to improve, and I worked on this daily for the remainder of my life.

I had many other training runs on Pikes Peak in preparation for my summer in Leadville in 2010. I learned how to run through shaded areas without slowing. I learned how to roll with an ankle twist so I didn't injure myself. A friend had told me about how he started wearing weight-lifting gloves when trail-running. This protected his hands from getting cut up and having gravel get lodged in his palms when he fell. This trick has saved me many times, as I fall often.

As I continued running Pikes Peak, I learned that mountain running requires nimble feet. Short, quick steps enable you to climb and descend safely and swiftly. If you have the choice between one or two steps, take three. As I ran more and more trails, I learned there are "lines of descent"—the paths of least resistance. When running extreme distances on trails, economy is important. There is no reason to step over or onto rocks if there is a smooth path around the obstacle. The former approach only saps energy. I learned to follow the "water path"—the smoothest path down the trail. Usually, this path was cleared of rocks, roots, and tripping hazards. It is impossible to run trails and avoid all hazards, but it was important to me to minimize these hazards.

Every time I fell, it was very hard to get back up and keep going. It was like taking a punch to the solar plexus, and it was demoralizing. After weeks of forcing myself to run on trails, I began to enjoy the experience. I looked forward to the freedom and nature I experienced, instead of fearing the obstacles that my failing eyesight wouldn't detect. I developed confidence slowly that I could overcome whatever might come my way. I pushed myself, but not over the edge. I was in a very delicate place, needing to build endurance and confidence for the Leadman events, but I didn't want to push too hard too quickly and feel like a failure due to a poor experience on the trail.

The more time I spent in the mountains and on the trail, the more at peace I was with myself and my situation. I ran for hours, getting lost and getting found in the woods. My family was melting down, and I returned back to Denver after these day-long ramblings to an empty house, devoid of life and my children. I had defined myself by my family, and now it was gone. I ran, and ran, and ran. My grief was different than any other grief I had experienced in my life. I was going through all of the stages of the grieving process from moment to moment—anger, sorrow, bargaining, denial, isolation, and acceptance. When I could be with my children, I made the most of it. I felt guilty, and still feel guilty for the struggle my kids experienced as a result of living in a broken family. More than that, I feared that somehow I might have inherited a genetic defect that would render me a derelict father. I couldn't let my kids down. They were, and continue to be, everything to me.

As I ran, I thought about the changes I needed to make in my life. No longer would I be able to accept high-paying, high-power, high-responsibility jobs. I had a choice of having a nanny raise my kids while I worked all day and night, or I could find a flexible job, which would probably be lower paying, and have the flexibility to be a father when I did have my kids. I decided that my kids needed a father much more than I needed a big paycheck. For the year following our return from Puerto Rico, I didn't work, and dedicated myself to my kids, training for Leadman, and self-care.

My Leadman experience was disappointing. I was trained and able to take on the trail marathon that went from 10,000 feet in Leadville to the turnaround point at Mosquito Pass which topped out at 13,186 feet. Next, I chose to tackle the fifty-mile mountain bike race, instead of the fifty-mile run. This presented a lot of obstacles. I could climb fine, as my cardiovascular fitness was good. However, I couldn't descend like other riders. I couldn't see where I was going, and I wiped out, crashed, flipped a couple of times, and even hit a tree during that fifty-mile mountain bike ride. I also got lost a lot as I wasn't able to see route markers when travelling so fast.

I was able to finish the race; however, I only had twenty-six minutes to spare. I was near the very back of the pack, and I knew mountain biking wasn't my thing. I had one month to get better on the bike before the famed hundred-mile mountain bike race. My brother had a friend who had attempted that ride and was a veteran mountain biker. He told my brother pointblank, "That ride is going to kill Jason." I didn't know if he meant it figuratively or literally, but I was going to give it a try.

As with all these Leadville events, my mom went to support me. As I waited nervously in a sea of fifteen hundred mountain bikers at the start of the hundred-mile mountain bike race, I heard that all-too familiar voice whispering in my ear. The *doubt* was back, and she was singing to me. The gun sounded. I had twelve hours to ride a hundred miles in the mountains of Colorado on an out-and-back course which had total elevation gain of 11,000 feet and included a 3,000 feet climb to the turnaround point at Columbine Mine.

As I went out on the course, I knew I had no business in this race. I wasn't a mountain biker, and, like the fifty-mile ride, I continually crashed. I was making the time cut-offs by mere minutes. If a rider was unable to reach a certain checkpoint by a certain time, they were removed from the race and not permitted to continue. The thought was that the rider wouldn't have a chance of finishing the race in the allotted time, and the risk of injury increased significantly as the rider might not have the skills necessary to be out on the course. In my case, I didn't have the skills to be out on the course.

By the time I reached the halfway point atop Columbine Mine at over 13,000 feet, I was spent and ready to quit. I had been on the course for just over six and a half hours. My chances of getting back to Leadville in five and a half hours for an official finish were somewhere between slim and none. I remember turning around, and, as I descended from Columbine Mine, I heard another rider crying who was trying to descend the mountain. I stopped and asked her what was wrong. She said she was scared—all the other riders were yelling at her to go faster, and they careened around her, causing her to have near accidents with each pass. I knew this woman's pain, as I had experienced this in the first fifty-mile mountain bike race I took part in just a month before. I told her I would ride behind her and block for her. She could go as slow as she needed in order to descend the 3,000 feet to a more manageable part of the course. Meanwhile, I followed her and blocked other riders from riding her wheel. She was grateful, and we worked our way down the mountain together.

This actually worked very well for me since I was following a rider who was descending at a safe speed for my eyesight. Neither one of us crashed on the descent. When we safely reached a flat section, I asked if she was okay. She said she would be fine and thanked me for helping her. I sped off, peddling as hard as I could, hoping to somehow reach the finish line under the twelve-hour cutoff. When I did reach the finish line, the sun was setting, and my time was thirteen hours and eight minutes. The finish line was being dismantled and nobody was around to bring me in. Then, I saw Mom screaming my name. She was worried about me, and was about to start running the course backward to find me.

Her actions spoke volumes of her love for her child. We hugged and knew my dream of an official Leadman finish was done. The next day was Sunday, and the fourth event of Leadman, a 10K run. I decided to participate as I was in Leadville for the weekend anyway. I ran, and was surprised to struggle badly on the run. My legs were destroyed from the prior day's hundred-mile, thirteen-hour mountain bike race. I finished the 10K, but had no idea how I would finish the hundred-mile trail run the very next weekend. I didn't train for the next five days, and focused on rest and recovery. Before I knew it, I was back at a start line in Leadville for the final event of the series—the Leadville hundred-mile trail run.

The race began on Main Street in Leadville at 4:00 a.m. At that time of year, the sun doesn't rise until 6:30 a.m. All of the other Leadman events took place in daylight, so I didn't need to confront my night blindness. The hundred-mile run was different, however. I had pre-run the first part of the course in the daylight, and knew I wouldn't be able to do it without a guide in the darkness before sunrise. There were just too many rocks, scree, and roots around the single track trail around Turquoise Lake, a magnificent jewel. Sunrise here is like no other on earth.

During the packet pick-up for the run, I had inquired about having a guide help me at the beginning of the race until the sun rose. The staff looked at me like I was crazy. I explained that I had bad eyes, and they laughed at me and said I should speak with the race doctor. I found the race doctor, and explained I had retinitis pigmentosa. At least the doctor knew of the condition, but he questioned me and asked, "What are you doing running this race?" I told him I was competing in Leadman and this was the final event. His facial expressions contorted even more than before. I didn't realize at the time that the doctor was really asking, "Why is a person who can see barely anything running the Leadville 100 Trail Race?"

The doctor found me fit enough to run, and I suppose he assumed that if I somehow made it through the preceding four events with my bad eyesight, I would have enough eyesight to not be a danger to myself in the run. The doctor directed me to a gruff old man in the corner and said, "Ask Ken if you can have a guide until the sun rises."

I walked over to this mountain of a man. His hair was long and gray. His face was weathered, leather-like, and bore the characteristics of a hard life of over six decades. His body, however, was muscled like a thirty-year-old, he was well-proportioned, and he just looked *tough*. This was the famed Ken Clouber, one of the founders and current directors of the race. I introduced myself, explained my eye condition and my night blindness, and asked for an exception to have a guide at the start of the race. Ken looked me straight in the eye and said, "Everybody will have headlamps . . . there's gonna be plenty of light." Then he turned his back to me as if to say go away, quit whining, and stop bothering me.

What I didn't realize at the time was that no other blind people had ever attempted to do what I was doing. As far as I know, I was the first and only blind person to even attempt a hundred-mile race. What I was doing was inconceivable to the doctor and Ken. This course had a DNF (did not finish) rate of more than 50 percent for sighted runners. Competitors DNF for a variety of reasons. For some people, the altitude suffocates their bodies until they can barely move, then they vomit and are usually debilitated with a paralyzing headache due to lack of oxygen. For others, the huge mountain climbs and descents beat runners' bodies into painful submission. For still others, the inability to eat and drink consistently while running causes their forward progress to halt due to insufficient fuel supplies. Finally, some are just too slow and don't make the time cutoffs to finish the race. Regardless of all these factors, Ken and the doctor seemed to be telling me with their eyes, "You don't have a chance, buddy."

In the Leadville 100 Trail Run, you are permitted a "mule" for the last fifty miles. That means the runner can be accompanied by one person who can run in front, beside, or behind the competitor, and she or he can carry supplies such as water, food, and clothing. I was asking to be treated differently than any other runner by having a guide to follow during the first thirteen miles of the race (which would take roughly two and a half hours to complete). I wouldn't use this person to carry anything for me. The person would only be there so I could follow their feet, not get lost, and avoid falling. Because neither the doctor nor Ken actually used the word "no," I took that to mean I could have a guide. The fact is, I didn't have a choice but to use a guide. I wanted to keep my plan as far under the radar as possible, since I didn't want to upset Ken and be disqualified from the race. He looked like the kind of guy whose bad side you did not want to be on.

At 4:00 a.m. on race morning (Saturday), Ken fired his shotgun into the air to start the stampede, as he had done for the preceding thirty years of the race. He would also fire that same shotgun at

10:00 a.m. on Sunday morning, to signal the end of the race, some thirty hours later. As the start gun sounded, I had one of my college roommates, Jay Flynn, guiding me. One of the knuckleheads who had lovingly helped me to laugh at my eye condition in college was now leading me through the first couple of hours of the Leadville 100 Trail Run. Jay wasn't a trail runner, and actually not much of a runner at all. He was in so-so shape, and the altitude had inflicted headache pain akin to a migraine on Jay. He was moving slow, and I had been cautioned by many veterans of the race about going out too fast. Many of the people who don't finish hundred-mile races go out too fast. Their bodies cannot sustain the speed, then as biological changes occur with bodily fuel consumption, the body can revolt in fits of lethargy, nausea, diarrhea, bloating, etc. When I first considered running an ultra-distance race (longer than a marathon), I asked a veteran ultra-runner how he ran so many ultras. His response was simple, and spot-on. He said, "You start slow, and get slower."

Jay and I were following that advice. I soon realized that Jay wasn't moving slowly because of his headache or fitness level; he was moving slowly because he didn't know how to guide me. I had no advice for him, because this was the first time I had ever been guided by another person. I had always run on my own in training, and I never ran in the dark. I wore the brightest headlamp I could find, and I pointed it directly at Jay's feet. I tried to step wherever Jay stepped. There were reflectors on the back of Jay's shoes. It was easy to see when Jay picked up his feet to avoid a rock, stick, root, log, or railroad track. Jay was also calling out everything, and kicking rocks out of my way so I wouldn't accidentally step on one of them and twist an ankle. We were shuffling, barely faster than a quick walking pace. People were ducking off to the side of the trail vomiting their morning breakfast. I couldn't see what was happening, but I could hear it all around me. I was frustrated trying to get Jay to jog faster, or even run. Jay spoke to me in a calm voice, and reassured me that we had plenty of time, and I could run faster when it was light out.

After five miles of this, we were at the Turquoise Lake single-track trail. This trail is riddled with obstacles, uneven surfaces, and moderately technical areas. Jay was having a tough time with his foot placement, not having trail-running experience. This was also the location of a big traffic jam on the race course. There was only enough room for one person on the trail. If we tried to pass anybody, I'd be bushwhacking while we passed. The same was true for people who were passing us. Jay was very concerned about me tripping. In my opinion, he was overly concerned with me falling. He took my safety personally, and if I tripped and fell, he would take that as a personal failure on his part. Jay had attended West Point for a year before receiving an honorable discharge. His discipline, loyalty, work ethic, and friendship are second to none. This was a far cry from our college days where we had fun with my blindness. Now, each of us were working together in tandem to overcome it.

After a couple of hours, the sky seemed to be getting lighter, the sun making its way around our giant orb called Earth. After about fifteen more minutes, I started to faintly be able to make out the trail. Jay guided me too slowly around the lake. We were passed all the time by other runners. I hate getting passed. Finally, I felt like I could go at it alone. We were still a couple of miles from the checkpoint, where my mom, kids, and crew would be waiting. I was ready to run, and I told Jay I needed to get going. Jay agreed, as he knew his lack of experience on the trail was forcing us to move at an unusually slow pace. He stepped aside, and I took off. Because I'd moved so slow for the first two hours, I was well-rested and almost sprinting. I felt free and knew I had over twelve hours of sunlight to run independently. It was so freeing to start running again. The joy of unbridled loping on a mountain path was exhilarating . . . then it happened.

I tripped. Before I could react, I found myself flat on the ground in a pile of rocks. I had badly twisted my ankle. It was the kind of ankle twist where you end up in the fetal position, trying to hold and protect your ankle as you rock back and forth, as if that would somehow numb the pain. This wasn't good for my race. I was barely over ten miles into the Leadville 100, and I didn't know if I'd be able to stand on the ankle again. Runners passing me asked if I was okay. My pride was hurt pretty bad, so I just waved them by, and insisted that I was fine. I tried standing, but was unable to put weight on the foot. Could I hop the final ninety miles? Were Ken and that doctor right to not believe I could complete this race?

That thought was all I needed to get me moving forward. I grabbed trees to lean on as I stepped on the sprained ankle. I played with a galloping running technique that enabled me to put as little weight as possible on the ankle. After a while, I played with moving back to my normal running gait. I was limping, but able to move forward. I did this for the next thirty minutes, and suddenly found myself at May Queen, the first aid station on the course. I found my mom, kids and crew waiting and cheering for me.

That morning, I discovered how vulnerable I was because of my eyes. Before that experience, I had existed in well-lit environments or had plans how to cope with and overcome the symptoms of my failing eyesight. The fact is, I didn't know what help I needed to run this type of terrain under the cloak of darkness. And, no other person had attempted running this type of technical trail who was legally blind. I was an explorer heading into the great unknown, not knowing what lay ahead of me. I just had to believe that somehow I would be able to overcome whatever adversity confronted me. Nighttime always had an uneasy grip on my psyche. It was as if that was the lair of the *doubt* that had attacked me so often in life.

I was able to run with a limp, and it seemed to be getting better the longer I ran on it; at least, that was what I tried to convince myself of. I winced, scrambled, and hobbled my way to the Twin Lakes aid station, forty miles into the race. Then, I crossed a raging river, holding onto a rope to keep from being swept away, and took on the 3,000-foot climb to the top of Hope Pass for the next five miles. Once at the summit, I began a 2,500-foot descent to the fifty-mile turnaround at the Winfield aid station. I felt horrible, and my ankle was only getting worse. My legs were like rubber from the prior week's hundred-mile mountain bike race. After taking down some nutrition that included watermelon and a peanut butter and jelly sandwich, I turned back to Hope Pass and crossed it again, climbing 2,500 feet on the Winfield side, then descending 3,000 feet and crossing the river a second time before arriving in Twin Lakes.

The sun was setting by this time, and I was still a couple of hours ahead of the time cutoff, but my pace was consistently slowing. I picked up another guide to help me as I headed off into the darkness with my headlamp, feeling beaten and battered. I was sixty miles into this beast of a course, and it was getting the better of me. The night was very difficult. I pointed my headlamp directly at reflectors I had placed on my guide's ankles. The concentration required to stare at my guide's feet to follow and detect objects on the trail was mind-numbing. I was going crazy in my own head, my ankle throbbed, and my body was being battered step by step into submission.

By mile 83, I had enough. The "grim reaper" or "the sweep" caught me. Leadville has race volunteers who sweep the course on ATVs. They ride the trail to ensure the course is clear at the back of the pack. It's an efficient way of rescuing runners who were too foolhardy to stop at the last aid station, or became injured and unable to continue moving forward. I was walking a few steps, then had to stop and catch my breath. I was hallucinating and saw the light from my headlamp slowly fade to black. I asked my guide for fresh batteries because my headlamp had died. He told me, "Jason, you're hallucinating. Your headlamp is perfectly bright." I pointed my head where I thought his reflectors would be and the area slowly became brighter until the light seemed to be back to full strength. The volunteers explained that I could try to continue on, but I only had thirty minutes to try to cover five miles to the next aid station. I was barely moving, and knew that, even in my best shape, on road and in the daylight, I'd struggle to achieve that distance in that time. I cried, knowing that I had failed.

After a couple of minutes of weeping, I realized my predicament and was thankful to have volunteers ready and able to take me back down. I was becoming hypothermic at 11,000 feet atop Sugarloaf Mountain, and my ankle was badly injured at that point. My dream of even an unofficial Leadman finish was dead. My race was over, and it was okay for me at that point. I was in too much pain.

My guide was Scott Gordon. Scott is an amazing ultra-runner, having completed Leadville eleven times, finishing in the top ten, and he finished runner-up at the Hardrock 100. Scott was gracious to me in my defeat. He said, "Jason, you never gave up. You came back on your shield." I think that meant I went into battle, and didn't stop until I had "met my maker". Scott explained that I had pushed to the edge. I had gotten an opportunity to look inside myself, and knew that, even though I thought it was over, I could still keep pushing. Scott explained that it was very rare for any ultra-runner to truly reach this point of delirium, exhaustion, and determination. Scott had reached this point during a solo Rim to Rim to Rim double crossing of the Grand Canyon in June. The fifty miles of distance didn't enable Scott to see the edge, but the scorching heat at the bottom of the canyon and lack of fluids had put Scott in a delirious and dangerous crossroads with his own mortality. He made it out of that situation, and I could feel Scott's respect for the torture I had put myself through.

But the shame of not finishing the race was overwhelming. I had dragged a hoard of people, including my kids, my mom, my aunt who lost hearing in one ear during the event, and friends from out of state, to follow me on this pipe dream through the Rocky Mountains of Colorado. Instead of us being victorious and celebrating, I was happy to just be off the mountain, in one piece and in a warm aid station. I felt like I had let everybody down. I felt like a total failure. It was hard to accept what had happened. As my crew talked to me, their sleep-deprived faces were adorned with smiles and positive, encouraging words. I hadn't failed in their eyes. It seemed as though I had endured a torture that they were happy to see concluded.

I think we all would have liked to have gotten to the finish line, and the suffering must have been difficult to witness. I mentally replayed that race over and over again for the next year, until I could get back to the start line. I vowed to complete that race which had defeated me. In the next three years, I toed the start line at the Leadville 100 Trail Run, and I finished the race three consecutive

11

Misunderstood

It's hard to appreciate a sunset when you're hiding in the closet.

After failing at Leadman in the Summer of 2010, I joined another Fortune 100 company as the Vice President of Global Core Operations, and shared an assistant who helped me with administrative matters. In my last five years at GE, I had the support of a full-time administrative assistant and relied heavily on this person to help me manage e-mail, which was difficult with deteriorating eyesight. I always asked this person to keep an eye on my inbox for important messages that needed immediate attention and response. There were times when lack of sleep, stress, or eye strain would prevent me from being able to read e-mails and spreadsheets. I was hesitant to share my eye condition or its symptoms with prospective employers until I had an offer in hand, as I was concerned they would label me "disabled" and I wouldn't be considered as competent for the roles I was pursuing.

In my new role, I received over three hundred e-mails a day from all parts of the world. The work never stopped, as it was always daytime somewhere in the world, and my internal and external customers needed my help. In order to fulfill my responsibilities, I often found myself on conference calls at 4:00 a.m. and 10:00 p.m. with people on the other side of the world. I was the proverbial road warrior when I had to travel. I tried to pack as much into a single trip as possible, in order to do the work required of me and be successful as a single parent.

After six months on the job, the company asked me to accept even more responsibility. I accepted the responsibility and was now handling the work of five VPs who had been laid off, and whose job duties had been consolidated into my job. I knew I was smart enough to handle the challenge, I was creative enough to come up with solutions, and my decade of experience and training at GE had fortified me into a "business machine" when it came to driving results in difficult conditions. I needed one additional support, however. I needed a full-time assistant to help me scan all the additional e-mails I would receive. I thought this was a reasonable request to accommodate my failing eyesight, and the fact that I was handling the work of five executives at this point.

When I was first hired, I explained my eye condition to my hiring manager and HR, but I also explained that I didn't want to be treated differently than other employees. I bought a larger monitor that I could use in my office, and I advised that I couldn't drive at night. However, my hiring manager accepted a payout and early retirement six months into my tenure at the company. I advised my retiring boss, new boss, and HR that I needed a full-time administrative assistant when I accepted the additional responsibility. HR advised that I needed to verify my eye condition with an eye doctor. This was strange to me as I had already advised HR and my previous boss of my eye condition, and I was performing at an exemplary level. I accommodated their request and made an appointment with an eye doctor. I hadn't been to an eye doctor for fifteen years, as I hated the experience of being examined and told I had an eye disease, and I was going blind with no hope for a cure. It was just too depressing to have to endure year after year. The doctor wrote a note to my employer confirming that I had retinitis pigmentosa, and I was legally blind, including tunnel vision with visual acuity of 20/200 and night blindness.

I felt emotionally defeated again, after having to endure another prognosis of hopelessness. I was deep in denial of going blind, and having to hear again what I feared most caused my bottom to drop out. I took the note to HR and let my boss know that I had provided the requested information. I thought that would be the end of the matter and I would continue on with the heavy workload I had agreed to take on. I was surprised to learn that a written diagnosis of RP and confirmation of legal blindness wasn't good enough to grant my accommodation request to augment my half-time administrative assistance to full-time administrative assistance. In my opinion, if doing the job of three VPs justified half-time admin support, adding an additional two VP jobs coupled with being legally blind surely justified moving my admin support to full-time. The HR manager handed me a packet of double-sided papers, with about fifty questions about whether I could do my job, and asked me to have my eye doctor fill out the packet of information. Her tone was curt and concise. I was confused, as I had been at the company for a year at that point, I was performing extremely well and had my level of responsibility doubled after my first six months with the company. Needless to say, I didn't stay with that company much longer.

This was the first time in my life I felt singled out because of my eyesight. It was the situation I had feared for my entire life, and why I had pretended to be sighted for three decades. I was afraid I wouldn't be given the same opportunity to achieve what others could, because society seemed to have lower expectations for blind people or because reasonable accommodations wouldn't be granted.

I took some time off work and resumed running. Eventually, I accepted a role as an Executive Director at a nonprofit that helped children with autism. I had been told by the board that the organization was primed and ready to grow. On day two on the job, I realized that the organization was in severe financial distress and would close in six months if drastic changes weren't made. After advising the board of the situation, and obtaining their approval and direction to make significant changes to save the organization and make it sustainable, I went to work. After two years of hard work at this nonprofit, saving the organization, expanding the operation to help more children in Colorado, and creating a sustainable financial operating platform for the organization, I moved on. It was bittersweet to leave. I was personally invested in the success and mission of this organization, as I knew at a very personal level how important this life-changing therapy and education was to children living with autism. I would have loved to have stayed there for the rest of my working years. However, as I had learned from my years with GE, there is always a time when you must step aside in order to permit the organization to continue its forward progress.

I had continued my running endeavors while I was in these positions. I ran hundred-mile races and more to raise money for different organizations including a Denver homeless shelter (Christ Body Ministries), a foundation that was working on a cure for blindness (Foundation Fighting Blindness), and an early childhood school for blind children (Anchor Center for Blind Children). I also ran to support the nonprofit organization I worked for. At the suggestion of my VP of Development, I agreed to compete in a three-day race in Arizona for my nonprofit. This was a timed event, a different kind of race than I'd competed in before. I had previously only competed in distance events, where I ran a set distance and tried to record the fastest time. In a timed event, you tried to run as far as you could in a set amount of time.

I was reminded of Uncle Ted when I first saw him competing in a six-day race on a one-eighth-mile track. I ran my race around a one-mile loop in Arizona, starting on the morning of December 29th and finishing on the morning of January 1 the following year. The race was appropriately named Across the Years. I quickly learned that the faster you ran, and the less you slept, the more miles you were able to accumulate. At the beginning of the race, I was mid-pack. By the end of day one, I was in the top ten. At the end of day two, I was consistently in the top six. And, at the end of three days, I had completed 205 miles which was good enough for third place. It was also good enough to raise over $7,000 for my nonprofit. The race was grueling and painful, and a totally different experience, having to learn about handling nutrition, sleep deprivation, pacing, and injury prevention while racing for multiple days on end. The complexity was much different, and more, than a hundred-mile race, and I loved it for that reason.

Whether I was turning around and saving a sophisticated business operation in Puerto Rico, consolidating global operations from Denver and developing strategic plans and key performance indicators for the first time, saving a financially unsustainable nonprofit organization, or running a long-distance race, I was able to adapt to new situations and solve whatever challenges confronted me. I seemed to have the ability to be unintimidated by the unknown. I actually thrived in jobs and experiences where I was asked to leap into the unknown and figure things out as situations unfolded. It was a skill and quality that made me unique. I didn't need certainty to feel comfortable. I felt constrained by the normal, routine and mundane. I was attracted to the complex, difficult and newness of an experience—whether it was a job, athletic endeavor, or personal relationship.

I attribute this ability to adapt and function in new environments to what I have experienced and learned as a result of going blind. My blindness was actually not a curse, it was a blessing. As my eyesight deteriorated, I had to continually adapt in order to continue on. At one time in my life, I could read a newspaper, then I needed reading glasses to read it, then I needed to use a computer to enlarge the text, then I needed to have the computer read it to me. These adaptations occurred as my eyesight deteriorated. Likewise, independent living changed. I went from being able to see things in kitchen cabinets and drawers, to not being able to see in these areas because of restricted tunnel vision, decreased visual acuity, and the weakened ability of my eyes to perceive light. Cabinets and drawers were just too dark to see anything, which meant I needed everything in my house put in an exact spot so I could find it.

My glasses, cups, plates, spaghetti noodles, cereal, chips, silverware, junk in the junk drawer, clothes, etc. all had to be in their place. When I was alone in the house, I couldn't see well enough to find items if they weren't in their proper location. My kids had to make significant adaptations to my deteriorating eyesight. When I was alone, I could easily keep things organized. However, when my kids were home, they might unknowingly put dishes in the wrong place, or my clothes in the wrong location. This caused me a great deal of anxiety when I was alone and not able to find what I needed when I needed it. It was difficult for my kids to understand why I had become so rigid in this area of my life. My deteriorating eyesight left me feeling out of control, and I had to go to extremes to maintain control where I thought I could.

While I was at the nonprofit, I continued to feel different because of my eyes. After receiving the offer but before accepting the position, I advised the board of my eye condition per my usual practice. They seemed accommodating, and again, I brought my own enlarged monitor for my computer. As with my experience at other jobs, I continually had coworkers make comments about the fact that I had such a large monitor. When I tried to explain I had poor eyesight, people would often respond, "So do I." I didn't feel the need to explain to people that I was suffering from a degenerative eye condition for which there was no cure, I was legally blind, I didn't want to be treated differently because of my eyes; and, in fact I purchased the monitor with my own funds. Instead, I just chalked it up to human curiosity, embraced the sting of the comment, and focused on doing my job.

My board president knew about my eyes, but he liked to communicate by e-mail. I had administrative support who would help manage my work e-mail, although he often would also use my personal e-mail for communication purposes. Sometimes, I missed messages to my personal e-mail from him. On one occasion, he had invited me to his home for dinner with him and his wife. I never saw the e-mail in my personal e-mail, and thus, never responded. After three weeks of not receiving a response, he brought up the incident, apparently wanting to know if I was blowing him off. I re-explained my eye condition, and that I use the eyesight I have very strategically during the day, as it might not last all day. In this case, I used my eyes to complete my job, and if they became too strained to be functional after work, I sacrificed managing my personal e-mail inbox for the day, or week, or whatever. I'm not sure whether he believed me. I was so good at faking being sighted, people just didn't believe I was actually legally blind.

I remember being at an annual gala fundraiser for the nonprofit one year. We had invited many dignitaries, including a former U.S. Secretary of State and his wife. I had spoken with this family previously, and they were exceptional people with huge hearts for our organization, and humanity in general. Apparently, I had looked directly at the wife and not acknowledged her as she waved to me from across the room. The fundraiser was held in a dark ballroom with hundreds of people. In this type of environment, I can't see much of anything, unless a person is one foot away from me and I am talking to them. I could usually recognize their voice, and the conversation could help me deduce who they were. The wife of the dignitary thought I had purposefully ignored her, not acknowledged her wave, and she was upset with me. Thankfully, a coworker of mine explained my eyesight to her so she understood. As my eyesight deteriorated more and more, and my ability to fake being sighted was also deteriorating. It was only a matter of time until something would have to give. My ability to fake it in the working world was coming to an end, and I knew it. I just had to accept it and, again, step into the unknown.

12

Finding Faith

Faith /fāTH/ noun - complete trust or confidence in someone or something.

I was raised in a strict Roman Catholic family, and felt like I was force-fed structured religion. In my college years, I rebelled and moved away from Christian beliefs to be more of a "spiritually aware" person who did good because that's what we are supposed to do. All of this changed on November 12, 2011, at 3:00 a.m.

I was living in Denver, Colorado at the time and was divorced. My kids were with their mother on this particular night. I loved to decorate my home with lights, ornaments, and inflatables for the holiday season. In 2002, I won the inaugural house decorating contest for my neighborhood. In 2011, I decorated my home with a couple of twelve-foot inflatables, one of Frosty and two of Santa, one riding a motorcycle. My fence was lit with LED lights, and the bushes, columns, and my entryway were exquisitely illuminated with a mix of soft white and multi-colored lighting. I had even braved a 25-foot ladder to put lights on the rain gutters to complete my Griswold-like masterpiece. The finishing touch was a six-foot homemade wreath which was adorned by hundreds of red mini-lights nestled in plastic faux pine clippings. I was proud of what I had created, and so were the neighborhood kids. People used to stop in front of my house just to view the decorations. I loved the Christmas season, not because of the religious aspects, but because of the joy and happiness that seemed to be so readily shared during this time of year.

On the evening of November 11, 2011, a cold front and windy storm had overtaken the city. By 3:00 a.m. on November 12, the wind had beaten my inflatables into submission. They were literally flapping in the wind, so I decided to go outside and check on them to ensure they weren't torn. They were all deflated, and the electrical cords had become unplugged due to the whipping wind. If their safety strings hadn't been staked into the ground, the entire inflatable would have been blown blocks down the road. I plugged the inflatables in one by one. The last inflatable I plugged in was a twelve-foot Frosty the Snowman. My home is a corner lot, and I have a street light that faintly illuminates the area around my home. Because Frosty was white, it was easier to see than the other inflatables which were darker in color. In its deflated state, Frosty was slumped over with its head on the ground. I traced the cord with my hands and connected the plug and the extension cord. I heard the whir of the fan come to life, and I knew Frosty would soon be standing upright. I carefully shuffled backward so as not to trip in the dimly lit yard. What happened next is unexplainable.

As I turned to look at the inflating Frosty in the dim light of the overhead street lamp, I was awestruck. I saw the inflatable come to life from a slumped-over position of lifelessness, to standing erect with its arms outstretched. At that moment, I felt something. I started crying uncontrollably. All I could think of was Jesus on the cross, then rising again from the dead. At that instant, I knew that Jesus wasn't a fairy tale. Jesus wasn't like fabled characters such as the Easter Bunny or Tooth Fairy, and not just another person who walked the earth like Moses, Cleopatra, or George Washington. Jesus was the son of God. Jesus was God, who walked on this earth. Time as we know it as well as our calendar is based on the birth and death of this man.

As I cried, I fell to the ground, overwhelmed with emotion and not even knowing what I was feeling. I made it inside after a considerable amount of time. I remember lying in my bed, being overwhelmed with what I had just discovered and accepted. It was much more than an intellectual experience. Everything that I was mentally, spiritually, physically, and emotionally had been affected by what I had experienced. I have been very reluctant to share this story with people, as it just doesn't make sense to me intellectually. Also, if I heard this story from another person, I would probably think they were off their rocker. When I was a skeptic, I would have probably thought the teller of such a tale was ripe for a one-way ticket to the cuckoo house.

I know what I experienced, and it was real. I share this experience as part of this memoir, because it truly changed my life and was the pivotal factor for what eventually happened to me.

For some reason, watching Frosty inflate at that moment at that particular point in my life made all of the above snap into place for me. I invited Jesus into my life at that instant, and I dedicated the rest of my life to God. Whatever God wanted for me, I was willing to accept. It was a wonderful feeling to have this breakthrough. Many things that I had struggled with in my life now made sense. I knew why it was so important to help others. We are commanded to love each other. We are supposed to help the poor and less fortunate. Being wealthy shouldn't be our goal. And, I had often heard the saying, "It is easier for a camel to fit through the eye of a needle, than it is for a rich person to get into Heaven." I never realized that saying came from the Bible. I also never knew that the saying, "What does it profit a person who gains the world, but loses his soul?" also came from Biblical scripture. The more I read, the more I was astonished.

This section of my book isn't intended to be proselytizing. I realize that each person has their own journey of faith and belief. And I'm not here to pressure anybody to believe anything. I have learned that faith is a choice. Truly believing in the unknown, and that for which there is no evidence, is very scary. What if we lived our entire life because we believed in something, and when we die we discover we were wrong? What if we *don't* believe in something, and when we die we discover we were wrong? What if we lived our entire life because we believed in something, and when we die we realize we were right? We are all blessed with free will and the ability to choose what we want to believe.

For me, it's scary to talk about the unexplainable things I have experienced. I have been ridiculed for my belief system, and my approach to life has significantly changed since having this experience. Previously, I rarely discussed God and Jesus with my children. Since this experience, I explained to my children my beliefs and why I do the things I do. If I am having a conversation with a stranger, and I am asked about my motivations for being a good community citizen, I ask them if they really want to have that conversation. When, and only if, the answer is "yes," I share the Frosty story and what I have since learned from reading the Bible and growing in my faith.

As I talked about this crazy experience with close friends, one of them referred me to a book by Bob Buford called *Halftime: Moving from success to significance*. The book was spot-on for my situation. It told a familiar story of how people chase a dream of success in a material world for much of their lives. For some lucky people, they actually achieve material and societal success well before the age of retirement. For some of these folks, they realize that material success really is a false summit, and not the true goal. They realize that material success, the accumulation of wealth and power, is hollow and insignificant in and of itself. The book explores ways to move one's focus to improve and gain meaning by contributing and giving which leads to *significance*.

Buford notes that many corporate executives who have experienced this "Halftime" phenomenon in their lives, had a profound faith experience like the one I had. It was nice to know that I wasn't alone. However, I really didn't know what to do next with my life, and my wish was that I would one day receive a letter from God telling me what I should do. I would willingly open that letter, read the instructions and pour myself into whatever God wanted of me. The problem was, the letter never came. Also, despite what the movies showed, I never heard God's voice. I also never had dreams where angels talked to me and gave me some divine message from

God. What was I supposed to do with this new found faith in Jesus, the son of God? I pondered this question for days, weeks, months, and years. All the time, the amazing feelings I had during the Frosty experience were fading. I still believed, although I was frustrated about what I was supposed to be doing.

And then, it happened and my question was answered.

13

Hitting Rock-Bottom

It is darkest just before the dawn.

I n May of 2014, I left my last paying job at the nonprofit. After a couple of years of hard work there, it was time to turn the organization over to a new leader. I decided to take the summer off and spend time with my kids before starting to look for another job. My kids and I spent the summer by the pool, visiting the zoo (one of my favorite places), and my mom and I took a road trip together to Yellowstone and Glacier National Parks. I finally felt like I was getting my energy back and recharging my batteries. I didn't do a significant amount of running, or attempt any major races during that time. I was running mostly for fun, and not really training to compete.

I was able to obtain a driver's license with the help of a licensed optometrist. I have never been able to pass the eye exam at the department of motor vehicles (DMV). I always had to get a form from the DMV, have my eyes examined, and find an eye doctor who would sign the form and say it was safe for me to drive. The eye doctors would never permit me to drive in the dark, as I have severe night blindness. Once I had the form signed, I had to pass the written test, and take a driving test to prove that I was capable of driving safely with a visual impairment.

During that summer, I drove into the Colorado mountains to pick up my girlfriend from one of her races. The race was the Georgetown half-marathon which went from one small mountain town (Georgetown) to another small mountain town (Idaho Springs) along a frontage road which paralleled the Arkansas River and I-70. We met at a gas station in Idaho Springs which was central and made it easy to locate one another. She had a tough run, and wasn't feeling that great. We had plans to go to Winter Park, Colorado for a quiet weekend and enjoy some relaxing time together. I loaded her up and got her comfortable for the forty-five-minute trip deeper into the Colorado mountains.

I drove through the small town, navigating the narrow streets en route to the entrance ramp for the interstate. In these small towns, many main streets can barely fit parked cars on both sides of the street and still permit two-way traffic to flow. The town was crowded with all the racers and their supporters, so I drove carefully, tapping the acceleration and brake pedals of my car many times. I encountered an intersection with a four-way stop so I came to a full and complete stop. I waited patiently for my turn to proceed through the intersection. When it was finally my turn, I looked both ways and checked mirrors to ensure there were no bikes or pedestrians overtaking me. Then I slowly tapped the gas pedal. Just as I entered the crosswalk, something darted in front of my car. A father, mother, and two children ran at top speed right in front of my vehicle as my car was accelerating. It felt like I was inches from them as I slammed on the brakes, and the vehicle came to an immediate halt, whipping my girlfriend's body into the seatbelt as it locked to hold her in place.

The family laughed and finished their sprint to the other side of the street, unharmed and untouched by my car. They waved at me, seemingly unfazed by the experience, and went about their business as if nothing had happened. I, however, was far from unfazed. I was shaking and overcome with nerves. All I could think about was the fact that I looked directly where they came from and failed to see them. It was possible that they weren't there when I looked at the corner where they originated their dash, but it was also possible that my eyes failed to observe them standing on the corner.

I was overwhelmed, and a million thoughts raced through my mind as it played out scenarios where the family wasn't so lucky, and ambulances with EMTs performed life-saving procedures on the family. Both of my hands gripped the steering wheel, and my knuckles were totally white due to the rigor with which I was gripping the wheel. I needed to breathe, to become unfrozen, and stop my legs from shaking. I didn't even know if I could continue operating the vehicle. All I could think about was, *What if I had unknowingly driven into that family?* The ensuing and underlying thought that was tearing me apart was centered on whether my eyes had deteriorated to such a point where it was no longer safe for me to operate a vehicle.

I knew my eyes were getting worse. I was told that my retinas would die from the outside in, causing me to experience tunnel vision. It happened so slowly over decades, I didn't even realize that it was happening. When I was younger, I had my peripheral field tested, and I had blind spots here and there. The fact is, many people have small blind spots where their eyes don't perceive an image. During a recent visual field test, I discovered that my retinas had deteriorated on the periphery, and I had no peripheral eyesight. My eyes were only able to see what was directly in front of me. It's like looking directly through two cardboard toilet paper roll cartons taped together. I am told that, as the retina deteriorates, it would seem like I was looking through two straws, then two pin holes, then I would see nothing.

I am terrified to go blind.

I'm scared of the dark. I'm claustrophobic. I've had claustrophobia attacks when I've been in strange places that are dark and I'm disoriented and can't find a light switch. This used to happen a lot when I would travel for work from one small European hotel room to the next, on minimal sleep. I remember the terror of being all alone in darkness. The only strategy I had to solve my panicked situation was to feel the walls for a light switch, and try to calm my breathing so I wouldn't hyperventilate. Eventually, I would find a light switch, and voila, I was okay again because I could see and understand my surroundings.

What would happen when flipping that light switch would no longer take away the darkness? What would my world be like? How could I survive? Did I want to survive?

As I calmed my breathing in that small mountain town after the near accident, I looked at my girlfriend and casually said, "That was a close one." I tried to brush off the incident as if it was nothing. It had shaken me to the core. I don't think she even realized what I was going through, as she was beat up from her run and I was trying hard to fake like things were okay. Things definitely weren't okay, and this was the beginning of a downward spiral that would eventually break me into thousands of tiny pieces.

After a short two months of contemplating what had happened at that intersection that day, I decided that I was no longer safe to drive a vehicle. As I had done with all major life announcements, I needed to let my kids know about my decision to stop driving. I took them to Buffalo Wild Wings to talk to them, as I had done when I changed jobs, or a girlfriend entered my life, or something significant had happened. As we sat down on the patio of Buffalo Wild Wings and ordered a feast of wings, I spoke.

"You guys know about my eye condition and how it is getting worse."

"Uh huh," they mumbled as they chomped on the tiny morsels of spicy chicken.

"Well, I decided that I need to stop driving," I said nonchalantly.

The kids didn't seem to be affected at all and they just kept eating. Then, my oldest asked, "When are you going to stop driving?"

"Now," I responded.

Time seemed to stand still. Everybody stopped chewing, and you could have literally heard a pin drop. It was like a bomb was exploding in each of their heads as their mouths stopped chewing, their faces changed to blank stares, and they were unable to process the information I had just shared. My son Sage broke the silence and asked, "How are we getting home?"

All of our lives changed dramatically and instantaneously when I stopped driving. I didn't know how to use public transportation, and it wasn't financially viable to take taxis everywhere. I had no plan for how I would get the kids to and from three different schools, nor did I have a plan for how I would grocery shop for a house of four people. I had no idea how this would impact whether I would be able to work, given that public transportation to some areas of Denver can take up to two hours one way. I hadn't thought about how this would affect my kids' experience of living with me 50 percent of the time, and whether they would want to be with me if we really didn't do anything but hang around my house on the days when I had them. I hadn't thought about how I would be able to maintain a relationship with my girlfriend who lived twenty-five miles away. None of this factored into my decision. I just knew it was time for me to stop driving.

I remember one occasion shortly after I quit driving. My youngest daughter, who was eight at the time, had been invited to a birthday party. We needed to get her friend a gift, and our neighborhood Target always had a good selection of decent-priced gifts for this age range. Like it was no big deal, I told my youngest daughter, "Let's go to Target and get a gift." My daughter asked me, "But how are we going to get there?" I told her, "Let's ride bikes." She erupted into tears, saying, "I'm scared to ride my bike." I calmly explained that we would just have to learn some different ways of getting around because I had stopped driving. I was doing the best I could to help her adapt to the change that we were all going through. Then, she astutely said, "But Dad, it's snowing!"

I felt less than human and like a failure for being insensitive to how my eye condition was impacting my children, and the ones I loved. I tried to just deny and ignore what was happening, but my denial was no longer effective. I finally had to face what I feared most in life. The darkness was upon me.

The more time I had alone, the more time I had to think about my failing eyesight. I tested my peripheral eyesight by closing one eye and looking straight ahead at a specific object. Then I extended my arm out to the side and would point one finger and wiggle it. I slowly moved my arm and wiggling finger toward the object I was looking at until I could see the wiggling finger. Then I would do the same test, but bring the finger in from the other side, the top, and the bottom. I then did the same test for the other eye. I was shocked to learn how little I could visually perceive. I sat in silence for hours on end, wrestling with my emotions and anxiety. I felt alone and like nobody cared or could understand me.

My biggest question was, how I would work? I had very high-level and high-paying jobs that were extremely competitive to get. How would future employers view a blind person? Would I be shunned and forced to endure the same "verification of lack of eyesight process" that I had experienced at the last public company I had worked for? I know it is illegal to discriminate against people because of disabilities, but the fact is, it happens. Would my needed accommodations be viewed as unreasonable and burdensome? Could I be open about my blindness, or did I need to continue hiding it and faking being sighted in order to earn a living? I had heard horror stories of blind people not being able to land jobs for multiple years. After some research, I discovered that 70 percent of blind people are unemployed and live on disability income. In fact, at this point in my life, the federal government had sent me a letter saying that I was "permanently and totally disabled" because of my poor eyesight and eye condition. Because of this, I was able to receive social security income and gain health care coverage through Medicare. I wasn't working and according to my income level, my earnings were below the federal poverty level. What had happened to my life? Was I going to lose my house? Would I lose my kids?

My once-jovial spirit and enthusiasm for life was slowly sapped away, and darkness descended on every aspect of my being. I found myself glued to my bed, staring at my ceiling. I wasn't showering. All I wanted to do was sleep. I had no enthusiasm or desire to talk to anybody. I isolated myself and withdrew. I didn't return phone calls from friends or family. One of my college roommates, Jay Flynn, even went so far as to call my mom and leave me messages threatening to show up on my doorstep if I didn't return his call. I felt hollow, as if nothing mattered. It was as if the knot in my balloon of life had become untied, and my life had deflated as I lay limp and lifeless in my bed. One day in bed became two, then three, then a week, then two weeks, then three weeks. I smelled disgusting and was unclean. There was nothing to eat in my house. When I had my kids, I did the bare minimum, and wasn't being a true father to them. I was a liability. I wasn't necessary. I was headed toward a very unhappy ending and spiraling deeper and deeper. I felt so empty.

After weeks of being unresponsive, Mom showed up at my house and came into my bedroom. She sat on the side of my bed, petting my head. I could see the despair in her face. There was nothing she could do for me. What I was experiencing was beyond her pep talks, or words of encouragement, or challenges to be courageous. She suggested that I needed professional help from a psychologist. I agreed, and asked her to help me find somebody.

In two days, I found myself sitting in a psychologist's office. The office had a recliner and a couch, just like I had imagined it would. The psychologist was named Marty, and he stood about five feet, four inches, had gray hair, and a welcoming voice. I remember that first conversation like it was yesterday. He asked me about ten questions, to all of which I responded "yes." It was obviously a checklist for diagnostic purposes. He told me I was depressed. In my head, I responded, "No shit; that's why I forced myself to get out of bed after three weeks, shower, and show up in your office on the other side of town." But I said nothing. I listened. Marty added that he wanted me to start taking medication. At this point, I spoke up. I had never believed that life's ills could be cured with a pill, or that a night time infomercial held the secret to losing weight or whitening teeth or developing the ability to speed-read massive amounts of text. My mom had taught me that hard work and determination were the correct and consistent ways to achieve goals.

I told Marty that I wanted to explore other options of dealing with my depression before jumping straight into medication. I think he was startled by my vigorous response, which was at a much higher volume than my previous lethargic responses. Marty sat back, and took in my statement. He said, "There is another thing we could try." I waited on his every breath, and wanted desperately to know what else might work.

Marty went on to say, "If you can exercise to the point where you are panting heavily four times throughout the day, we might be able to avoid the medication." I asked, "Are you saying I need to exercise four times a day? And when I exercise, it needs to be vigorous enough so that my breathing and heart rate is elevated?" Marty responded in the affirmative. I told him that I liked to run, and at this point I had graduated to ultra-running (running distances longer than the standard 26.2 mile marathon). He explained that vigorous exercise causes the body to produce and excrete certain chemicals and hormones that directly combat the chemicals that cause feelings of depression. Apparently, Marty wanted me to do this consistently throughout the day so I didn't slip back into a depressed state, and get stuck. He said we could try that approach, and see how it went.

The rest of our hour was spent getting to know each other. Marty asked me a lot of questions about myself. As I explained my situation of being a single father, unemployed, living on social security, not driving, and going blind, his expression and tone seemed to wane to empathy, and at some points it felt like pity. I knew the situation I was in was rough, but I never thought about how all these factors had converged on me all at once.

I had hit rock-bottom. All of the education and work experience I had worked so hard to develop didn't matter one bit, as I didn't work. All of the running successes I had didn't matter as nobody was calling me to run with them, and I didn't really didn't want to run with other people at that point. My fun and jovial sense of humor and parenting style didn't matter, as I was empty, unenthused, and really snappy with my kids. My relationship with my girlfriend was being strained significantly and I wasn't able to adequately explain to her how I was suffering. I could foresee that my savings and financial security would dwindle to nothing, I would lose my house and I didn't know how I would care for my kids. All I could see in life was the worst-case scenario.

The day after the appointment with Marty, I started running again. It was short distances at first, and I gradually built up. As I ran, I cheated and didn't do it four times a day. I just made sure that I was on my feet for one to two hours per day, spread throughout the day. If I ever felt like I was getting down, or thinking negative, I put on my running shoes and bounded out the door. This running wasn't like the running I had experienced previously in my life. Before, when I ran, I tried to go fast. I tried to push to the edge. I tried to make myself suffer, as if that suffering somehow would forge me into a stronger person. The running I was doing for my plan with Marty was just running. There was no purpose, no race to prepare for. It was the simple act of putting one foot in front of the other, and I ran because, when I wasn't running, I felt empty and unworthy of love. I also had to learn a new way to get around town since I wasn't driving. I decided I would just run wherever I needed to go. That could be a one-mile jaunt to Home Depot, or a six-mile trot to my mom's house, a fourteen-mile meander to my counseling session, or a twenty-six-mile venture to my girlfriend's house. Wherever I went, I ran.

Because I had hit rock-bottom, I constantly thought of another place where I knew many people were experiencing the same feelings. When I first returned to Denver from Puerto Rico, my neighbor had invited me to volunteer on Friday mornings at an inner-city homeless shelter—Christ's Body Ministries. A group of about ten retired men had pulled together and committed to fund, cook, and serve a pancake and sausage breakfast every Friday morning for Denver's homeless population. The group regularly donated money to buy food and supplies. Then, on Friday mornings at 7:00 a.m., the first volunteer showed up and started mixing pancake batter and cooking sausage. As more and more of the group arrived, the work area in the kitchen came to life. People talked, laughed, and worked hard to serve and joke with people who are truly less fortunate.

They prepared pancakes and sausages, and stored them in large foil pans to remain warm until they were served. This wasn't a cook to order operation; it was cafeteria style. We needed to be prepared to start serving at 8:30 a.m. sharp, when hundreds of very hungry people crowded the line, wanting to put something into their barren bellies. I loved the energy of this group of guys. Everybody seemed to come from a different walk of life. One of the guys was a successful attorney at a high-powered law firm who just walked away from it all one day. Another was a retired school administrator who had worked his whole life helping kids, and now was working for a local airline cleaning planes so he could get travel benefits. Another owned his own landscaping and snow-removal company, and he regularly organized service trips to Haiti and South America to build schools and orphanages. Yet another was a writer, who was writing a book about people with unique and interesting stories. On the side, he was a meditation guru and traveled the world instructing multi-week Buddhist meditation seminars. Then there was a writer and college professor, an engineer at a large defense contracting firm, and so on. This group was very eclectic, but they were also very kind, in the truest sense of the word. There was no ego in this group. These men were all about serving others. I was inspired every time I would go and help out.

My favorite part of the pancake breakfast was to speak with our "customers." I discovered that a lot of homeless people feel dehumanized and are just trying to survive. Each one of them has undergone and experienced extreme and dire hardship. Some have been abused, raped, and worse. Many have varying forms of mental illness. And yet others are just like many people in suburbia who lived a charmed life as a middle-class citizen, until some unexpected crisis intersected their life and they suddenly found themselves without a roof, without their kids, and on the street. These were the people I could relate to at this point in my life.

I had spent almost every Friday morning at Pancake Breakfast when I was going through my divorce, and then when I was between jobs, and now I was back when I was at my lowest of lows. After a few years of volunteering, I wanted to do more to help the shelter. I asked the Executive Director, Pastor John, what more I could do to help. The shelter had a volunteer opportunity on Thursday mornings for showers and laundry. On weekday mornings, the shelter opens its doors at 10:00 a.m. When the doors open, people come flooding in to get a hot breakfast, and to take a hot shower and do laundry—all free of charge, of course. My volunteer job was to take down names, get people in and out of the showers in a timely manner, and ensure the washer and dryer were being used appropriately since they were available on a first-come, first-served basis. The job wasn't difficult or complex in its nature; however, interacting one-on-one with our customers was eye-opening and inspiring. I fell in love with my Thursday job.

I made so many friends, and we talked about everything. Sometimes we talked about how they slept behind, or in, a dumpster the night before. Sometimes, I heard stories about far-off travels, or high-school success stories of winning state championship football games. Other times, I couldn't understand what the story was about, or how it began or ended, but I gave them my undivided attention. They just needed a friend, and to be recognized as a human being. I made a lot of friends there. I used to run to and from the shelter on Thursdays, about a twelve-mile round-trip endeavor. Sometimes, as I ran home, my friends I had served at the shelter would make fun of me and call me Chicken Legs. My legs are admittedly very skinny, but they can run a decent pace and pretty long distances. I always laughed when I was out on a run and one of my friends pushing a grocery cart full of their life's possessions yelled out, "Hey! It's Chicken Legs!"

The shelter was very important to me. It helped me. And, for some reason, I kept finding myself back at the shelter whenever I hit a trough in life. The depression I experienced when I hit rockbottom was no different, and I asked if I could volunteer on Thursday mornings again to help with showers and laundry. Pastor John must have noticed the sorrow in my voice, because he told me to come down and do "whatever I needed."

I remember the day I received my "Calling" like it was yesterday. It was a Thursday morning, and I needed to get to the shelter to help with the showers and laundry. I threw on some running clothes, laced up my shoes, and grabbed a running pack, then I was out the door trotting six miles to the shelter. I crossed a couple of busy streets before making my way through City Park, Denver's biggest park. Then, I snaked through the urban jungle of the Capitol Hill neighborhood, where hipsters and young people lived in turn-of-the-century homes that had been carved up into chic condos with pitched roofs and cool architecture. Then, I passed through Cheeseman Park, a beautiful jewel of a park right in the city that was strangely known as a hangout for the LGBT crowd. I'm not sure how or why this is, and frankly I just notice people whenever trotting through Cheeseman Park. As I turned west out of Cheeseman Park, I ran several blocks on 9th Avenue, then arrived at the shelter.

It was a beautiful day, and the run was nothing out of the ordinary. I entered the shelter and greeted Pastor John with a hug and other volunteers with hand-shaking, smiles, and jokes. As we got ready for our 10:00 a.m. opening, I had all my ducks in order—the showers had fresh towels and washcloths, and travel-sized bottles of shampoo, conditioner, and soap. The doors opened, and my list of people who wanted showers and laundry was full within five minutes. I let the first two people into the showers, reminding them they had twenty minutes to be in and out, then helped a customer load his laundry. The other volunteers were in the kitchen next door serving oatmeal and fruit, chatting up a storm. A faith-based movie was playing on the TV in the eating area, as was customary on any weekday. I remember looking at the list on my clipboard, and trying to mathematically figure out whether there would be enough time for all the people who had signed up to take showers. As I did this computation, I was overcome by something.

My mind suddenly went blank. Every thought I had in my head was erased, and everything became silent. I didn't hear the showers, or conversation in the kitchen next door, or the sound of the laundry machine that was just five feet away from me. Within seconds, I felt something that I cannot describe. It was like being hit by a big wave in the ocean. When that wave hit me and submerged me, time stood still. When I emerged to the surface after the wave passed over me I could only think of one thing:

I AM GOING TO RUN ACROSS AMERICA.

I was stunned. This wasn't my thought, want, or desire. I had never even contemplated it as an item on my bucket list of adventures. I felt adrenaline surging through me. I didn't hear a voice or anything, but this thought was shoved into my head somehow. The thought was not that I *needed* to do this or that I was going to *attempt* it; it was factual, as if my very existence, fate, and destiny hinged on me crossing America on foot.

Suddenly, my mind came back to the hallway and I heard people talking. I heard the washing machine making a loud noise because of an uneven loading of clothes in a spin cycle. I heard my customers singing in the showers. Fear suddenly washed over me. What had just happened? Was this one of those self-imposed thoughts that I had previously had of running a marathon, or the Leadville 100 or some other race? Was this something that I should just put on a bucket list, and wait for it to possibly occur when the timing was convenient? Was this my thought or a dream? Or, was something else telling me I would do this?

I didn't know the answer to all of these questions, but I did know what I had just experienced. I couldn't explain it, and it really wasn't necessary to explain it to anybody. I just knew that I was going to run across America. In order to prevent my intellect from undermining and methodically analyzing this Calling into a farce or self-created fantasy, I immediately texted my mom, knowing that I had to tell somebody to hold myself accountable for what I knew had happened. I texted my mom the following message: *I am going to run across America.*

Within five seconds, she texted back, *I'm in.*

Points to Ponder

The following questions are inspired from Part I of my story. There are no wrong answers. There are only your answers, which are right for you.

1. How has your first memory shaped the person you have become?
2. What hardships have you overcome, and what strategies did you use?
3. When will you choose to stop feeling shame?
4. Who was your earliest inspiration? Why?
5. When have you done your best, and still failed?
6. What dreams have you not pursued?
7. Are you vulnerable and open to letting a person love you?
8. Do you talk about insecurities with others?
9. Is your job your passion?
10. What do you believe in?

PART II

Leap

14

Telling My Kids

How do you tell someone you love that you must leave them?

Left to right—Sierra, Jason, Sofia, and Sage

I was truly alive, and every cell in my body was surging with adrenaline. I needed to start running . . . right away. In my mind's eye, I saw the scene from *Forrest Gump*, where he leapt from his porch and began running. He ran to the edge of town, then across the state of Alabama, then to the ocean, then to the other ocean. He just ran. People followed him. People felt hope. He grew a beard and just ran. I started thinking about when I could start the "transcon" (transcontinental run). It was November 2014 when I felt the calling, and I thought it could be possible to start the transcon as early as March 2015.

My biggest concern with the run was leaving my children. We had never been apart for more than two weeks, when their mother took them on summer vacation trips. I didn't know how we could be apart for two months, or more. There was no good solution to this. I considered the possibility of bringing them with me, and doing the run in the summer. Then, I thought again. This would be a very difficult ordeal, and it would have been selfish for me to force them to spend two months of their lives following me across America at five miles per hour. My youngest daughter Sofia was nine, my son Sage was thirteen, and my eldest daughter Sierra was fifteen. Even if they wanted to come, I knew there was the issue of trying to convince my ex-wife to let them come with me. Before anything else, I needed to sit down and talk with my kids about my need to run across America.

As was customary in my home, when I have my kids, we all sit down at our kitchen table and eat together. Before we eat, we say a prayer for our food, our time together, and we pray for friends and family who may be suffering. I considered taking the kids to Buffalo Wild Wings to talk, a lively place where a serious topic can be broached, and humor can easily be folded into the conversation. But this conversation was too serious, and the stakes were too high to have in a setting like that, so I chose to have the conversation in the quiet of our home.

I had all kinds of feelings leading up to this conversation with my kids, and most of the feelings were negative. I was angry that I was being Called to do something that would require me to leave my children. I didn't want to. They are at the center of my life, and everything I did, I had done for them. I was scared that I might be injured, or even die on this run. I didn't know what it would do to me. Would I even be able to walk after such an expedition? I also knew that pedestrians are hit and killed by cars on a daily basis. Would I be a casualty? What if something happened to them, and I wasn't around to help or save them? I was sad that I wouldn't be able to support them at their events, during their highs and lows of life, and just be there to give them a hug when they needed it most. I had so many feelings about leaving my kids. I just didn't want to do it. I wanted this Calling to be rescinded. I wanted it to go away. I wanted to pretend like it never happened. I didn't want to run across America. I couldn't bear leaving my kids, and risk never returning to them.

As I sat down for dinner with my kids that fateful evening, I tried to make it like any other dinner. I didn't want them to be alarmed or feel the nervousness and fear that I was feeling. Once we sat down, I said a quiet prayer to myself that my kids would be accepting, supportive, and not scared of my need to run across America. After our meal was done, and our conversations had wound down, I told the kids I had to talk about something. I nervously looked down at my lap, took a deep breath, then raised my head and opened my eyes. My body language must have said a lot, because the conversation that had been overtaking the table faded to nothing, and it seemed like there was only silence.

I started the conversation by telling my kids about volunteering at the shelter. My kids had also volunteered there fairly regularly, and I thought it could help give them context for the story I was about to tell them. I told them the story of how I felt I had been called to run across America. When I finished, they seemed unfazed by the story. Sierra immediately said, "Cool! You should do it!" Sage seemed unsure, and appeared to be processing what I had told him. Sofia cracked a joke and made light of the story and my need to run across America. As we continued the conversation, I explained that this would require me to leave them for at least two months, maybe longer. I could see the concern in Sofia's eyes, and it felt like tears might soon follow. Sierra must have noticed the situation, because she immediately became a cheerleader and tried to point out all the positives of such a run. Only, there weren't really any positives, except that it was something really hard and it would be cool if their dad could actually accomplish it.

Sofia's spirits rose as Sierra spoke. The kids started firing questions at me about the run. They asked if it was a race, and who else would be doing it. I explained that it would only be me. They asked if somebody would go with me. I said I didn't know. They asked how long it would take, I said I didn't know. They asked about a route, and I said I didn't know. Their minds immediately saw scenes out of *Forrest Gump* as well. They asked if I would grow a beard. Then, they opined that I would be like a rock star when I did the run and I'd have a bunch of groupies following me as I ran, just like in the movie. Their faces and spirits seemed happy. They supported me and accepted my crazy proposition to run across America. They didn't understand and couldn't comprehend the actual genesis of this expedition and Calling, and neither could I.

As dinner and the conversation ended, my heart was melancholy and broken. I just didn't want to leave these children, but I knew I had to.

15

Picking a Start Date

A journey of 3000+ miles begins with "doubt" and ends with "doing."

I settled in on the date of March 25th, 2016 to start my run. I chose this date for one simple reason—it would minimize the amount of time I would have to be apart from my children. Every other year, my children rotate their spring break holidays between their mother and me. In 2016, my kids would be with their mother for ten days. In my head, I rationalized that if I could run across America in sixty days, I would really only be forcing an additional fifty days of separation from my children. It was illogical math, because, regardless of how I tried to rationalize it, I would be apart from my kids for sixty days, and probably longer. Because of my chosen start date, I had roughly eighteen months to prepare for my crossing.

I was a team of one setting out to figure out how to accomplish this goal. I had told my mom of my intention to run across America in text, but there was no more discussion with her. I think she thought it was just a bucket list item that I would get to sooner or later in my life. I told no one else about my transcon intentions for the first few months.

I had to figure out what exactly I was taking on with this endeavor. So, like with everything else in this day and age, I jumped on the Internet and Googled, "How to run across America." Much to my surprise, a list of pertinent website links popped up on the screen. There was an article from *Outside Magazine Online* that was a few paragraphs in length. It gave some tips on the journey of a couple of people who had walked across the US. I also found a website (USACrossers.com) that actually tracked how many people had crossed the US on foot, and gave links to their websites and causes, as well as statistics on the crossings. The website was created and managed by John Wallace, III, a man who had crossed America on foot in 2005.

As I read his website, I saw links to a lot of other websites for people who had crossed America on foot. Most of these links had a brief summary of the crossing—where it began and ended, total miles, and number of days. For about half of the websites, the summary would give an explanation for why the crossing wasn't successful, and would say things like "aborted," "postponed," or "need funding." The list included both well-known and unknown runners. As it turned out, only 252 people had ever crossed the US on foot! The other thing I noticed was that my goal of running fifty miles a day was extremely aggressive. The site reported that, in 2014, three people had completed transcon crossings. One had completed a crossing in 107 days, another had completed in 1,095 days, and another had completed a crossing in 1,103 days. As I scanned a few pages of the website, I didn't see anyone on this site who had successfully completed a crossing in sixty days, averaging fifty miles a day or more. Even the fabled Marathon Man, Dean Karnazas, took seventy-five days to cross America on foot with an entourage of support crew and an RV—and he brought along his wife and kids while being filmed by Regis and Kathy Lee. As I looked deeper into the site, I saw that Marshall Ulrich, the American icon of ultra-endurance athletics, had successfully completed a transcon in 2008. He had run 3,063 miles in 52.5 days and averaged 58.5 miles a day. After a quick perusal of the website, I realized

Marshall was the only person there who had exceeded my own personal goal of averaging fifty miles a day. I was very nervous, and quickly learning that my goal might have been too foolishly aggressive. I just picked the number fifty out of thin air, and when I divided it into three thousand miles for a crossing, it netted sixty days. I figured two months was the longest I could tolerate being away from my kids, and even that was an intolerable amount of time.

As I scoured the Internet more, I found a website for a New Zealander, Perry Newburn, who had also completed a transcontinental run in a little over fifty-one days, averaging fifty-five miles per day. It appeared that Perry's time was faster than Marshall's, but Perry's daily mileage and total distance were shorter. In my mind, both men had completed the unthinkable and were incredible athletes in mind and body.

I had purchased an autographed copy of *Running America* by Marshall Ulrich at my very first Leadville 100 Trail Run, so I sat in my living room by myself and put the movie into the DVD player. The movie was about Marshall's crossing and chronicled his experience. Another well-known ultra-runner, Charlie Engle, attempted the crossing with him. Charlie had actually run four thousand miles across the Sahara, averaging around forty miles a day. As I watched the documentary, I saw two incredible athletes set out to run from San Francisco City Hall to New York City Hall. Each man had a support crew of five people, including their significant other, a doctor, experienced crew personnel, and other experienced medical professionals. Each runner had his own RV and additional support vehicle. The men were setting out to break the world record for a transcontinental foot crossing. The record of 46 days, 8 hours, 36 minutes was held by Frank Giannino, and was set in 1980.

At the beginning of the run, the film showed a lot of smiles, and bantering between the two runners. As they logged seventy mile days, day after day, I watched these men wither, both physically and mentally. After only one week of doing this, both men were severely injured, suffering, and contemplating whether a crossing was going to be possible. As I continued watching, it struck me that each man's body was revolting against him with injury after injury; however, the body was recovering from each injury only to give rise to a different one.

What I found gripping in this account was the mental agony that each runner was experiencing. These men who had each won epic races like the Badwater Ultramarathon and Eco-Challenges, and had summited the highest mountains in the world, were being broken into tiny pieces. These men were crying, not because of pain or fear. They were crying and doubting themselves because of being overwhelmed at having to get up day after day and put in insane miles with no end in sight. Charlie quit before the halfway point due to injury. Marshall continued on, but had to take days off, reduce his daily mileage, and change his focus from breaking a world record to just making it across without quitting. Marshall was successful in running across America. He is also quoted as saying it was the hardest thing he had ever done. That statement scared me.

Marshall has summited all of the tallest mountains on each continent, including Mt. Everest. He has competed in all the Eco-Challenge adventure races around the world, run across Colorado multiple times, run the Badwater Ultramarathon course four times back-to-back-to-back-to-back—a total of 586 miles. His list of accomplishments goes on and on. And he consistently stated that his run across America was the *hardest thing he had ever done*. My resume of endurance accomplishments was decent, but nothing compared to the great Marshall Ulrich's. He had taken a lifetime to get to the point where he was able to cross at the pace he did. Was my goal of fifty miles a day totally out of reach, and would the cumulative daily mileage crack me in half, as it had done to The Running Man, Charlie Engle?

Marshall had also written a book about his crossing, *Running on Empty*. It had great insight into the highs and lows of his expedition. It also recounted a lot of things that the movie didn't seem to address. As it turned out, the movie was commissioned by Charlie Engle, and he was a part-owner in the documentary. The crossing was planned for forty-six days or less; and, despite having hundreds of thousands of dollars in funding, the group ran low on money in the final ten days. As I finished reading Marshall's book, I realized that organizing and orchestrating the logistics of my own transcon was going to be as difficult as the run itself.

I had heard about a Race Across America that was taking place in 2015. Apparently, this was an attempt to recreate the Bunion Derbies of 1928 and 1929, where a group of athletes raced across America on foot. In the Bunion Derbies, the men averaged forty-some miles a day, and their crossing took over seventy days. When I looked at the website for the Race Across America, I discovered that the runners had to apply and be selected—a process that had already taken place. They also had to pay a fairly significant sum of money to participate. In return, the race director had plotted out a course, and lodging and food was provided. Although it was still a significant expense, most of the logistics had been taken care of. The race was set to begin on January 15, 2015, and it would take close to four months to cross, and the runners were only going to average about thirty miles a day. The Race Across America was no longer an option because the daily mileage was just too low, and the time commitment was too long.

The more I researched running across America, the more I came up empty-handed. There was no book or instruction manual on how to do this. The brave few souls who had attempted individual expeditions had taken months on end to complete it, and almost nobody had run across America averaging fifty plus miles a day. The other thing that became apparent was the fact that no blind person had ever attempted a crossing. When I ran 205 miles in a three-day race on a contained one-mile loop, I had run farther in one continuous effort than any other blind person in recorded history. So, I would have a whole additional set of issues to contend with in my crossing due to my lack of eyesight.

I needed to figure everything out on my own, and I would have eighteen months to do it. As near as I could tell, there were six major things I had to focus on in these eighteen months:

1) train my body and mind,

2) fund the expedition,

3) strategize and innovate to neutralize my lack of eyesight,

4) plan a route,

5) get the word out about the run, and

6) create a team and support plan for the run.

16

Mind Over Matter

The body will quit before the mind will quit.
— Arnold Schwarzenegger

U p until this point, my ultra-running career had included a seventy-two-hour race, four one-hundred-mile finishes (including three at Leadville), some fifty-milers and 50Ks, and a solo double crossing of the Grand Canyon. I had some knowledge about running longer distances, but I was wholly unequipped for the challenge of completing a transcontinental crossing on foot. Most of my training had been for foot races that lasted thirty hours or less in duration. I knew how to log base miles, how and when to incorporate altitude and speed work, and when and what to eat and drink at different points of these races. I had also learned to vomit and keep on running. I had experienced physical and mental meltdowns. I had learned that I could push through these dark points in races, and eventually the pain would recede and I would be able to run again at top speeds. I had learned that running ultra-distances was a great metaphor for life—there are always going to be ups and downs, and the greatest lesson is to never stop trying and always make relentless forward progress. As long as I didn't take myself out of the race, generally speaking, I had the physical and mental ability to finish it. I believe we all have this ability, just by virtue of being human—it is woven into the genetic fabric of our biology and survival instinct.

I had absolutely no idea how to train for a transcontinental run. I believed I could build my body and mind into something that could withstand the torment and torture that I was sure to experience, but I couldn't stop replaying a scene from *Running America* where the great Marshall Ulrich had his head down, was surrounded by his wife and crew, and he wept as he muttered, "I just don't know how I can do it. I just don't know how I can do the miles." This impenetrable force of a man had experienced ultimate suffering—physically, his orthopedic doctor said he had sustained more injuries than the entire running field at any Western States 100 race (the oldest hundred-mile trail race, where this doctor was also the race doctor). Marshall had experienced a slew of injuries including Achilles tendonitis, plantar fasciitis, a dislocated fibula, diarrhea, infection, a tendon tear, blisters, sleep deprivation, muscle cramping, and heat exhaustion.

He was doing fine suffering through the physical pain; however, it was the mental fatigue and pain that had stripped this mountain of a man into a hopeless, slumped-over, crying and pitiful person. As I replayed that scene, I just wanted Marshall's suffering to stop. The only way for the suffering to stop was to quit, or to reach New York. If he quit, his immediate suffering would stop, but he would have a lifetime of regret, and Marshall knew that suffering would be much more severe than anything he was experiencing during the run. The other option was to continue trudging forward across America, and endure the physical and emotional torment of an agonizing dream. Of course, Marshall chose the latter.

I knew my physical training would need to be more demanding than I'd ever experienced. I also knew I had to intentionally make myself suffer physically, mentally, and emotionally. I already knew that my biggest adversary in life—doubt—would be making daily appearances until, and if, I somehow reached the Atlantic Ocean on this run. The devil of doubt would whisper and sing excuse after excuse, in an effort to make me quit. Sometimes it originated from my own thoughts, like when I thought about the fear of leaving my kids. Sometimes it came from others and I would grasp onto negative thoughts, like when people told me my ex-wife would take this opportunity to pursue full custody of my children, or that I would end up in bankruptcy and lose my house as a result of not working for almost two years in order to prepare for and complete the transcon. Whether the negativity was grounded in fact or not, doubt had a way of making the threat seem real and made me want to quit every day for almost two years, but my Calling required that I do it.

I thought it would be best to have a lot of hundred-mile races built into my training schedule, in order to have many build-ups and increase my body's ability to endure and not break down despite long grueling miles. In addition, each race would permit me to stretch myself mentally, make me run in different environmental conditions, and make me suffer in new and different ways. Then, for the six months immediately before the transcon, I would train specifically for the run, building and logging an insane amount of road miles. My training started with a hundred-mile race in Arizona.

Javelina Jundred
100 miles—trail
Phoenix, Arizona
November 2014

First on my list was the Javelina Jundred hundred-mile trail run in Arizona. Javelina, as it is known in the ultra-running world, is a party in the desert held on the weekend nearest to Halloween. A bunch of kooky runners have a tradition of gathering in the desert and running a fifteen-mile loop on the Pemberton Trail through the desert just outside of Phoenix. There are some technical parts of the trail, although it is mainly rolling single-track trail that is lined with shrubs and huge Arizona cacti. Javelina had a reputation of beating its runners into submission as the sun rose and baked them on a fully exposed trail. This race was intended to help me build base miles, and the plan was to run at a relaxed easy pace. I had lined up a guide, Robert, to help me run when it was dark. I intended to use my strategy of putting reflectors on my guide's ankles and pointing my headlamp directly at the reflectors.

When I arrived at race check-in, it was the party I had anticipated. Everybody was pumped up and ready to party in the desert. Some of the well-known ultra running personalities were in attendance like "The Jester," Ed Ettinghause. Ed lived in San Diego and wore a jester costume when he ran races. Ed was in the process of setting a world record for the most hundred-mile races completed in one year (forty), and Javelina was one of many. "The Dirt Diva," Catra Corbett, was also in attendance, a tattooed vixen who had run over one hundred hundred-mile races and substituted an addiction for booze and drugs with an addiction for a runner's high. I also met some Tarahumara runners, the fabled Mexican "running people" who ran incredible distances as a way of life, and lived in the harsh Copper Canyons deep in the heart of Mexico.

My guide and I had made plans to meet up before the start of the race. He graciously offered to help me run roughly fifty miles in the darkness. We just had to coordinate where and when we would meet up so I didn't get caught in the dark in the middle of a fifteen-mile loop. I called him up and he suggested that he would bump into me during the daytime, and we could figure out how to meet up when it became dark. I was confused, and explained that I only needed his help when it became dark. He told me he was running the entire hundred miles. I wasn't sure how I felt about that. From past experience, I knew that a guide needed to be pretty fresh in order to guide me on trails in the dark. It takes a lot of energy and focus to run fifty miles on trail and call out every obstacle and undulation of the trail for a blind runner. The more he and I talked, the more concerned I became. He had never finished a hundred-miler before, and he had DNF'd (not finished) several shorter races of fifty miles and fifty kilometers. He had a huge giving heart, but he had overcommitted in offering to help me, while he was trying to finish his first hundred-miler. I told him he needed to focus on his own race, and I would just figure out my own.

I immediately went to the race director and told him about my predicament. He knew about my visual impairment, as I'd raced for seventy-two hours at one of his prior events. The search began for guides, but by the start of the race, I had none. I decided to start running and see how far I could get before darkness fell upon me, and halted my forward movement. I ran and ran, checking every loop to see if we had found a volunteer to help me out. I had finished three loops, and realized the sun was going to set on the next loop, but I still had no guide.

I decided to just go for it and run as fast and as far as I could until it became too dark for me to run solo. My plan was then to follow other runners' feet as they passed me for as long as I could. Maybe there would be a group walking and I could just power hike, following them in the darkness. I was able to reach the midway aid station, Jackass Junction. When I arrived, the sun had tucked beneath the horizon and the all-too-familiar darkness enveloped me and my spirit. I leaned over to refill my water bottle from a cooler. As I did this, a race volunteer asked me if I needed anything. I told her, "Yeah, I'm night blind, and I need a guide to follow; otherwise, I'm stuck here with you for the next thirteen hours until the sun rises." Another racer, Phil, was standing next to me, and he said, "I'll guide you." I turned to him and explained I'd need him to wear reflectors on his ankles and I'd shine my headlamp on them. I'd also need him to call out rocks and other tripping hazards. He said, "Sure," and we took off running.

A complete stranger had come from out of nowhere to help me. All I had to do was ask. As I ran with Phil, we chatted. I came to learn that my guide was Phil Nimmo, a very experienced ultra-runner who was well-known for his jaunts of more than a hundred miles. I was really humbled to have a racer as experienced as Phil offer to help me. He had given up his own race and slowed his pace just to help me get back to the start/finish area of the loop.

When Phil and I reached it, I received even more good news. I had a couple of people volunteer to guide me for one loop each.

That should enable me to get through the dark of night. Apparently, they were at the race to pace other runners; however, both of their racers had dropped from the race for one reason or another. With the help of three total strangers, I was able to navigate the darkness at Javelina. By the time I had finished the sixth loop, the sun had risen and I had bagged ninety miles of desert trail. I only had to run a ten-mile shortened loop to finish. My body felt great since I was forced to move so slow during the dark of night. My mind wasn't good, however.

I hate running in the night. I am constantly reminded that I am losing my eyesight, and it is extremely difficult to see anything in the dark. I had thirteen hours of dark to have doubt feed negative thoughts into my head. As soon as the sun rose, I had renewed energy. I was again capable of being independent. I was ready to run. I needed to run hard, to rebel against the torment that I knew would someday overtake my eyes and permanently negate my ability to perceive light. I took off like a jackrabbit, passing runners, bounding over rocks, and descending technical terrain swiftly. As I passed a couple of runners, they mocked me and said, "Dude, you're not Killian Jornet!" The comments didn't matter. I wasn't racing anybody. I was running to exert all of the pain, fear, and anger that had welled up in me that night, as I was reminded that I am going blind. I finished Javelina within twenty-six and a half hours, and received another belt buckle—the award every finisher of a hundred-mile race receives.

I returned to Denver after Javelina with newfound confidence. From this race, I learned that there are really good people out there. If you're vulnerable, share your needs and ask for help—you will usually get the help you need. I had also won a big battle with doubt. Doubt had served up the challenge that darkness signaled a time when I shouldn't even try. I should just throw in the towel and not attempt to run because I couldn't see. A headlamp, a couple of reflectors, a few strangers, and determination snuffed out doubt's flame.

My next long run was going to be a solo, self-supported hundred mile run (The Relentless 100) around a local park in Denver,

Colorado. I had contacted Anchor Center for Blind Children in Denver and asked to run a hundred miles to support the school. The school gladly obliged, and I had the run set for the second week of December. The weekend before the run, I was in Sacramento for the US Blind Marathon Championships. After catching a red-eye flight, I was somehow able to pull off a first-place victory, clocked a personal best time, and became the US Blind Marathon Champion for 2014. The paralympic world marathon championships were going to be held in London in April 2015, and in the back of my mind, I hoped I might be asked to represent the US with my win in Sacramento.

Relentless 100
100 miles—packed gravel
Denver, Colorado
December 2014

My mom and I had discussed our plan for the self-supported hundred-mile run. We would start the run at sunrise at Washington Park, which has a two-and-a-half-mile loop on a packed gravel path. We would set up a card table with food, drink, and first aid. Mom would park her car in the park by the card table, and it would be our makeshift aid station. All the other races I had run were "pay to play" races. In other words, I paid a registration fee and the race organizers took care of all the logistics like timing, planning the route, and providing water and nutrition. I had no idea how much water I drank during a hundred-mile outing. I also had no idea how much food I ate. This was going to be an all-new experience.

A local TV news station caught wind of the run and came out to interview me to promote the story that a blind man was running a hundred miles for blind children. I felt honored to finally be open about my failing eyesight, and the thought that somehow my disease was helping others was fulfilling. A lot of people came out to support me, some friends and some complete strangers. I was working a half day a week at the Boulder Running Company, just to get me out of the house and expose me to different people. A bunch of my coworkers showed up to run some laps with me, and I learned that one of them, Taylor, also had an interest in film-making. A lot of other stellar runners came out to share laps and support me like Pat Sullivan ("average-Joe" winner of a local Denver marathon), Karen Kantor (a phenomenal para-athlete), Brandon "The Stank" Stapanowich (Nolan's 14 finisher, Colorado Trail record setter, Pikes Peak Quad finisher, Leadville/Western States/Hard Rock 100 top-ten finisher), Mike Hewitt (local doc and Leadville 100 man-imal), and Zach Miller (former Nike Trail Elite and current North Face team member). The fact that I was visually impaired seemed to attract a lot of people to want to help me. I was able to complete a hundred miles in a little over twenty-two hours, had lots of fun, and learned a lot about food and water quantities that are required to run a hundred miles. I also realized that my mom was the most experienced person I knew in ultra-distance crewing.

In ultra-running, usually the runner has a crew of people that support him or her. The crew is usually comprised of people of various talents and relations to the runner. In my crew, I like to have a nurse with medical training, a couple of runners who can act as guides and complete other miscellaneous tasks, my girlfriend (who is also an ultra-runner and the best guide I have ever had) and kids for emotional support, and a person in charge of logistics who is very detail-oriented—the latter is usually my mom, who also doubles as the crew chief. Mom is an expert in knowing me and reading my ability to run hard and push through difficult situations when they arose. She knew things about me and my running that I wasn't even aware of, like my dependency on Mountain Dew to bring me back from the brink of implosion. So, I knew she was going to have to make the trek across America with me. After the hundred-mile run around the park, I revisited the obscure text I had sent to her a few months prior, stating my intention to run across America. The conversation went something like this:

Me: "Hey, Mom . . . remember that text I sent you a while back?"

Mom: "What text?"

Me: "The one where I said I was going to run across America."

Mom: "Oh. Yeah, I remember."

Me: "I was serious."

Mom: "Okay."

Me: "Well, are you in to crew me? I'm planning to leave in late March 2016 when the kids are on spring break with their mother."

Mom: "Sure."

I expected her answer to be more thoughtful, or for her to ponder it for a longer time. She gave me a one-word answer, and I suspected that she didn't understand what she was committing to in that moment. I was happy to have an affirmative answer, so I didn't pepper her with additional questioning.

PR150+

183 miles—road

Roosevelt Roads to Rincon, Puerto Rico

January 2015

The next race I had to complete was a month later in Puerto Rico. I was ecstatic to be part of the PR150+. The race was in its inaugural year, and was intended to be a 183-mile, self-supported crossing of Puerto Rico, from the easternmost point to the westernmost point. There was a sixty-hour time limit, and 42,000 feet of elevation gain and descent. It was all road, and was sure to be hot, humid, and hard. I added heat training to my routine run training, which was averaging eighty miles per week at this point. I used the steam room at a local gym and did pushups and stairsteps for forty-five minutes per day. My thought was to make my body get accustomed to cooling itself while exercising in a super-hot and humid environment. I didn't know if it would work, and I consulted several ultra-runners I knew who had run in desert environments. All of my experts were stumped, as they had never run that long a distance in hot and humid environments.

This was a wake-up call for me. All of my mentors and ultra-running savants were puzzled as to how I should take on this new challenge in Puerto Rico. I was about to go beyond conventional ultra-running into the uncharted territory of extreme ultra-running. I was crossing over the line of being a "follower" in running, to being at the edge and being a "discoverer." It was exciting and scary, all at once.

I approached Taylor, my film-making coworker at Boulder Running Company. I asked if he might be interested in making a short film from pictures and video I planned to shoot while I was at the PR150+. I revealed my intention to run across America, and I hoped to use the video to gain sponsorship for my transcon. Taylor was excited to be asked to do the project, and he took it one step further. He asked if he could come to the race, and film it live. We brokered a deal that I would pay his way to the race, and whatever film he produced would be owned by both of us on a 50/50 basis.

In late-January 2015, I found myself toeing the start line of the PR150+ with the likes of Charlie Engle (Badwater winner, 4,000-mile crosser of the Sahara, and unsuccessful transcon attempt with Marshall Ulrich), Joe Fejes (multi-day phenom who had bested Yiannis Kouros in a six-day race and current six-day American record holder at 606 miles), Jared Fetteroff (boy ultra-running wonder—he had completed twenty-six hundred-milers at twenty-six years of age), Luigi Dessy (the greatest Puerto Rican ultra-runner in history), and then there were a few unknown people like Angel "Bacho" Vega, Antonio Borques, Vinnie, and me. Only eight runners were invited to attempt the race, as each runner would require one and at times two police escorts to help keep them safe from errant drivers. My crew was made up of my mom, my aunt who was a nurse, and Taylor who was filming and acting as a crew member.

The PR150+ course was straight out of a Stephen King horror novel. After climbing up a narrow, steep, rocky trail from the ocean, I began my journey toward the west. The group ran together for about five miles, then we entered the El Yunque rainforest, climbing and descending never-ending hills with steep pitches in humidity that neared 100 percent. After about thirty miles, the eight-man field was spread out, and the sun was steep in the sky. I exited the canopy and suffocating humidity of the rainforest, only to be greeted with a blazing sun and ninety-degree heat as I ran through the beach cities of Rio Grande, Loiza, and Pinones for twenty miles until finally making it to San Jorge Children's Hospital in San Juan, which was the fifty-mile marker. The sun was about to set, and I needed to keep moving. I started my run out of San Juan, which is on the northeastern shore of Puerto Rico. The route headed south to the center of the island and followed the spine of the mountains called "The Panoramic Route." This hundred-mile section in the mountains lowered in temperature to the seventies and eighties, although the humidity was still around 80 percent.

I was deep in the mountains at mile ninety-four when it began raining cats and dogs, as was normal in the tropics, and I chose to take a sleep break. It was 3:30 a.m., and I dove in the back of our van and stretched out on top of two coolers and numerous suitcases. Only Francisco, the driver, was awake. My mom, my aunt, and Taylor were sleeping at this point. After a short one and a half hours, the alarm went off, the rain had subsided, and I pulled my contorted body from atop the coolers and uneven sleeping surface from which I had slumbered. By mile one hundred, the sun was up and I was feeling beaten.

Over the police radios, we learned that three of the eight runners were out. Charlie had dropped out due to severe blistering, as he made the choice to not dry his wet feet in a humid environment. Moisture and friction are the cause of blistering, and on this occasion, Charlie hadn't chosen wisely. Luigi had dropped when he noticed that his urine was a dark brown, bordering on red. This is a sign that kidneys are shutting down, and a glaring red flag in ultra-running. Antonio had dropped from the race due to fatigue.

I ran up and down hills in the mountains, and felt as if I was on the verge of death from miles 100–135. We popped blisters, taped toes, and cut off the toe-box of my shoes with razors. My feet were causing me a lot of pain and problems. The rest of my body ached, and I thought I could even feel pain in my hair and fingernails. Every cell of my body seemed to be hurting. Then, in the darkness of the second night, something happened. I didn't feel pain anymore. I didn't feel fatigued. My body had been through hell, but it didn't hurt and I felt fresh—as if I'd just woken up. I wanted to run, fast. So I took off. I was running eight-minute miles up and down hills in the mountains of Puerto Rico. I even surged and overtook my lead car and police escort at times. For the next few hours, this unknown energy fueled me and I was able to gobble up twenty miles. As I exited the mountains, I had to run a bone-crunching, never-ending ten-mile descent to flat, exposed terrain. As the sun rose on the third day, I was around mile 175 when I realized that I could finish the race under the sixty-hour time cutoff. I shuffled and "wogged" (a combination of walking and jogging) for the final miles until I reached the finish line and was greeted with a hero's welcome.

It took me fifty-one hours to cross the island, and my mom and I learned monumental lessons from this experience. We learned that we needed to be extremely organized when crewing out of a van. Just like in my house, everything had its place. We needed to be able to access first aid, specific clothing, nutrition, and supplies on a moment's notice. The more people moved things around, the more difficult it became to support me. We also learned that I don't do well with multi-day sleep deprivation. I have heard that some runners can tolerate and do well on minimal sleep. This wasn't the case for me. I need sleep to let my body heal, and for my mind to make good decisions. We also realized that living out of a van for days on end was going to be torture. We learned that a large crew can be a blessing and a curse. It can be a blessing in that there are just more people to do the tasks that are required. It can be a curse if people are inexperienced or if the crew isn't working in unison. We were reminded that as the runner and crew wear down and become fatigued, the likelihood of conflict rises exponentially. Sometimes your own crew might be so focused on fighting with one another, they'd totally forget about the end goal of getting the runner to the finish line. The PR150+, or The Kraken as I like to call it, was the most difficult race I had ever competed in, and I felt like I'd earned some stripes for finishing. Taylor produced a topnotch documentary called *Running Vision* (RunningVisionMovie.com) about my run, entered it into some film festivals, and it now sells on Amazon.com.

On the way back to Denver from Puerto Rico, I received a call from the US Olympic Committee. I was invited to join Team USA and represent the US at the Paralympic World Marathon Championships in London in three months' time. I would be the first blind/visually impaired runner to represent Team USA for almost a decade. A contingency of this invitation was that I wouldn't run any ultras until I had competed in London. I was fine with this contingency, and dedicated the next three months to speed training at the marathon distance. Never did I imagine that I would be a paralympian, and as I ran in London in April 2015 at the International Paralympic World Marathon Championships, I experienced thousands of onlookers chanting "USA! USA! USA!" just like you see in the movies. I was overwhelmed and teared up several times during the run. I even slapped some kids high fives as I ran by. I finished in fourth place, just off the podium. I didn't care—I was forty-five, had just battled back from a deep depression, was going blind, and just had an experience that most people only see in movies. Being blind was actually opening doors which were previously locked when I was pretending to be sighted. Was my blindness a curse, or a blessing in disguise?

Keys 100
100 miles—road
Key Largo to Key West, Florida
May 2015

Next on my transcon training agenda was the Keys 100, a hundred-mile run on road from Key Largo to Key West in May. The run was more or less a self-supported run, on roads and bridges in the heat and humidity of the Keys. It was sure to be beautiful with the multi-colored blue ocean, and I knew I would appreciate whatever I could see of it. I was planning to meet the race director from the PR150+, Luigi, at the race. My mom volunteered to make the trip and crew me last minute, which I was thankful for. I also didn't have any guides lined up for nighttime, but I figured I could manage it if no volunteers came forward, as the course was road and I could follow a painted line with my headlamp. The Keys 100 ended up being difficult because of sun, heat, and humidity. It also turned out to be a fully self-supported race that year because the coolers of water and chests of ice that the race staff had put out were taken by passersby.

I was in good shape from my London training, and my legs felt fresh from shorter distance training. I ended up placing seventh overall with a time of twenty hours and thirty-one minutes. It was my fastest hundred-miler yet, and the conditions were fierce, causing many runners to DNF.

Badwater Ultramarathon
135 miles—road
Death Valley, California
July 2015

I had two months until my next big training run—the Badwater Ultramarathon (aka Badwater). Badwater is an iconic run that only a hundred runners from around the world are invited to on an annual basis. The race is a 135-mile race through the desert in Death Valley, California. The race is run on road, and is a point-to-point course from Badwater Basin (the lowest point in the contiguous United States) to the Portal Trail of Mount Whitney (the highest point in the contiguous United States). The race is run in July when the desert is the hottest, and temperatures routinely hit 120°. Runners run on the white line to keep the soles of their shoes from melting on the black asphalt, which routinely reaches 200°. The runners at Badwater are truly the best of the best. In order to be invited to compete at Badwater, a runner must have completed at least three races of a hundred miles or longer, and the applicant must answer questions about his or her character and explain what Badwater means to them. This race wasn't about glory-seeking self-centered individuals. One part of the application actually asked for the name of a Badwater veteran who the applicant admired, and why that person was admired. I gave the name of Phil Nimmo, the runner who offered to guide me without a hesitation while I was stranded in the middle of the Javelina Jundred. I also gave the name of "The Jester," Ed Ettinghause, a runner who I'd run with many times and had given me countless pieces of advice as I increased my mileage and frequency of hundred-mile races.

By the time the race rolled around, I felt very confident about my ability to run the race well, and possibly have a top-ten showing. I had significant mileage on my body, without injury. I had raced well in heat and humidity, and had gotten the hang of self-supported racing. I had prepared for the heat by spending an hour a day in a sauna, and running in the 95-degree summer heat of Colorado in four shirts, a rain jacket, and two down coats, with three pairs of sweat pants, a wool hat, and gloves—all black so as to absorb as much heat as possible. When I arrived in Death Valley, the heat was like I had never experienced before. It was just *hot*. It was windy, and felt like a hair dryer was about a foot away and blown on high directly at me. I could feel my body drying out as I stood outside in the baking sun. My throat became scratchy and my nose bled. Wherever my bare skin was exposed to the sun, it felt like it was being flash fried.

It was 120° when we arrived at the hotel in Furnace Creek. Some friends drove out to the start of the race at Badwater Basin, which is 282 feet below sea level. The ground is cracked and hard, and the landscape looks more like something from a moon landing with no signs of life. Upon their return, my friends were telling me that the temperature was reported at 130° at the basin. It was as if the hotter it was, the more excited we all became. I remember thinking to myself, *Is the purpose of this race to punish ourselves and suffer, and to see just how much we can endure?* Whatever the reason, I had allotted a day and a half to try to acclimatize to the heat. I periodically took fifteen-minute walks in shorts and a shirt to try to get used to the oven. There just was no escaping the heat. The only thing to do was to seek shelter in the safety of our air-conditioned motel room in Furnace Creek. When the sun set, it was still extremely hot. The ground had just baked all day, and was radiating heat, cooking me from the feet up. An eight-pound bag of ice was selling for $8.00. Gas doubled in price, as compared to cities just outside of Death Valley. I think the merchants knew that once you were inside Death Valley, you either paid their price, or you would "pay the price".

Due to National Park rules, runners weren't permitted to have a pacer for the first forty-two miles. The start of the race was in the dark, and I was going to have to run it alone. My trusty friend Luigi from Puerto Rico was also running Badwater and he agreed to get me out of the starting area, and onto the road where I could follow the painted white line on the road. With the eyesight I had, I was able to follow the line. I did get lost when I came to an intersection and the line disappeared. I had to slow down and shuffle forward until I could again pick up the line. Sometimes, I just stopped dead in my tracks and waited until another runner came from behind, then followed him or her until I saw the line again. I knew I was losing valuable time, but I didn't have any choice as I couldn't see anything other than the white line in that darkness.

As the sun rose the next morning, I had covered about forty miles and was on pace for a good race. I immediately changed into an all-white sun suit and covered my skin from head to toe. The sun suit had a Sun Protection Factor of 100—more than any sunscreen on the market. It had air vents to let cool air in. The only problem was, although the suit protected me from the sun, it added an additional layer of clothing that trapped heat around my body. We decided to dump ice water on the suit every mile, which worked to cool the suit and my body. After eight to ten minutes of running, the suit was dry again. Hence, my crew was required to meet me every mile or so in order to keep the suit wet, and my core body temperature down. At times, my crew was forced to not use the air conditioning in the van, to prevent overheating. This meant they had to drive in over a hundred-degree heat with the windows down, sweating and suffering.

At the beginning of the race, I noticed that I had plantar warts on the bottom of my right foot, by the heel. I didn't think much of it, and it only caused me a little discomfort as I had trained and competed in previous races. At Badwater, however, the nuisance of my plantar warts became a nine-alarm fire. As the blood rushed to my feet, and my lower extremities swelled from the heat and exertion, the ingrown warts became inflamed and extremely painful. They became so painful that I started limping as I ran, in order to not let the heel of my foot touch the ground. Each time my heel struck the ground, it sent shockwaves through my body and felt like my foot had been impaled by a galvanized nail. About two hours earlier, I had just passed Pam Reed (an icon in ultra-running). My plan was to run the first hundred miles easy, then in the dark of night, I would run a flat section from mile 100-122. I figured that would enable me to tuck in under thirty hours, and possibly a top-ten finish.

As my warts rebelled against me, and my run turned from limp to hobble, I knew my goal of *competing* in this race had changed to a goal of just *completing* this race. I took off my right shoe which housed my warts, and instructed my crew to cut a hole in the foot bed where the warts were located. Because that didn't cause relief, we cut deeper into the foam of the shoe, to prevent pressure from the inflamed warts. Still, there was no relief from the pain. The warts were about a dime in size; however, after a hundred miles of running on them in Death Valley in July, half of my foot had become inflamed. I dreamed about just cutting the foot off, and continuing on with a prosthesis of some sort. The foot just hurt too much.

As my physical pain continued to climb, and my forward progress slowed, doubt again revisited me. I wanted to quit. I wanted out. I wanted the pain to stop. I was more than a hundred miles into the iconic race that was dubbed the Challenge of Champions. I was still on track to set a new record for visually impaired runners, despite not having a chance at a top-ten finish. I realized at that point, my pain wouldn't subside before the end of the race. And, there was nothing I could do to make it go away. If I wanted to finish the race, I would just have to embrace the pain and keep moving forward. I hobbled as best I could, and in the cover of the second night, I actually started passing runners. I couldn't see much at this point, due to my eye condition, fatigue, and the distraction of the pain. Sometimes I wandered off the shoulder of the road onto sand and gravel. As I twisted ankles, it really didn't matter since the pain caused by the plantar warts had overtaken my entire being.

As the sun rose the next morning, I felt something. Actually, I felt nothing. The pain was gone. I could step on my foot, and I was okay. My fatigue had lifted, and the fog of being sleep-deprived for over thirty hours was having no effect on me. I started running, really running. I was putting down seven-minute miles and my pacer was unable to keep up with me. I ran and ran, feeling fresh and rejuvenated. I knew the sensation wasn't going to last forever, but it was real for me at that moment so I took advantage of it. I just ran, and ran. I was freed from the cage of my body, and any pain that I was feeling. After about five miles of pure exhilaration, I felt pain reenter my body. This time, the pain took hold and refused to let up. The last fifteen miles were absolute torture. I limped two miles into the city of Lone Pine, which is at the base of the thirteen-mile climb to Mt. Whitney Portal. Over that last thirteen miles, the elevation climbed some 5,000 feet as the sun again baked runners. At one point, I collapsed on the road, feeling like I couldn't take one more step. I remember a mountainous police officer in a kilt walking to me. As he stood over me, I think he said, "You're tiny." Then he picked up my limp body, moved me off the road, and laid me down in the shoulder of the road so I wouldn't get run over. I felt like road kill, and I probably looked more pitiful.

After 39 hours, 59 minutes, and 59 seconds, I reached the finish line. I was greeted by a BBC film crew that had been filming my race, and I had set a new record for visually impaired runners, beating the old mark by more than six hours. Badwater was extremely humbling, and we learned a lot from the race. My mom learned even more about crewing me in harsh conditions, and we both gained more experience about continuing on despite feeling hopeless and questioning whether finishing was even possible. We learned that a minivan was an adequate crew vehicle for self-supported expeditions, and we gained a lot of knowledge on how to better pack a van to make supplies easily accessible. Our crew was good, but we were reminded that picking the right crew becomes even more critical as the difficulty increases. In this case, I had a lot of hands to help, but I only had one runner who could run with me. Despite my agonizing race, I came in fifty-fifth out of a hundred racers. Badwater is definitely one of the toughest races in the world, for many reasons.

After Badwater, I returned back to Denver and went to see a podiatrist about the plantar warts. First, we tried to freeze them, but they had grown too deep for the treatment to be effective. So the second course of action was to use acid to burn them out. Apparently, beetles create a special type of acid that is extremely effective in combating plantar warts. With my next race, Spartathlon, only two months away, I needed to get the warts removed as soon as possible. After the acid was applied, the warts bubbled and burned, along with all the area around them. Basically, the acid burned a hole in my foot, including the plantar warts. I was free of the warts, but my foot had to heal from the hole that had just been burned into it. I was unable to run for a full month, and I was concerned. How could I take on Spartathlon if I wasn't in the best shape of my life?

Spartathlon
153 miles—road
Athens to Sparta, Greece
September 2015

Spartathlon is a race steeped in antiquity. Its roots come from the legend of Phidippides, the great Greek runner and messenger. The story goes that in 490 BC, the Persians were coming to invade Greece via the port city of Athens. The Athenians knew they couldn't defeat the great Persian fleet without help from the fierce Spartan warriors. The only problem was that Sparta was over 150 miles away, and the treacherous route could only be made on foot. For most, it would take well over a week to cover this distance. The Athenians dispatched their great runner Phidippides with a message and request to the Spartans to help fight the Persian army. Ancient lore states that Phidippides arrived the next day.

Almost thirty years ago, a group of four British runners studied the story, route, and lore of Phidippides's run . . . and that was the birth of Spartathlon. The race requires runners to run from Athens to Sparta, or 246 km/153 miles, in 36 hours. The race is like the Olympics of ultra-running as there are runners from all over the world. The field size is limited to 390, and the US is permitted to send only twenty to twenty-five runners, depending on the year. The Greeks and the Japanese always field the largest teams, and there are always strong German and British teams as well. In order to qualify for Spartathlon, you must be a "fast" ultra-runner. Examples of qualifying standards include completing a hundred miles in less than twenty-one hours, or a hundred kilometers in under ten hours. After a runner is time qualified, they must submit an application with their running resume and race performances.

Obviously, the more races and better performances a runner has, the better chance he or she will be invited to race at Spartathlon. I was selected to the US Team in 2015, and only the second blind runner to ever attempt Spartathlon. The other blind runner didn't finish the race.

When I was accepted, the race directors invited me, contingent on my being tethered to another runner for the entire race. A tether is a connective device such as a rope, string, or bungee, held between a blind athlete and the guide. It allows the blind runner to get information on which direction to run, and helps the guide "steer" the blind runner in the correct direction. This was a big problem for me. I had never run tethered to a guide, even in training. I begged the International Spartathlon Association (ISA) to not force me to use a tether. They were stern and stated that it was for my own safety. I sent the ISA videos of me running other races independently, running on roads and on trails. The ISA didn't care, and gave me an ultimatum—either run tethered to a guide runner or don't run Spartathlon. I chose Spartathlon, so I had to figure out how to run tethered to another runner for the entire race. The race was in Greece, and I didn't know any runners in Greece. The cost of bringing a guide to the race was prohibitive on my budget while unemployed and supporting three children. From my past adventures, I leaned on my lesson that there are good people out there who want to help—all you have to do is ask for it.

I logged onto Facebook and explained my situation, and half-jokingly asked if anybody wanted to or could guide me for 153 miles in Greece at Spartathlon. I didn't expect any responses, and assumed I would have to find somebody in Europe who could help me. Much to my surprise, I had a message in my Facebook inbox within a couple of hours of my post. An über-ultrarunner who had come out to help me at my Relentless 100 run contacted me—none other than Brandon Stapanowich offered to help me. In addition to being a physical therapist and a great runner, Brandon also founded the Pikes Peak Chapter of Achilles, an organization that hosts a weekly training run and guides physically and mentally challenged athletes. I knew of Brandon's running resume, and was sure he could cover the distance, despite never having ran farther than a hundred miles. Brandon was also going to cover his own travel costs, and use his valuable vacation from work just to help me. A part of me felt extremely guilty and as if I was imposing on Brandon. Another part of me felt extremely lucky and honored to have a person like him agree to invest so much to help me try to complete and compete at Spartathlon.

I had some unexpected things happen before Spartathlon. My month-long hiatus from running after my wart removal had made me question my fitness. I did what I could with biking and swimming, but it just wasn't the same type of workout to maintain my running fitness. Also, my mom and I decided that she wouldn't make the trip to crew me, due to some unforeseen circumstances. I arrived in Athens a few days before the race in an effort to adjust to the time difference. Athens was eight hours ahead of Mountain Daylight time in Denver. I now attempted to run my first Spartathlon self-supported, while being constantly tied to another runner.

The start of the race began at the steps of the Acropolis, where ruins over two thousand years old remain, including the mighty Parthenon. I had invented a hip tether which was made of two race belts, two elastic shoelaces, and two lobster-claw hooks. Brandon and I each wore a race belt with a shoelace tied to it. The other end of the shoelace was tied to a lobster-claw hook about one inch in size. When we needed to be tethered to one another, we could hook the claws to each other. When we needed to separate for a bathroom break or crowded aid station, we could easily unhook the claws from one another.

When the start gun went off at 7:00 a.m., the energy was electric. I was overwhelmed with all of the different languages I heard, and the thought of retracing a route that was run thousands of years ago humbled me into silent thought. As Brandon and I ran, I grabbed hold of his elbow since it was too dark for me to see, and there were masses of people running down a cobblestone street with periodic posts sticking a foot out of the ground. We held back and chose to run at nine to ten-minute miles for the first fifty miles. In Spartathlon, there are aid stations and checkpoints every couple of miles. If a runner doesn't reach the checkpoint before a predetermined time, the runner isn't permitted to continue running.

There are a couple of big checkpoints that runners aim to achieve by a certain point. The first one is around mile fifty at the Corinth Canal. Runners are required to leave the checkpoint in nine hours, thirty minutes or faster. I was having stomach problems since we started the race. It felt like I had to use the bathroom, and my stomach was gurgling. I needed to relieve pressure from the area, so I ditched my waist belt that held my water bottle. I also ran with a spare battery for my headlamp because I forgot to put one in the drop bag where my headlamp was located. If I didn't have light, my race was over. My headlamp could last twelve hours on two of the rechargeable batteries.

The first fifty miles wound through Athens, industrial areas, and ocean towns on small roads and highways. The pollution in the air was noticeable, but tolerable. I assumed I would be able to eat food from the aid stations, but soon discovered that raisins, potato chips, wafer cookies, and fruit juice couldn't sustain me for the entire 153 miles. The day heated up, and temperatures neared 90° and humidity rose as we followed the coast of the Mediterranean Sea for about a marathon, or twenty-six miles. Brandon and I reached the fifty- mile mark with over an hour to spare. We were moving good, and I was feeling strong. Brandon had struggled with the heat and jet lag, although he just kept moving through the pain as he couldn't stop running. If he stopped, my race would be over, and to Brandon, that simply was not an option. I came to discover that 50 percent of the field wouldn't make it past mile fifty.

Brandon and I kept running, although our pace was slowing from our planned pace. We needed frequent walk breaks, and soon the majority of our forward progress was walking. I felt the effects of my month-long hiatus from running due to the plantar wart treatment. Many of the runners were suffering from the pace of the race. In Spartathlon, the runner is required to run with limited walking in order to finish in the cut-off time. For most hundred-mile races, the cut-off is thirty hours. For Spartathlon, the hundred-mile cut-off is twenty-two and a half hours, and the race cut-off is thirty-six hours for the full 153 miles. There was no time for sleeping, resting, or long pit stops. If you had to puke or use the bathroom, you needed to be as efficient as possible so you could keep making forward progress.

As Brandon and I entered the cool of the night, I found the strength to run again. We were passing many runners who were fading. As we passed them, we offered words of encouragement, and they did the same. We were all feeling and fearing that the next checkpoint might be our last. I became obsessed with the time, and how much of a buffer we had. I was asking Brandon to do the math in his head, and he isn't great at math. My anxiety was causing Brandon anxiety. By mile ninety-two, I had accepted my fate—that my race would end by being timed out. At one aid station, I sat down and told them to take my bib. The aid station volunteers yelled that we were still twenty minutes ahead of the cut-off. That must have sparked something in me, because Brandon and I got up and started off into the darkness again. As we climbed from mile 95 to mile 99.5, the pitch of the road was so steep at points, it felt like we should have been on our hands and knees. By the time we got to the infamous Mountain Base, we were only seconds ahead of the cut-off. Brandon and I figured that my race was done, so we decided to run up the road to reach a hundred miles instead of turning into the trail that led over a treacherous mountain pass of single-track trail. It was raining, I was demoralized, and doubt had finally gotten the best of me. I had quit with seconds to spare. Who knows if I could have made it to the next checkpoint in time? I'll never know, because I refused to try. I had failed.

Brandon and I boarded the "Death Bus," a coach-style bus that carried the beaten and battered bodies of competitors. Brandon and I were delirious and we faded in and out of consciousness, being woken periodically by people vomiting and crying. By the time we arrived in Sparta, we witnessed runners making their way down the final six blocks of the course to a statue of King Leonidas, which was the finish line. When a runner finished, they kissed the foot of the great king, and were greeted by women in togas, and water from a sacred fount. The final honor was the placement of a wreath on the head of the successful runner. Brandon and I looked at each other and said nothing, but in our hearts we were saying the same thing: "That should have been us."

After the failed attempt at Spartathlon, my ego was put back in check and I was reminded that I was capable of failing at any time. I also questioned whether my body and mind could complete the transcon given my failure in Greece. Doubt was screaming loud into my ears and not letting up. I replayed the pain, and my ultimate decision to quit when I was still in the race, if only by less than a minute. I couldn't wrap my head around the fact that I had been beaten into submission. I would rather die than quit. However, on this occasion, I quit and lived. I never discussed how deeply that DNF at Spartathlon affected me, and I don't know if I have the words to describe it. Suffice it to say, it's like a pebble permanently mounted against your foot. It's always there, and is noticeable at random times. There are other times when you don't even notice it; however, the sensation of something not being right always returns. I suppose I'll have that pebble until I am able to finish that race.

After Spartathlon, I had six months to do transcon-specific training. I ran between seventy and a hundred miles per week by the time I ran Spartathlon. I needed to increase my mileage even more.

During the transcon, I planned to run 350 miles per week, or fifty miles per day. This was a 200 percent increase over the training miles I was putting in. I planned to have my training peak during the run. For many events, runners increase their training until they are a couple of weeks from the race day, then they drastically decrease their mileage in these two taper weeks. The idea is that they save their peak performance for race day. In my case, I was planning to use the first couple of weeks of the run as training, and be at my strongest when I was two to three weeks into the transcon.

From October 2015 to March 2016, I trained myself to run seven days a week, with no rest days. I wasn't planning to take any days off during my transcon, so I needed to train accordingly. Next, I made sure that I was always running on asphalt or concrete. I needed my bones to become as dense as possible during training in order to prevent fractures in my toes, feet, ankles, legs, and hips. I supplemented my diet with calcium as well. I also created a tire drag to increase running resistance training—a car tire attached to a rope which is affixed to a belt around the runner's waist. The friction of the tire on asphalt and concrete creates a significant amount of resistance. For me, it was a good way to simulate hill training and forced my hips and quads to engage for a more powerful stride. I couldn't drive to the mountains of Colorado for scenic hill repeats; however, I did have my tire which could inflict as much or more pain.

The months passed and I played mind games with myself. I forced myself to routinely run in the dark. I hated the dark because it reminded me of going blind. I tortured myself by running in the dark. I also had the benefit of running in hyper-cold weather as Denver experienced a few "arctic blasts" which caused temperatures to decrease to below 0° Fahrenheit. Anything I could do to make training uncomfortable was fair game. By December, I was running thirteen to fifteen miles per day, with a marathon on Saturday, putting my weekly mileage routinely at 110 miles. The last weeks of December, January, and February leading up to the transcon were my high-mileage weeks. In the last week of December, I ran a marathon a day for seven days straight, which was a 183-mile week.

17

Show Me the Money

Humility does not mean you think less of yourself.
It means you think of yourself less.
- Ken Blanchard

The reality of funding the run was a major issue for which I had no solution. I had read Marshall Ulrich's book *Running on Empty* where he recounted that he had a friend agree to underwrite his entire run. Then, when Charlie Engle became involved, they were able to recruit enough sponsorship dollars to underwrite their entire run. I always fantasized about that one super-rich friend who believed in me and my dream, and one day would call me and agree to fund this entire run; however, that wasn't to be my path.

The first thing I had to do was to figure out how much this expedition was going to cost. As I researched this topic, I soon discovered that there was a huge spectrum regarding budgets related to transcontinental crossings on foot. On one end, people who walked, maintained a low daily mileage, and were humble in their needs reportedly were able to cross spending $1 per mile. So, for a journey of 3,000 miles, they would spend $3,000. This seemed extremely conservative, and I didn't understand how a person could buy food .

. . and any motel stays were out of the question. For this type of crossing, I'd have to camp in fields, not shower, eat minimally, and walk at a slow pace. On the other end of the spectrum were the speed crossings. Usually, these people were averaging forty miles per day or more. The speed crossers routinely had a large recreational vehicle (RV) where the runner could sleep at night, go to the bathroom, rest during the day, and where the crew could prepare meals. These speedsters usually also had an additional support vehicle like an SUV or a minivan. A bike was also common to ride alongside the runner to keep him or her company. What was assumed with these speed crossers was that there would be a four or five person crew who would tend to the runner's every need, and take care of all the logistics of the run. Most of the time, these crews were provided a stipend (payment) for taking time off work to help with the expedition.

Marshall and Charlie's crossing seemed to be one of the best-funded expeditions I found in my research. I don't know for sure, but I guesstimated that their crossing effort with two RVs, two support vehicles, two crews of five people each, and an entire movie crew to film the entire effort would cost well over $300,000 for just under two months of running.

I knew that I couldn't run across America at fifty miles per day on a budget of $1 per mile. I also knew that my expedition would never be as well-funded as Marshall and Charlie's attempt. From my experience, I knew that I had to have at least one person with me. There was only ever one real option for who this person would be. It would have to be my mom. She was the strongest, most courageous person I knew. She was also the only person I knew who was crazy enough to follow me in pursuing a seemingly insane goal like running coast-to-coast across America. My mom barely stands five feet tall. She is just a hair over a hundred pounds.

In her early years, she liked to go out with my aunt who loved country music and dancing. They would frequent a place called the Zanza Bar on Colfax. A scene from a Clint Eastwood movie, *Any Which Way but Loose*, was filmed there. Mom was at a 7-Eleven, and while she was in line waiting to buy her cigarettes, the customer in front of her was also trying to buy a pack. The customer didn't have any money and only had traveler's checks. The clerk at 7-Eleven wouldn't accept them because the check was made out in Clint Eastwood's name. Mom intervened and bought the customer his pack of cigarettes, so he invited my mom and a guest to a party at his hotel suite in Denver. When my mom and stepfather went to the party, the customer really turned out to be Clint Eastwood. And, that is how my mom's smoking resulted in one of the coolest stories I've ever heard.

Mom stopped smoking when my stepfather passed away from cancer in 1991. She also started working out with weights and a personal trainer, bicycling and running a bit. She became very fit. I remember one time when I was in law school, I came back to Denver and wanted to work out with Mom at her gym. I thought it was cute that she was working out and had a personal trainer. We went to her gym and the trainer started us working out. Within five minutes of starting the strenuous workout, I found myself running out of the gym to the nearest dumpster I could find, and I puked my guts out. This little lady meant business. She didn't look like much physically, but I knew she was physically fit and was mentally stronger than anybody I had ever encountered in my life. She was the only choice for a crewperson, and I felt like I had to have her with me if I was going to be able to make fifty miles per day.

When I chose my mom, however, that also affected my anticipated budget for the trip. My mom doesn't eat much; however, at seventy years old and living a comfortable lifestyle, I knew she wouldn't be up for roughing it and camping out to conserve money. We would need to stay in hotels and motels, which would increase the expense of the venture. Mom loves to drive, and prefers to drive over being a passenger, so I knew she could handle being behind the wheel for an extended period of time. However, I couldn't imagine her trying to drive a large RV over mountains, through deserts, on highways, etc. Also, she wasn't going to drive the RV to refuse stations to unload human excrement. If an RV was going to be in our future, I would need other crew members to volunteer for the trip. I had no money to pay them, so it would be on a strictly volunteer basis. No volunteers or crew members materialized, and the expedition was turning out to be just my mom and me.

From a budgeting perspective, this seemed to help keep the costs down. I sat down at a computer to try to create a budget for the sixty-day expedition. What I came up with was as follows:

Motels: 60 x $120 = $7,200
Food: 60 x $200 = $14,400
Gas: 60 x $20 = $1,200
Miscellaneous: $ 500
Shoes: $5,000
Recovery Supplies: $2,000
ESTIMATE TOTAL: $30,300

I knew my estimated budget was very rough, and there were a lot of things I hadn't even thought of. I was shocked to even think that a transcontinental expedition would, at a minimum, cost $15,000 per month. I wasn't working and I was living on social security disability income when I was preparing for the transcon. I was humbled, at times I would say I felt humiliated, to be relying on my social security distribution at such a young age. I still remember when I applied. First, the government had to verify that I was disabled. This is a very stringent process, and I was required to submit eye doctor's reports, sign releases, and submit to an examination by a government eye doctor. I remember going to that eye appointment, being interrogated, having my eyes tested, and being treated with skepticism. I was again told I had RP, I was going blind, and there was nothing I could do about it. I was ripped to shreds again, and I went to my girlfriend's house and lay there, destroyed and crying. I was told by many people that applying for Social Security Disability Income would be a process. I was told that I would probably have to hire an attorney and that almost nobody was approved on their initial application and evaluation. I wasn't relying on it, as I had some savings from when I was working. However, all of that was significantly decreased when I divorced and chose to keep the house in order to provide stability for my children. Most of my assets weren't liquid, and consisted of equity in the home I would still be paying on for the next twenty plus years.

A couple of months after the government eye appointment, I received a letter in the mail from the Social Security Administration. I expected to open it and read that I wasn't approved, and I was already thinking about which of my lawyer friends worked in Disability Law. I opened the letter, and don't remember anything the letter said except the following words, ". . . you are permanently and totally disabled." My world was turned upside down, again. How could the government label me like this? Most people I knew had no idea I even had a degenerative eye condition. I was faking it with employers, friends, and family. My eyes, however, couldn't fake it. Whenever I go to see an eye doctor, they always treat me like I can see before they look into my eyes. Then, they look into my eyes at my retina and their whole demeanor changes. I feel their pity after they look into my eyes and tell me there is nothing they can do for me.

For the first time, having a degenerative eye condition played in my favor. There could be no faking my eye disease, or the stage of its progression. The Social Security Administration labeled me as being disabled. *So what does this mean?* I wondered.

It meant I would receive a monthly check paying me for the social security contributions I had made during my working career. I later found out that my monthly payment was one of the highest permitted. I suppose this was because I was contributing at very high levels when I was a highly compensated executive. To put the amount in perspective, I was compensated at near the highest payout allowed; however, I was well below the federal poverty level. Luckily, I was able to buy health insurance through Medicare. I remembered watching the fictional movie *From Prada to Nada* with my kids and having a good laugh. The movie was about a couple of sisters who were very well off, and through a series of events found themselves living a meager existence. My life wasn't fiction—it was real for my kids and me. My income was meager, and I lived according to a tight budget so I could maintain savings and my retirement plans. Life for my kids and me had dramatically changed because of financial changes in my life.

With a fixed income, I didn't think there was any way for me to fund the run on my own. I didn't want to deplete all of my savings since I still had three kids to put through college, and there would be unforeseen expenses I would need to handle for them. I also knew I couldn't get a second mortgage on my house—no lender was going to give an unemployed disabled guy on a fixed income a loan of $30K to go and run across America. I did have credit cards, but that would be a last-ditch way of funding this expedition.

The next thing I had to figure out was the vehicle. I wanted to have an RV to bring down motel expenses and decrease the need to drive to and from motels on a daily basis. I viewed this driving time as non-value-added time. I should either be running or resting. I shouldn't be sitting in a car being driven to a place to rest. When I looked into RVs, they were renting at $6,000 to $10,000 per month. No RV company was willing to give me a discount or donate the use of an RV. A friend of mine had offered us the use of his RV; however, my mom wasn't comfortable borrowing a friend's RV. She counseled me against this, since a wreck or problem could cause the demise of a friendship. She always thought about people first, and knew how people can get weird about money and material possessions. The only way an RV would be feasible would be if I found an extra crewperson, because Mom couldn't and wouldn't drive it.

Eventually, Mom and I discussed using a minivan as a crew vehicle for the transcon. We had used a minivan to crew me when I ran across Puerto Rico and when I ran Badwater. With minimal crew members, we thought a minivan could be a perfect vehicle. When I looked into renting a minivan, the cost was around $1,500 per month, without insurance. My brother had a twelve-year-old Honda Odyssey minivan with only 50,000 miles on it. He volunteered its use for the transcon. Although it was low in miles, it was well broken in. My brother's kids who were in high school used the van to commute to and from school and sporting events, and there were probably some great party stories associated with this vehicle. I jumped at the opportunity to use the van, as it would decrease expenses significantly. There were some mechanical repairs that needed to be done, and after the run, the transmission totally died. Hence, the expense of renting or using this donated minivan became a wash in the end.

I had decided on my crew and crew vehicle. I had a rough number in mind for total expenses—$30,000 on the cheap end, and $50,000 on the expensive end. But I had to figure out a way to raise this amount of money in the eighteen months leading up to the run.

I had heard stories about Erik Weinmeyer, the blind mountaineer, who had summited Everest some fifteen years prior. I remembered watching a film about his summit and he told a gripping account about how he had gotten a telephone conversation with the President of the National Federation for the Blind, and within a short time he was on a plane with his dad to DC to meet face-to-face with the President of the NFB. Erik said the NFB funded his expedition, and then he just formed his team, trained, and set out on the expedition. In return for funding the expedition, Erik promised to put a NFB flag atop Everest and take a picture with it.

I figured the NFB was a good partnership opportunity. After all, according to Marshall Ulrich who has run across America and summited Everest, a transcon run is much harder than an Everest summit. Numbers seem to tell the same story. Since the 1950s, Everest has been summited over 4,000 times. Since the 1800s, less than 300 people have ever crossed America on foot. Marshall recounts that many of his days on Everest were spent journaling, and joking at different camps while he waited for his body to adapt to the altitude. When he did ascend into the Death Zone, above 24,000 feet, his body was assaulted and the game was to get to and from the summit before his body consumed too much of itself, in order to make a safe descent.

While the physical demands of climbing the great mountain were significant, they were nowhere near what was required to run across America. When Marshall was climbing, he also noted that there were always team members there with him on the rope undertaking the same challenge as he was. He never experienced the extreme isolation that a person running across America experiences. Regardless of whether a crew is there or not, it is upon the runner's shoulders to take those six million steps to run 3,000+ miles. I thought a transcon run by a blind person seemed at least as impressive as an Everest summit by a blind person. Accordingly, I thought the NFB would be a great partner to help fund my transcon expedition.

When I called the NFB and asked for sponsorship, I was asked to postpone my start date for a couple of years so more of a marketing effort could be made about the run and NFB's sponsorship. It was only a few months to go before the start and I knew my mental and physical preparation for the run couldn't withstand a one or two year delay. I had to start on the date as planned, and I told the NFB the same. The NFB decided to not sponsor the run, and I was back to paying for the expedition on my own—where I had started.

I moved on and reached out to other organizations I knew that served the blind, including the Foundation Fighting Blindness, the American Foundation for the Blind, and Guiding Eyes for the Blind, although none of them were willing to give me money to cover expenses for me to run. All of them were very excited to have me use the run as a fundraiser for their nonprofit organizations. I wanted to use this run to help blind people, but not to fill their coffers while I emptied my own pocketbook to the tune of tens of thousands of dollars. I couldn't understand why these significant "blind organizations" wouldn't get behind the run and put a little skin in the game. I knew they could afford it. Perhaps they just didn't believe I could actually run all the way across America, or there were financial constraints I wasn't aware of, or this was but another challenge that was put in front of me to test my faith in this Calling.

I remember staying up many sleepless nights trying to figure out how I was going to pay for this extremely expensive endeavor. After coming up empty-handed from all of my efforts to get the run sponsored, I resorted to the fact that I was going to have to ask for help from friends, family, and strangers, if I was going to maintain the standard of living I had established for my kids and me. In the middle of one of these sleepless nights, I got up and went to my computer. I had heard of a guy named Adam Kimble who was going to attempt to break the transcon world record beginning in February of 2016. Adam was young, in his late twenties, and relatively new to ultra-running. He'd run a few ultras with average finishes, excepting one. He had won one race called the Gobi March in China. The race is a seven-day footrace covering roughly 155 miles. Adam said he was cross training and not running a lot to minimize the wear and tear on his body. In a podcast interview, Adam said he thought he had a 60 percent chance of breaking the world record for a transcontinental foot crossing. It seemed like a cocky, uninformed statement, but it also seemed like the attitude a person would need in order to break the record that had stood for over three decades. As soon as Adam publicly stated that he was going after the record, there was a media frenzy and Adam became an overnight semi-celebrity.

I didn't intend to make a brash statement about trying to go after the record. I did go so far as to submit an application to Guinness (not the beer) to have a record created for the fastest transcontinental foot crossing by a blind person. Guinness denied my application to create a new record category, but said my application was sufficient to try to break the same record Adam was chasing, and Marshall and Charlie had chased. Adam's strong online presence gave me an idea. I thought I could get people to donate to my cause if I could get the word out online about what I was going to attempt.

I decided to build a website. The only problem was, I had no clue how to create one. First, I discovered that I had to find a domain name, or a name for my website. I needed it to be catchy and related to some blind guy running across America. I settled on VISIONRUNUSA because it fit my criteria and the .com domain name was available. The way the word "vision" contrasted with the word "sight" was very important to me. I had come to grips with the reality that I was losing my sight and there was no amount of denial or treatment that was going to change that fact. Vision, however, was different. I remembered being a young executive at GE and having a vision that my organization would be world-class and a center of excellence for the company. After eighteen months of innovating, failing, recovering, and ultimately succeeding, I had fulfilled the vision I had set out to accomplish. I realized that *one doesn't need sight to have vision.*

Vision is what could be and should be with each and every one of us. It is about pursuing dreams relentlessly in the face of ultimate adversity—despite doubt, pain, and fear. Vision is driven through our head, into our heart, and is an inspirational explosion when it is unleashed into the community at large. This run would free me of my fear that going blind would wreck me as a human being. If I could accomplish this run, I knew I would be able to go on with life in a good way, regardless of whether I had sight or not. In the end, this run wasn't intended to give my life meaning, it was a Calling from something much larger than myself, and, if I could somehow see this through on faith alone, I knew my blindness would be healed, even if I still couldn't see.

Before long, I had a website up and running. I also found a nonprofit organization that helped blind people and was willing to help me. The US Association of Blind Athletes (USABA) is a member of the US Olympic Committee. They are responsible for building, developing, and supporting the US Paralympic Goalball Teams—a sport that was developed specifically for blind athletes. In addition to goalball, the USABA hosts the US Blind Marathon Championships in Sacramento, which I won in 2014. The same man who steered me toward running in the Championships in 2014 also suggested that I ask the USABA to help support me with the run. I looked at USABA's Form 990s and realized that they weren't in a position to financially cover the expenses of the run. However, perhaps we could strike a deal that I would raise money for USABA during the run, and any money raised would first go to cover the expenses of my run. All additional money would go to USABA.

Their executive director, Mark Lucas, was a man of his word with amazing integrity and humor. After a thirty-minute conversation with Mark, we had all the details hammered out. This arrangement was good for the organization as they would get publicity from the run and any donations in excess of my expenses would go directly to them. The donations were also tax deductible to the donor.

I still remember how horrible I felt when I wrote the post on my Facebook timeline saying that I was accepting donations for my run. I felt like a failure, again. I wasn't able to independently take care of myself, or my dreams. Some people told me that nobody was going to give me money for my run, and if that was my dream, I would need to fund it by myself. I hoped they were incorrect. Within thirty minutes of posting my plea, I had a friend text me and say she was giving me $1,000. I told her I felt guilty, and wasn't sure I could accept such a donation. She told me I had to accept it, and every other nickel that was given to support the run. She went on to explain that this wasn't just my run—it was an attempt by someone to do something truly incredible, and that was why she was supporting it.

I was speechless as I lay in bed that night, not knowing what to think or expect. I know I felt like I was begging for money, and that was very humbling. But I had to set aside my pride if this run was going to happen. The only difference between the guy who stands on the street corner with a cardboard sign and me was that my sign was a website and I was hiding in my house. I felt ashamed to have to ask for help.

I did keep calling on companies for sponsorship, although none were willing to financially sponsor the run. Some were happy to donate their products for my use during the run, and I was extremely thankful. My product sponsors included KIND Snacks, Oberto jerky, Zensah compression clothing, Pearl Izumi running clothing, HOKA ONE ONE shoes, Smartwool Socks, LED Lightvest reflective safety vest, NoxGear reflective safety vest, PrincetonTec headlamps, Gem Elixirz aroma therapy recovery scents, NormaTec compression boots, Denver Sports Recovery services, Chiropractic Solutions services, RockTape kinesiology tape, and DJO Global mobile icing solution.

I called hotel chain after hotel chain, and tried to get them to sponsor me. As it turned out, many hotel and motel chains are franchised businesses in the small towns we would be passing through. We weren't even sure of our route, or the pace we would be able to keep. It was a daunting task to try to line up hotels and motels in advance of the run. The effort it would take, the logistical precision, and time to sell and negotiate with each hotel and motel made this a task I had to abort. I also considered homestays. These were also logistically difficult. It sounded like a good idea—people would open up their homes, feed us, let us sleep in a room, and we would be able to shower, then take off early in the a.m. But there was the logistical problem of planning with precision exactly where we were going to be on any given day. People who would host us would naturally want as much advance notice as possible. And, what if we changed the route last minute due to weather, or we found a more desirable way of crossing a geological formation, like mountains? I didn't want to disappoint anybody. Finally, we considered that we would have to exchange pleasantries, visit, and tell stories about the run. After all, people would be interested to learn more about the run. I would barely have energy to walk, let alone talk. I needed to conserve every ounce of energy I had. A homestay strategy was more appropriate for a runner who was going to try to cross America without any speed goal in mind. Because I was going to attempt a speed crossing, I had to be as efficient as possible. In this case, choosing efficiency was going to cost me at least $7,200 in motel expenses.

My attempts to get a big sponsor to fund my expedition had failed miserably. I didn't have the luxury or an all-expense paid expedition like Weynmeir's Everest expedition or other transcons. I did, however, have credit cards. And, I was going to violate the cardinal rule my mom had taught me about the use of credit cards. Mom always told me, "Credit is for convenience only. If you can't pay for what you want in cash, you don't buy it." Between all the credit cards I had, I figured I had enough to fund the expedition. I wasn't looking forward to dealing with the 20+ percent interest rates of the debt, but I decided I would just have to figure that out after the fact. That little devil of doubt sang sweetly into my ear on a daily basis, telling me what a bad father I was—putting myself in debt with this run, and making my children's futures more difficult because of the strain the run would put on my finances. I wanted to abandon the run almost daily for the eighteen months leading up to it for the solitary reason that the financial burden was crippling.

After exhausting all my resourcefulness to get the run funded, I was left begging for people's money via a website, and my credit cards. I would just have to have faith that everything was going to work out somehow. Money couldn't stop a Calling. And, if in fact this really was a Calling, I had always heard in church that "God will provide." I'm not sure I really believed that, and since I hadn't received a check from God for the $30,000+ that it was going to cost to run across America, I had to rely on faith alone for this part.

18

A Stranger to the Rescue

Unexpected kindness is priceless and free.

In October of 2015, Taylor had completed the documentary about my run across Puerto Rico. The documentary was called *Running Vision* and debuted to a crowd of family and friends at my church. The event was great, and it was strange to see myself on the big screen. More than anything, I was proud to have my philosophies on life, running, and my eye condition documented for my children, and their children. Some running fans also came to the event. One of those running fans was a young lady named Carly. She must have been in her late twenties, and I remembered her from Achilles, the running group that guides blind runners. She was the guide I ran with the first time I ever ran at Achilles, almost one year prior. After the movie, there was a question and answer period and I noted how I hated running in the dark. I think Carly thought I was saying I needed a guide or help running in the dark. I actually didn't because I was running on streets in Denver that I had memorized during daylight hours. I had memorized every curb cut and pothole on my routes. Carly was hoping to run more in the pre-sunrise hours and I needed to put in more miles. Carly offered to run with me one time per week, and that turned into a couple of times a week.

As Carly and I ran, our conversation naturally turned to the transcon. The longest distance Carly had ever ran was thirteen miles, and she had no experience in terms of ultra-running, crewing, or supporting this type of expedition. She did, however, have the same faith as I did, and she had many complementary skills to mine. At the time, her job wasn't too demanding, so she also had time. I called her Coach Carly, because she was the first person who dedicated a significant amount of time to the transcon, other than me. During our runs, I debriefed Carly on my fundraising attempts, injuries sustained, upcoming training schedule, ideas for minimizing expenses, etc. She was a master at details and getting things done, and had the time to help. I often felt bad, as this virtual stranger was dedicating so much of her time to help me with the transcon; but she would often say that she was getting more out of it than she was giving. This was an interesting discovery—there really are some people in life who truly and genuinely just want to help you and take nothing in return. I think she was attracted to being part of something that was so crazy and out there, and her organizational and technical skills were coming in very handy.

I had been trying to develop a route for over a year. In fact, I had reached out to Charlie Engle, because I had met him at the Puerto Rico run. Charlie told me he really didn't remember the route, but that the film company probably had it and he'd get it to me. This struck me as odd, as I didn't understand how he wasn't part of the route development. It was becoming clearer and clearer that my expedition was going to be like no other. If I could figure out this entire expedition, fund it myself, and have one seventy-year-old crew member help me, it would be a run like no other. Although it would be the seventh fastest crossing in history at fifty miles per day, it would be in a category by itself since other expeditions were so well-funded, crewed by so many people, and the runner wasn't figuring out every single facet of the expedition. On top of that, I had this eye condition that added an extra level of complexity to the entire project. I was truly going where nobody had dared to go before. And, it wasn't even for my personal motivation. I felt like I had been given an order and that it was a destiny I needed to fulfill whether I wanted to do it or not. So, I chose to be obedient, and do what I had been told to do.

This was a dramatic shift in how I had chosen to live life previously. In my professional careers, I was always a nice guy trying to help people out. However, my motives were to rise to positions where I could use my gifts and be paid significant income to take care of my family. My worldview stopped at the edge of my microcosm, which was my family and the organizations I supported. I was obedient to myself and my own needs. When faith entered my life, I was no longer the center of the universe. I became obedient to an entirely different set of values and objectives. Had I not had faith, I would never have, and could never have, even attempted a transcon. Now I was absolutely terrified at what I believe my belief system was telling me to do. I was doing it anyway, despite fear, reason, and logic. To this day, I'm not sure anybody would fully understand my motivation to go through with the transcon if they didn't have a strong belief system. I literally planned to run across America because of blind faith.

Blind faith, however, wasn't getting my route done any quicker. I also reached out to some other folks to see if they could help me with a route. I found Perry Newburn, the Kiwi who had crossed a few years prior at fifty-five miles per day. Perry didn't have the best memory of his route, and wasn't able to provide a map or spreadsheet of towns. He did remember a few towns on the route, and I jotted down the names. I also reached out to Adam Kimble who was about to start a transcon attempt. I didn't receive any response back from his camp at the time, and I assumed they were busy with their own preparations. I had also heard that Lisa Batchen-Smith was going to run across America. Lisa is an icon in American ultra-running, having won the *Marathon des Sables* in the Sahara and the Badwater 135, plus she ran fifty miles in fifty states in fifty days. Lisa was super responsive when I reached out to her; however, like Charlie, she had other people working on her route, website, and logistics. They had yet to settle on a route, and there was nothing to share.

I decided on Santa Monica Pier in Los Angeles, California as the starting point and Fannuel Hall in Boston, Massachusetts as my stopping point. I chose to start in Los Angeles because one of my running heroes, Adrian Broca, said he wanted to run some miles with me during my transcon. Adrian is legally blind and consistently wins or is on the podium for the blind marathon championships. On top of his running, Adrian is just a very nice person. Since Adrian lives in Los Angeles and Guinness World Records rules stated that a legitimate crossing went from either Los Angeles City Hall or San Francisco City Hall to New York City Hall, I picked LA as my start point. I planned to go through New York to City Hall so I would comply with Guinness; however, I intended to continue on to Boston.

There were two reasons why I wanted my run to finish in Boston. First, there is an organization called Team with a Vision which is organized by the Massachusetts Association for the Blind and Visually Impaired (MABVI). MABVI pioneered a recognized division for visually impaired athletes at the Boston Marathon. The division was groundbreaking, and just by virtue of having this division, more and more blind and visually impaired runners were competing in marathons. I wanted to celebrate Team with a Vision and MABVI, and Boston is where they are located. The second, and more important, reason I chose Boston was because of the woman I was in love with. I had been in one significant relationship since my divorce, and by the time the run had come onto my radar, I had been with this lady for almost four years. We both had children, and we ran together a lot. Our first couple of years together were amazing, and we had all kinds of adventures.

Then, we entered a rocky season of our relationship—her father became ill with cancer and I was trying to deal with deteriorating eyesight and career changes. We had some short break-ups and make-ups; however, I truly believed she was the one. We were both trying to get through difficult seasons in our lives, and they were coinciding with one another. I figured we just had to stick it out and when things got tough, we needed to hold tight to one another. Instead, on many occasions, we attacked one another. It was hard and heartbreaking. She was from Boston, and I'd gone back east to visit her family many times. We ran the Boston Marathon together in 2013 when the bombings occurred, and we were stopped just blocks from the finish line. We spent many weeks on multiple occasions on the Cape where her family had a home. We ate pastries and scrumptious Italian food in the North End of Boston which is famous for Italian cuisine and pastries. Her idea of a perfect afternoon was eating at Il Panini, followed by a cannoli at Mike's Pastries, and finishing off with a cappuccino at Vittoria's—all within steps of one another in the North End of Boston.

It was time again to swing for the fences, and the hopeless romantic in me dreamed about a finish in Boston that included her standing at Fannual Hall with arms outstretched, beaming with pride, and we would live happily ever after. Boston was important to her, and she was important to me, and I wanted to go to the end with her, so Boston would be the end of my run across America.

So, if I was ever going to reach Boston and a fairytale ending, I needed a route. I sat at my computer, pulled up MapQuest, and entered my starting point and ending point, and pressed "Directions". A route appeared; it was about 3,000 miles and looked good. Upon closer inspection, I realized that the route included interstates. From the little research I had done, I knew that running on interstates wasn't permitted, and illegal in most states. Usually highways and smaller state roads were legal to run on, although some states and municipalities ban running on highways as well. I saw that MapQuest had walking directions, so I clicked on that button. I saw the route suddenly shift, and about 600 additional miles were added. I also noted that the route was going over the Rockies in my home state of Colorado. I am acutely aware of spring snowstorms and knew it would be a big risk to pass through Colorado at this time of year. Putting in a final start and stop point into MapQuest was just too generic. I was going to have to plot a route in fifty-mile increments day-by-day.

I chose to go south of Colorado into New Mexico, then head

northeast through St. Louis until I hit New York City. Boston was about two hundred miles north of New York and there seemed to be some fairly natural routes. I plotted a route with fifty-mile intervals into MapQuest, and the program kept freezing after about 2,000 miles. I tried to plot and replot three times, over a span of three weeks. It was painstaking and tedious work. My eyes would "go out" after about three hours of plotting, and were just so strained, I couldn't read anything anymore. I spent the rest of the day training and caring for my kids. Routing was a major issue, and I wasn't successful in overcoming it. I asked a friend to hold me accountable and check in on my routing work on a daily basis. I was responsible to tell her whether I was was procrastinating or had made forward progress on the task.

During our morning runs, Carly also asked me how the route was coming. I would give the same old response, "Well, it's going okay, but I can't get it done." I had so many excuses for not finishing it. I was failing again, just like I had failed in my effort to raise funds to pay for the expedition. If I continued to procrastinate, I knew I had very big problems. There was no way I would be able to route on the fly with only one crew member. I would waste a ton of time, get lost numerous times, and the mental strain of not knowing where I was going would eventually crack me like a walnut. I had to establish a route somehow.

With about five weeks to go, Carly took the bull by the horns, showed up at my house one day, and announced that she had plotted a route for me. I was flabbergasted. She sat down at the computer, logged into a website, and voila. There was a route she had built from nothing. It had some of the cities that I was thinking about going through, and other routes I hadn't even thought of. We sat and talked about how she had created the route and what assumptions she had used to build it. She tried to stay off interstates and plot as direct a route as possible. She hadn't taken desert miles, weather, or elevation gain and descent into account. Carly didn't have experience with extreme running; however, she had technical savvy, a heart to help, and absolutely no ego.

After we talked, Carly said she would plot a different course based on what we had discussed. Within a couple of days, another route magically appeared. What she had completed in days, I had struggled and failed to complete in weeks. She had a complementary technical skill that I needed on my team, and it had arrived just in time. We talked more and determined that I would run due east out of LA until I reached Highway 54, then cut northeast across the central part of America through New Mexico, Texas, Oklahoma, Kansas, Missouri, and Illinois. After exhausting Highway 54, I would head due east, choosing terrain as flat as possible. By making this third and final modification to the route, we reduced total elevation gain by over 100,000 feet for the transcon route. We were proud, and we shared the route with other runners in the hopes that it might be able to help them with their routes. Secretly, I think we were hoping to get some sort of validation from other expeditioners that our route was sound and legitimate. We never received feedback from any other transcon expeditions, and by the time I locked down my final route, I was only three weeks away from my start date. I was out of time, and had to commit to the route regardless of the uncertainty I had about it.

19

It Takes a Village

Alone we can do so little,
together we can do so much.
— Helen Keller

Afters months of hard work, I felt like I wasn't making enough progress for the expedition to succeed. Between all the physical training, trying to fundraise, planning a route, keeping my weekly counseling appointments with my psychologist, and raising my kids, I was overloaded and overwhelmed. I had committed a classic error that I consistently coached my subordinates through when I was in my professional careers.

I was trying to do everything myself.

At GE, I learned the real value and importance of teams. It didn't matter that I had a cool title, or that I was receiving a coveted expatriate compensation package, or any other me-focused criteria. I would have been out of a job and my company would fail if I wasn't focused on my people and my customers. It was up to me to lead my teams, and I relied on the following tenets to do so:

1. **HIRE & PROMOTE THE BEST.** Surround yourself

with people who are better and smarter than you at their respective functions/disciplines/jobs. As people thrive, push them up into roles above your own.

2. BE HUMAN. Be vulnerable with your team as it builds trust and connection.

3. VISION. Constantly communicate where your team is going, and how the team will achieve their goals. Give them a road map of the future for the uncertainty you are leading them into.

4. BE A DOER. There are people who talk a lot, and there are people who do a lot while others are talking. Action speaks louder than words. I had no problem picking up trash in the parking lot or unclogging a toilet to make my team's work environment pleasant.

5. COMMUNICATE. People need to know what is on their leader's mind, and why things are happening. A workforce subjected to poor communication from its leader is like a scared child who feels abandoned.

6. EXPECT THE BEST. Have higher expectations for your employees than they have for themselves. People often underperform because of low internal expectations. Exceedingly high expectations can be stressful, but they can also be very satisfying when people accomplish their dreams.

7. HAVE FUN AND REWARD. Humor and laughter is great medicine for the human spirit, especially when times get tough. Recognize each and every accomplishment. Celebrate all successes, little and big. Always be on the lookout to give a compliment for a task well done. This creates a culture where people want to do good because they are appreciated and recognized.

8. EXECUTE RELENTLESSLY. Plan your work, and work your plan. Most organizations, leaders, and projects start strong and fizzle out as time goes on and other fire drills happen. Have a plan, and follow through on that plan to completion.

9. INTEGRITY. Do the right thing all the time. Behave the right way, even when others aren't looking. This value permeated GE, and I think that's why I felt like I belonged there.

10. RISK AND FAILURE ARE PART OF SUCCESS. My innate desire to swing for the fences and take big, calculated risks fit perfectly at GE. GE wasn't for overly conservative leaders who permitted fear and pain to paralyze their vision. GE rewarded courageous risk-taking. I learned that failure is part of succeeding; and more importantly, I learned to dissect and learn as much as possible from each failure to prevent it from happening again and to perform better in the future.

I needed to put these tenets into practice to build a team for my run across America since I was failing as I tried to do it on my own. I knew I needed my mom to crew me, and come with me if I was going to try to do a speed crossing of fifty miles a day. Nobody knew me better, and as far as I was concerned, Mom was a one-person "wrecking crew" who could handle known and unknown demands of the transcon. She had single-handedly crewed me in some of the harshest environments on the planet. But I didn't know if she fully understood how much of the transcon was unknown.

Mom committed to go with me because she was retired and had the time, but also because she wanted to be supportive. At one point, she told me that she wasn't willing to crew the entire two months and that she would need to come home for a week to take care of her home, bills, and life. That threw a big wrench in my plans. If I couldn't rely on her, I knew that I wouldn't be able to rely on anybody for the full two months. My plan was to try to get two people to fly out to help me when my mom took a week off. I didn't have these substitutes identified, and it was a lot to ask of anybody. Worst-case scenario, I planned to run with a baby stroller filled with my supplies and just go as fast and far as I could. I really got my feelings hurt when Mom said she wasn't going to stay with me for the entire expedition. I felt like I was one person going after an insurmountable goal. And, it was true. This was *my Calling*. It wasn't Mom's Calling. I would just have to figure it out, and I was thankful to have her support for as long as she could give it.

The next person to join my team was Carly. She had already helped with training and routing. While the run was taking place, she would handle the website and logistics from Denver. I also had a couple of different GPS tracking devices which would show my whereabouts at any given time. This would enable people to find me, come out to run with me, and follow the run virtually. She was committed, and in a role that suited her skill set.

I also have a couple of neighbors, Gary and Lori, who have become extremely good friends and supportive as I went through my rollercoaster of ups and downs in life. Lori was semi-retired and continuously asked to help me with the run. She always saw me running and training, and she was relentless in her quest to help me. I didn't know what skills she had, but I knew she was committed to this mission. As I learned when I was at GE, sometimes you have to create a job when you have a highly talented and committed person who wants to be on your team. So, I put Lori in charge of making motel reservations and backing up Carly on logistics. Lori's job was critical, because if we didn't have a place to go at the end of the day, the whole run could fall apart. The art of Lori's job was to try to find places for us to stay that were cheap and as close as possible to my daily stopping point. If the motel was thirty miles away, that would mean it would be about forty-five minutes of driving time one-way, plus another forty-five minutes to that location the next morning. That equated to a decrease of one and a half hours of sleep that I would be deprived of because we couldn't afford and didn't have the people power to manage an RV. Lori could only make reservations two days in advance, at best.

I had already recruited the US Association of Blind Athletes (USABA) to help me with public relations and media. They were going to be the beneficiary of the run, and would help promote it. I wanted to bring awareness to at least three issues affecting the blind and visually impaired:

1. A 70 percent unemployment rate,
2. A 66 percent obesity rate, and
3. Two times the rate of depression as the general population.

I was beginning to understand at a very personal level why blindness caused many of its victims to be plagued with low to no employment, and an unhealthy body and mind. Something needed to change, and awareness was the first step. The USABA also printed up some shirts, hats, and jackets for Mom and me to use and distribute during the run. The USABA had a small budget, and was going far beyond its comfort zone to support the run. It was people-focused, and it started with their leader, Mark Lucas. Mark is a humble man who believes in people and the power of the human spirit. He is sighted, but has helped the blind and visually impaired for the majority of his career. Mark and the USABA were integral parts of my team.

For emotional support, I needed my kids and my girlfriend to be on the team. My kids would be in school and wouldn't be able to see me physically, but we could talk on the phone and FaceTime each other. I knew they were my biggest fans and I had their love, regardless of how hard it would be for us to be apart. My girlfriend had a lot going on in her life, being a single mom and a full-time teacher, but she supported me as best she was able. She said she was going to visit me as I passed through New Mexico during the run, and I was counting on her being at the end of the run when I got to Boston.

I also had friends, family, and virtual strangers wanting to support me and the run on some level. A friend bought me a volleyball that looked like "Wilson" from the movie *Castaway*. In the movie, Tom Hanks's character is stranded on an island, and he befriends a volleyball. He names the volleyball Wilson, because it is a Wilson-branded volleyball. I had all my supporters sign my volleyball and I intended to carry it with me as a reminder that I wasn't alone.

I had overcome my foolish pride of thinking I had to move a mountain on my own. I was finally asking for help, and, more importantly, I began to accept it when people offered it. This was a very hard lesson for me to learn—a prideful person who had been stripped of jobs, titles, and fancy vacations to become a jobless, blind person who was investing every ounce of his being to pursue a Calling (something that caused many friends to question my very sanity).

My team was small, but we were mighty. When I asked Lisa Batchen-Smith to offer up her thoughts on my expedition and advice for success, she had only one suggestion. She said I needed at least one more crew member to help my mom support my needs. But I didn't know any people who could or would take off life for two months. Lisa tried unsuccessfully to help me find another crew member. In her voice, I could hear her thinking that she didn't want to see my transcon attempt fail due to lack of support and crew.

I also had the pleasure of meeting the great Marshall Ulrich face-to-face for lunch. After months of corresponding via e-mail with him, he agreed to have lunch and go over my transcon plans. He was extremely gracious and drove to my house, because he knew I didn't drive anymore due to my failing eyesight. I still remember when he rang my doorbell. I was star-struck. It was as if Michael Jordan stood at my door. Only, the person standing at my door was dressed in casual clothes, drove a normal vehicle, and didn't stand out from any of my neighbors who routinely walked their dogs past my house. Marshall looked normal; however, he was anything but normal. He had run across America, and had climbed the seven summits on the first attempt. He had been in every Eco-Challenge. He had won Badwater, and crossed it four times back-to-back. He was the first person to have completed the Leadville 100 Trail Run and the Pike's Peak Marathon on the same weekend. He is *The Man* when it comes to extreme endurance. He is also the man who said "Running across America is the hardest thing I've ever done."

Marshall is a tremendous listener, and is filled with a vast amount of information on extreme endurance pursuits. I asked Mom and Carly to join us for lunch. I knew that I wouldn't be able to absorb all of Marshall's wisdom, and more heads were better than mine. If this was the one time I had to pick the brain of this endurance icon, I didn't want to miss any pieces of advice.

We all went to a local pub where we could have lunch and sit and talk. Marshall first asked about my training. I told him about the racing I had done over the past eighteen months, and my buildup to a 300-mile training week. Although he didn't say anything, he seemed to approve. I think the first question in his mind was, "Has this guy physically prepared his body for what he is about to go through?" Next, he asked about my crew. I told him my mom was going to follow me with a minivan. There was silence. Then, more silence. And more silence. Marshall seemed concerned with such minimal support. He didn't come right out and say it, but I believe he was thinking, "You're making a big mistake."

The conversation then turned to my daily mileage goal. I advised Marshall that I was aiming for fifty miles a day or more. He explained that only four crossings had averaged fifty to sixty miles per day, and only two crossings had averaged sixty or more miles per day. He explained that my goal of fifty miles a day or more was "world class," and that a crossing of fifty to fifty-five miles per day assumed a 50-60 percent chance of serious injury, fifty-five to sixty miles per day assumed an 80 percent chance , and sixty plus miles per day assumed a 100 percent chance. He also said nonchalantly, "Anybody can cross at forty miles a day or more." He wasn't being cavalier, but noted that a fit person could easily walk thirty miles per day, and with consistent extra effort could probably figure out how to get in another ten miles per day.

However, in order to reach fifty miles per day or more, that person would have to either run day after day, or endure extreme sleep deprivation to walk twenty-hour days or more. In his eyes, fifty miles a day or more was a very, very high standard. Marshall had run 3,063 miles across America, averaging 58.5 miles per day, the third highest mileage per day crossing in history.

He gave me countless nuggets of advice. He told me about a break-in period my body would go through in the first two weeks. As I forced my body to do high mileage day after day, it would revolt against me. It would become injured, and I would have to endure more pain than I'd ever experienced in life. His advice was that I just needed to go through it, almost as if it was a rite of passage for anybody who was going to undertake a speed crossing. He told me there would be multiple times that I would feel depressed and as if I was the only person on earth. Marshall had his wife to help him with these feelings. I wouldn't have my kids or girlfriend with me, but I would have to just find a way to get through it. He also said I was signing up to go through extreme physical pain, but not to fight it. The pain would always win, and it would distract my focus from running safely on the roads. When the pain came, he told me to just embrace it. Just tell it, "I know you're here. I'm not going to fight you. Now I'm going to keep on running." It was a mental trick to overcome my physical being. I had done this in the past subconsciously, but I had never tried it at a conscious level. This tip would come in very handy.

Marshall told me about how he overcame Achilles tendonitis and cut a "V" notch into the back of his running shoe. This modification allowed the shoe to flex and not put pressure on his Achilles tendon. During Dean Karnazas's transcon, he called Marshall in pain and complaining about the same injury. Dean used Marshall's advice and was able to continue on and complete his transcon in seventy-five days, averaging around forty miles per day.

Marshall was confused by whether I was in fact legally blind. I had spent over four decades faking being sighted. Hence, it isn't uncommon for people to question whether in fact I have a degenerative eye condition. I don't think Marshall was questioning my condition, however; he was about to give me the most important piece of advice that anybody has ever given me about a transcon. He told me that the most dangerous part about running across America was the vehicles on the road. He had almost been run over while he was running in the breakdown lane. He almost had his body severed in half as a semitrailer with a wide load passed him in the dark of the night. He had people swerve at him to force him off the road. And, all of these things were happening at highway speeds.

Marshall's message was kind, but stern—"Only you know if you have enough sight to do this safely. Make a good decision." As he'd adventured through life, Marshall chose not to pursue those adventures where he could have died. To Marshall, those were extremely selfish pursuits. By this time, our conversation had naturally been steered toward my children who were all under the age of eighteen and living with me half the time. That lunch with Marshall gave me a lot to think about. I had to ask myself a lot of questions—was I prepared? Did I need more crew? Was this safe? Should I take this risk? Could I withstand the pain? Was my daily mileage goal too aggressive? Was this really my Calling? After that conversation, it seemed like I had even more reasons to just throw in the towel. Here was this icon who had told me how difficult this was going to be—in his eyes, summiting Everest wasn't even in the same category of difficulty as a transcon.

What am I doing? Why am I doing this?

I needed to take my lack of eyesight into consideration for this expedition. This wasn't a one or two day race on a marked course. This was an expedition where I was going headfirst into the unknown, and I was going to be armed with only four fully functional senses. The sense I was missing was the one I probably needed the most to guarantee my safety on roads where cars and semis would be travelling at seventy plus miles per hour.

20

Facing the Facts

I seldom think about my limitations and they never make me sad,
perhaps there is just a touch of yearning at times;
but it is vague, like a breeze among flowers.
— Helen Keller

I spent over four decades in denial that I was going blind, until I could deny no longer. Then I spiraled into a depression because of the changes this disease was forcing into my life. Each and every day I rose from my bed in defiance of imminent change was a miracle. We have all gone through difficult times in life, and we all know this feeling of making a decision to not give in or give up. At times, we must make a conscious decision to take just one more breath and think one more positive thought, which then becomes the beginning of curing smallpox, flying to the moon, or running across America.

An oak tree begins with only a seed.

I had to come to grips with the fact that when I opened my eyes, I didn't see what Marshall Ulrich, Lisa Batchen-Smith, Perry Newburn, Frank Giannino, and Adam Kimble saw. My run across America on its highways and open roads would be different from any other person who had ever attempted the feat. I was sorely underfunded and under-crewed; however, I was also lacking the sense of sight. I never like to play down how much I can see, because I think I can see okay. I think I've been faking being sighted for so many years, sometimes I can convince myself that my eyes function just fine. It is obvious that they don't; otherwise, I'm sure I would have never voluntarily stopped driving and caused undue hardship on my kids and me as a result.

I remember sitting at the kitchen table in my home, and asking myself the question, *What accommodations do I need to make for my eyes during this transcon?*

I had run on open roads in the past at Badwater in the desert, at Spartathlon in Greece where driving can be chaotic, and across Puerto Rico where curvy roads, speeding cars, and rum and Cokes are plentiful. I'd survived all those running experiences without ever being clipped by a car. Sure, I'd had close calls, but hasn't everybody? I forced myself to remember that I had been hit nine times by cars while running or biking. These included "love taps" with side view mirrors by a passing car cutting it too close, and resulted in my famous jump-tuck-and-bounce technique. Right before I am about to get hit by a car, I jump into the air and make a ball with my body. I try to elevate my body above the bumpers so I will first be impacted by the hood or trunk of the car, then I usually hit the windshield, and by that time the driver is usually braking; finally, I bounce in the opposite direction the car was travelling and skid across the ground. The driver is usually mortified, thinking that they have killed me. As I pick myself up off the ground and dust myself off, I usually share a monologue which ultimately has the intent of communicating, "You need to be more careful when you are driving."

The nice drivers apologize profusely and ask to take me to the hospital, or give me a ride somewhere. The bad drivers yell at me. Recently, I was in a pedestrian crosswalk and a lady on her phone in an SUV clipped me with her side mirror. After the impact, I was in shock at what a close call it had been. The lady, who was professionally dressed, slammed on her brakes, backed up, rolled down her window and started yelling at me saying, "Why did you hit my car?

I'm calling the police." I pointed out that I was wearing a high visibility yellow vest with six-inch black capital letters that said BLIND. I also pointed out that I was standing in a crosswalk that was painted for pedestrian crossing. Finally, I pointed out two signs that forewarned drivers to yield to pedestrians in the crosswalk. I asked her to call the police because I wanted to report the incident. She rolled up her window and sped off. I wasn't able to see her license plate or the model of her vehicle due to poor eyesight. Overwhelmed with disappointment in humanity and the shock of yet another near miss left me deflated. I started walking back home.

After about a minute, a different SUV slowly pulled up and the window rolled down. I heard a woman's voice saying, "Are you alright? Do you need anything?" She had witnessed the entire interaction, and just wanted to make sure I was okay. All I remember is babbling about the fact that I shouldn't get so upset when I nearly get killed by an errant driver. The woman's face went blank. It was obvious she had never experienced what I just experienced. As opposed to having anger toward the hit-and-run driver, I chose to be grateful to be able to make it home to my kids for joking, playing, and laughing.

This is the risk I take on a daily basis when I run independently in and around my home city of Denver. Regardless of whether I'm on sidewalks, in bike lanes, or on a bike path, there is always a possibility of collision with a vehicle, biker, or another person. As I train year after year, I have become all too aware that collisions do occur when you put in as many miles as I do. I can either not train as much, waiting for a guide's schedule to accommodate my training, or just go out and train on my own. The fact is that most guides don't have the time to train with me, and most guides couldn't train at the same speed and distances that I train at. I've been told by sighted and unsighted people that I shouldn't be running or biking independently. When I hear this, I hear them saying what they would choose to do if they were in my shoes. It saddens me to think that people would stop trying just because of losing a little thing like eyesight.

But they make me think, and I know it is the devil of doubt

speaking through my friends, family, and strangers, trying to make me quit. I always smile, and just keep on running, biking, and training. I have always said that God must want me to do something else in life, because He has yet to let me die despite all the close calls I've had in my life.

Regardless of my faith or my luck with city drivers, I knew I needed to be more vigilant and take more precautions during my run across America. My jump-tuck-bounce technique wouldn't work if a semi hit me at highway speeds . . . I would be nothing but a pancake on its grill and it would surely be the end of me.

I was constantly asked if I would have guides help me run across America and I knew the person asking didn't have an understanding of what I was setting out to do. There aren't many people on this earth who can run fifty miles day after day on open roads. A runner would have to take time off work and find me on the highways of America in order to guide me. Then, there would be the logistics of trying to get volunteers and organize these guides, as my daily mileage might ebb and flow. I was setting out to do a speed crossing of America, and that just didn't permit the use of guides. I did think it would be a good idea to have one, but it just wasn't realistic. I did throw up a Hail Mary, and I sent a message through a website to one person who I thought could guide me across America— Scott Jurek (an American running legend who had experience guiding blind runners). I never heard back from my website submission, but figured if he wanted to go for the three-thousand-mile jaunt along the roads of America, I'd gladly accept his help and company.

I knew from my prior racing and training experience that I should run against traffic, on the shoulder of the road, if there was one. I would use what sight I had to know when I had to get farther into the shoulder to avoid being hit. My eyes have dramatically different visual acuity. My left eye is a blurry 20/400 and my right eye is a crisp 20/200. This difference in acuity causes me to have no depth perception. I constantly get in trouble with moving vehicles as my eyes cannot judge how far away they are, or how fast they are closing in on me. I figured that if I could see an object and couple that with my hearing, I could try to deduce distance by judging the increasing volume of the oncoming vehicle and adding in the visual information I had from my eyes. It was the best I could do, so that was my plan.

I also knew there would be times where there might not be a shoulder on the road or there could be blind curves and it wouldn't be safe for me to run against traffic. In these instances, I would switch to the other side of the road, and only run with traffic when there was enough of a shoulder for my crew vehicle to follow behind me and block traffic. I figured that if a car was coming at me and I was running against traffic, I could jump off the road and had a chance at surviving. If a car ran me down from behind, I wouldn't even have a chance at surviving. My mom and I learned this "block from behind" technique when I ran across Puerto Rico. As we passed through the curvy mountain roads of the Caribbean island under the cover of night, the vehicles overtook and swarmed around me like gnats. I ran with traffic and had a police escort usually following me at a distance of three feet, and I was tucked in against the white line. There were no shoulders on these roads, and cars would zip by us and cut in front of the police car, usually missing me by just feet. They didn't realize that a person was running in front of the police car, and if I wasn't using the car as a blocker, I would have been hit on multiple occasions. The car and the runner had to work as a team for safety reasons when the runner was running with traffic.

I calculated that I would usually have between thirteen and sixteen hours of daylight each day, depending on the month and where I was at in America. I was starting in LA, a southern latitude and early in the spring, so I would have less daylight. Toward the end of the run, I would be at a more northern latitude and in late spring so I would have much more daylight to play with. I planned to complete fifty miles in twelve hours or less each day.

When I spoke with Marshall, he told me he preferred to run in the dark. It was easier mentally for him to be out there. There would be fewer cars to dodge, more calm and peace, and the weather would be much more moderate. Perry Newburn said he ran all desert sections at night in order to avoid the heat and storms.

I knew I wouldn't have the luxury of running in the dark of night. I had my best chance of not twisting an ankle, and avoiding wild animals and car collisions during the day. This didn't make me totally avoid running in the dark. I have super bright headlamps that were donated by PrincetonTec. At 300 lumens and a five-hour burn time, I felt like I could safely put in a couple of morning hours of running in the dark before sunrise. Usually, cars aren't on the highways at this hour, and if there was a shoulder and Mom could block for me, I could also use the light of her vehicle to illuminate the road.

One of my friends, Bob Weber, who had guided me during a Leadville 100 race, saw a high-visibility lightvest at a Ragnar Race he had attended. Bob contacted the manufacturer, LED Lightvest, and got them to donate one to me. It had high-visibility reflective material everywhere and white LEDs on the front and red LEDs on the back. There were flashing mode options for the lights, and it was impossible for cars to avoid seeing me when I was wearing it. Curiously enough, when I called the manufacturer to thank him for his donation, he went on to tell me that he felt he was Called to make the vest and his daytime job was working as an engineer for a big company. What a coincidence . . . or was it?

If I wore the high-visibility vest, used my headlamp, and ran in front of my crew vehicle's headlights, I thought I could do some early morning running in the dark, assuming there was a shoulder to run on. Mom and I discussed the possibility of running past sunset and into the evening hours. We both agreed that this wasn't safe. The more fatigued I am physically, the less my eyes function. After a full day of running fifty miles, I expected to be very fatigued, and didn't know how well I could expect to see. I also realized that my other senses would be dulled from fatigue, and their ability to help compensate for poor eyesight would be minimal. Mom and I agreed that sunset would be the end of the day, regardless of what mileage we had achieved. If we were short miles for the day, I would just have to make them up on subsequent days.

I knew my crew vehicle would be out of sight most of the run. The fact is, once it was about two hundred feet from me, I wouldn't be able to make out any unique features, and could only tell it was a vehicle on the road. I couldn't distinguish it from a car, truck, or mini-van with a cargo carrier on the roof.

My mom was going to be my only crew, and we would have responsibility to take care of one another. She would take care of my needs as I ran. I would care for her safety in the event something happened. There were a myriad of concerning scenarios I had dreamed up, like her pulling over on the side of the road and being struck by a car from behind, or crossing the highway and being chased or attacked by wild animals, or accidentally ditching the van on a shoulder of the road, and so on. A multitude of things could happen, but Mom is intelligent, street-smart, and a survivor. I had confidence she would be able to take care of herself; however, we both knew that neither of us had a clue of what we were getting ourselves into.

In order to stay in communication, we brought along walkie-talkies. We had used them in prior trail races where it wasn't possible for the crew to get to me. We used them to call out to the crew in advance of reaching the aid station to let them know what I needed. Usually the walkies had two miles of distance in the mountains. We hoped they would have at least five miles of distance on the open road with no obstructions. I also planned to carry my cell phone in a small backpack. We knew there would be areas where there would be no cell phone service, and in those areas, we would rely solely on our walkie-talkies. Our strategy was to have Mom crew me every mile, assuming there was a shoulder for her to park on. With good communication, we could be nimble, fast and use our under-supported expedition as an advantage for speed. We had less complexity and fewer people to accommodate, so we could move quickly across America.

Based on speaking with Marshall, I knew a goal of fifty miles per day was stretching myself well beyond my physical and mental breaking points. When doubt softly whispered all of those things that could happen to inhibit me achieving my daily goal, I fought hard to not listen. Doubt continued to attack, and it was overwhelming. If I continued to listen to that siren's song, I would shut down and only be aware of all the bad that could happen.

I had to just commit to my goal, understand and respect my safety rules, and make relentless forward progress toward the Atlantic Ocean. If I could run, I would run. If I couldn't run, I would walk. If I couldn't walk, I would crawl. And, if I couldn't crawl, I would have to find somebody to drag me. I just had to keep moving forward. It was at this point that I chose my battle cry. I needed a single word that could silence that devil of doubt. I found it almost instantaneously. My battle cry would be *ONWARD!*

Regardless of injury or pain, I must move *ONWARD*. Regardless of weather or limited support, I must move *ONWARD*. Regardless of blindness and depression, I must move *ONWARD*. Regardless of being underfunded, I must move *ONWARD*. Regardless of how isolated I might feel, or how much I might miss my kids, I had to move *ONWARD*. Regardless of whatever doubt or obstacle would cross my path, I must move *ONWARD!*

A goal of fifty miles a day, or almost two marathons a day, was a big enough goal to keep me moving forward with no easy days. I couldn't take any rest days or days off. When questioned why, I responded that I said I was going to run fifty miles per day from the beginning, and I would follow through with that commitment regardless of how much discomfort and pain it caused. It was a reminder of my days at GE, when I had expectations of my employees far beyond what they thought they themselves were capable of. It was now my turn to set cosmic and mind-bending expectations for myself that I knew would cause me more pain and suffering than I'd ever experienced before.

I rested upon confidence that I had developed during a life of overcoming deteriorating eyesight, performing at high levels in difficult working environments, and continually pushing myself physically and mentally in endurance sports. My entire life had led up to this point. I knew that when things looked the bleakest, I would just have to find a way to get the job done.

The USABA had suggested getting a fancy marketing wrap for the crew vehicle. The shirts and coffee tumblers I had made for the run were cherry-red. We figured if we wrapped the minivan in a cherry-red logo, passing cars would be sure to see us and it would help with visibility. As the USABA and I researched the cost for a wrap, we realized that it would cost around $3,000. We couldn't justify asking people to donate to my run and spend their money on a wrap that would only last for two months. It just seemed like really poor stewardship of people's hard-earned money. I chose instead to make some magnets, to the tune of about $100. The magnets had the logos of the companies that had donated products for me to use during the transcon, and I tried to take as many pictures with them as possible to give their brands visibility.

I also had a couple of magnets that said "BLIND RUNNER." The signs were about 24 inches x 24 inches and had red lettering on a white background. We affixed these magnetic signs to the minivan so that passing vehicles would note there was a blind runner somewhere near the minivan and hopefully be more vigilant. It wasn't an easy decision to keep using the word blind. I hate being reminded of it, but I needed to embrace this as an asset and hope that people would use more effort to avoid hitting me on the open road. I needed all the help I could get, so we used the signage. It was cheap, and seemed like it would be effective.

My mom also had blinking lights on magnets that were easily attached to the outside of the van. They had the ability to be always on or blinking. They would help me identify the van from a greater distance than 200 feet. This strategy only worked when there was dark cloud cover, because my eyes were better able to perceive the blinking lights in a darker environment. During a blue-sky day, the blinking lights were irrelevant and not bright enough for my eyes to perceive.

I routinely wear +3.00 magnifier glasses to help me see my phone or text. For smaller print like a newspaper, I also use a 5x handheld magnifier with my glasses. I can just make out newspaper-sized text, although it strains my eyes and I can only use this strategy for about five minutes before my eyes can no longer see the text. We had a route book with maps and an atlas. Mom is pretty good with maps; however, she hadn't participated in the painstaking routing process. In order for me to see a street sign, I need to stand right next to the pole, get on my tiptoes, and wear my glasses. When we had places along the route where there were a lot of turns, I knew I would need the ability to navigate. In order to prepare for this, I decided that I would run with a lightweight running pack where I could stow some glasses, a magnifier, a map, and my phone. I needed to be self-sufficient if I was going to be the route finder out on the road. Mom would be busy enough just trying to keep me nourished and hydrated, and keep herself out of harm's way. Navigating and route finding was going to be a big issue for us. I was the person on the road who knew the route the best. But, I couldn't see road signs and I would be in a mental haze, making navigating while running extremely difficult. I would have to study and memorize the next day's route the night before.

21

Walking to the Gallows

There is always a calm before the storm.

S ome friends had arranged to have a going-away party for me a few days before Mom and I were scheduled to start driving to California to start the transcon. They chose one of my favorite local watering holes, the Lowry Beer Garden. It has great burgers and beer—one of my favorite meals. Mom, my kids, and I drove to the restaurant to celebrate the eighteen months of preparation. All of us in the van wore our cherry-red VISIONRUNUSA shirts. We even drove the van, aka the Silver Bullet, with magnetic signs to the restaurant. As we arrived, we were the only people in the restaurant. After about an hour, it seemed the entire restaurant was overtaken with people supporting my run. My girlfriend and her kids came. There were uncles and aunts and cousins. There were friends from grade school, middle school, high school, college, and law school. There were people from boards I served on. There were people from Achilles, the group that guides blind runners. There were people from USABA with their organization's signage. There were even some runners I didn't know, but they heard some Denver guy was going to attempt a transcon and they wanted to come out and see what was going on. It was a huge party with a couple of hundred people who were there just for me. I never had people look at me like they did that day. I received stares from people I had known for decades, as they tried to process what I was about to attempt. I remember a lot of the comments I received:

"Well, good luck."

"Give it your best."

"You can do it."

Behind each one of these well-wishes, I heard that devil of doubt whispering into the well-wisher's ear. The well-wisher tried to blurt something positive out, while they thought, "He's crazy," or "He'll never be able to do it," or "What should I say?" Even the most enthusiastic and optimistic well-wisher couldn't convince me they believed I would be able to run from one coast to the other. I understood their feelings. What do you say to someone who is setting out to attempt something only a handful of people had ever done in the history of the world? Oh yeah, and that person is legally blind. I got it.

I'm not sure it felt so much like a party as a premature wake for a friend who had met his demise. We all told stories of the past. We joked and hugged. It was almost like I was getting to enjoy my funeral wake, but I was alive to participate in it. At one point, I was asked to say some words to the crowd. People wanted to hear from me. I wasn't prepared to speak to the crowd. I was just focused on the run. I said what came to mind. "I am doing this because it is a Calling. I want to bring awareness to three issues affecting the blind —high rates of unemployment, obesity, and depression. We need to do something about those issues." I stopped talking as quickly as I could.

As quickly as the party had mushroomed into an overwhelming event, it had shrunk down to just my kids, my mom, and me and we drove back to my house.

My kids and I spent our last night together. I remember having so many emotions and trying to only think positive thoughts. We talked about calling each other every day. I tried to keep our normal routine, and not be clingy, since I feared this might be the last time I would see them. I had life insurance and a will in place in the event something terrible happened. I had to continuously force those thoughts out of my head. Once I had my kids in their beds and I had spent one-on-one time with each of them, I went to my room and cried until I eventually fell asleep.

Points to Ponder

The following questions are inspired from Part II of my story. There are no wrong answers. There are only your answers, which are right for you.

1. What is your Calling?
2. How do you help others on a consistent basis?
3. When have you doubted yourself, and still done something?
4. Do you finish what you start?
5. Does pride prevent you from accepting needed help from others?
6. Do you give without the expectation of receiving?
7. How do you prepare for something important?
8. Does lack of resources ever hold you back?
9. How do you think it feels to beg for money?
10. Who is on your "team"?

PART III

Run

The Man in the Arena

It is not the critic who counts; not the man who points out how the strong man stumbles, or where the doer of deeds could have done them better. The credit belongs to the man who is actually in the arena, whose face is marred by dust and sweat and blood; who strives valiantly; who errs, who comes short again and again, because there is no effort without error and shortcoming; but who does actually strive to do the deeds; who knows great enthusiasms, the great devotions; who spends himself in a worthy cause; who at the best knows in the end the triumph of high achievement, and who at the worst, if he fails, at least fails while daring greatly, so that his place shall never be with those cold and timid souls who neither know victory nor defeat.

— Theodore Roosevelt

22

Driving to the Start

Monday, March 21, 2016, was the day that Mom and I had chosen to start driving to Santa Monica Pier in Los Angeles, California, the start of my run. I woke up that morning before my kids rose. I went into each of their rooms and stared at them as they slept. It would have probably been pretty creepy if they woke up and saw me looking at them. By 6:00 a.m., they began to stir. Sierra woke up first, and we met in the hallway. As per our usual routine, I asked if she wanted coffee. She smiled, said yes, and headed to the bathroom to start getting ready for the day. I scurried downstairs to the kitchen and proudly started preparing her coffee one more time. She doesn't like sugar, and only half-and-half in her coffee.

By the time I had her coffee made, my son, Sage, had come downstairs to have cereal for breakfast. I ran Sierra's coffee upstairs to her, so she could have it as she did her hair and got dressed for school. I ran back downstairs to sit with Sage as he served himself cereal. Sage likes his cereal dry, with no milk. I asked if he wanted juice, and he said he did. Sage isn't a big talker, but we did chat a bit. I tried to make normal conversation. I asked about school, and talked about their upcoming spring break trip with their mom. They were planning to visit San Francisco, and take a train to and from there. Sage had never been on a train for that duration of time. We talked about different things he could do to occupy his time, and we imagined what things he would see when he looked out the window of the train. It seemed like an instant, and Sage was done with his breakfast.

He darted upstairs to start getting ready and Sierra came downstairs. I made her favorite breakfast sandwich—a bagel with a poached egg, cheese, and a little mustard. I wanted to see my kids happy and without concern before I left. I was trying to give them anything I thought would make them happy. I wanted them to remember our last moments together as happy ones. Sierra and I hugged, I gave her a kiss on the forehead, and we told each other we loved one another, then she headed out the back door to the garage, started the car, and drove off to school. My heart was ripped from my chest. I had to hold it together until I got Sage and Sofia off to school.

It seemed like moments, and then the same sequence of events happened with Sage as he prepared to depart for school. Sage and I hugged one another. I kissed him on the forehead, looked him in the eye, and told him I loved him. I also told him that while I was gone, he was the man of the house. He needed to be strong and loving for his sisters. I knew Sage was more than capable of being a strong male figure for his sisters. Sage is a kind, respectful young man who people look up to. In a blink of an eye, Sage was off to school on the bus and it felt like I couldn't breathe.

My youngest daughter, Sofia, had woken by this time and was getting ready for school. She is a diva and it takes some time to get ready for school. She moves at her own pace, and often is on "island time." After all, she was born in Puerto Rico. Eventually, Sofia had gotten ready for the day, and we sat at the breakfast table together as she ate the breakfast I had prepared for her. We talked about all kinds of things, and she was the most interested in the run. She told me, "Daddy, I'm going to call you every day." Sofia's school was a short walk away from our house. She grabbed her backpack and we walked to her school, joking and laughing about all kinds of things.

We held hands all the way to school, like we always do. When we got to school, the bell was about to ring and she hurried off to line up so she wouldn't be late. Before she ran off, I hugged her and kissed her on the forehead and told her I loved her.

I was standing alone as the bell rang and I watched her walk with her classmates into the rectangular brick school building. I stood there in silence and took a couple of breaths. This thing was really about to happen. All the talking and preparing was over, and it was time to do what I had been Called to do.

I switched my focus instantaneously to the run. I believe in being 100 percent present in life. While I was with my kids, I was thinking only of them. I was absorbed by being with them and sharing with them. As soon as the last one was safely and securely into their daily routine, I switched my focus intently to the run. There could be absolutely no distraction or multitasking if I was in fact going to run from the Pacific Ocean to the Atlantic Ocean.

Without a tear, I walked home. I thought I would be a complete mess after seeing my last child off. I wasn't, however. I could only think about how to repack the van. My head was swirling through a checklist of items and reevaluating whether I had forgotten anything.

Do I have enough variety of shoes? Should I have gotten even bigger shoes in case my feet swelled like Uncle Ted's did during his six-day run?

Do I have enough clothes for the weather I will encounter?

What did I forget?

What injuries will I get, and do I have enough first-aid supplies to keep me moving forward?

Is Mom properly packed?

Will the van make it all the way across the country?

Did I make a mistake by not having more crew members?

Did I train enough?

What will happen to me?

Can I actually do it?

This is insane!

The chatter in my mind exploded on the walk home from Sofia's school. I arrived at my house and looked at the neatly organized gear that needed to be packed into the van. I had removed the middle row of captain's chairs and put down foam padding so we could pack supplies and I would have an area to lay down during the run, if needed. Mom came over at about 10:00 a.m. I was frozen and couldn't do anything. I was just overwhelmed. It was as if I was going to the electric chair. I had said my good-byes to my children, and my mom was coming to take me to my doom and destruction. I summoned all the courage I had to not show my fear. That devil of doubt was screaming into my head, my heart, and my spirit. I was wracked with fear.

Mom is a doer and she started repacking the van. I stopped her, and felt like I needed to control the packing. She could sense my nerves and remained calm. We went really slow. She only brought a small carry-on size bag and a yellow duffle bag. I had one carry-on size bag half filled with day clothes and the other half filled with jackets for different types of weather conditions. I had a huge duffle bag with twenty pairs of shoes, about ten small plastic see-through bins filled with gear, including headlamps, batteries, reflective vests, first-aid equipment, headphones with iPods and satellite radio players, a small sterno burner to heat water, KIND bars, and duct tape and scissors. Each bin was neatly marked with its contents. Then, I had a large Normatec Recovery bag that contained a pair of air compression boots for my legs. It was bulky at about 18 inches x 18 inches x 36 inches. We brought a scale so I could weigh myself to ensure I wasn't losing too much weight, and a five-gallon bucket with a toilet seat that would be my makeshift port-o-let when there were none to be found and Mother Nature was calling.

In the back of the van, where the back hatch raised, we had two square seven-gallon ice chests for food and a five-gallon cooler that would only hold fresh water. The five-gallon cooler sat on a plastic dresser that contained my running clothes. Other bins held shorts, shirts, socks, and compression gear for my calves, thighs, and arms. In the roof-mounted cargo carrier, we stowed a collapsible gravity chair that Mom envisioned we would use for me to nap on during a daily break. A baby stroller Thule had donated was also stowed in the rooftop cargo carrier. The Thule stroller was my Plan B. If for some reason Mom wasn't able to continue on with me, I planned to load it with as many supplies as I could carry, and continue my run across America pushing the stroller. I prayed that it wouldn't come to this, but in a worse-case scenario, I had a plan to cross America on foot self-supported. We loaded the rest of the rooftop cargo carrier with toilet paper, paper towels, baby wipes, disinfectant wipes, and other supplies.

The passenger-side sliding door wasn't functioning properly, probably due to one too many van parties by my nephew or niece. We decided to duct-tape the door handle so we wouldn't accidentally open the door and have all our gear fall out. We neatly stacked and packed gear in the van so the area behind the passenger seat to the rear bench was filled with luggage and gear. We rigged a cargo net to hold the gear in place, as we feared that one quick turn or braking would send our packed gear everywhere. The back bench was loaded to the hilt as well. The only vacant area was behind the driver's seat to the back bench. There was barely enough room for me to lay down and almost stretch out. This would be the place I would rest, if I needed it.

After three hours of packing, unpacking, and repacking the van, we were ready to leave. My dog Doug (the Pug) was in his kennel in the house. My neighbors and friends were going to split time taking care of him. Doug was a faithful dog and I wondered what he thought. He must have sensed something was going on. I have left so many times before for multi-day racing trips, I'm sure he just assumed that I'd be back in a couple of hours, days, or maybe a week. I gave Doug a treat before I left, then I closed the door to my home and locked it.

It was about 2:00 p.m. before we got on the road. I jumped into the van with an icepack on my right foot. About a week before we were scheduled to leave, I began having a sharp pain on the outside of my right foot. At first, I hoped and assumed I had bumped my foot against something and only bruised it. The pain didn't go away, however, and it increased with continued running. I made an emergency appointment with a podiatrist to have the foot x-rayed. If I had the beginnings of a stress fracture, I needed some advice on how I could get it to heal while I ran on it. My son had an air boot from when he broke his toes, and I pulled it out and was ready to use the boot for the first few weeks, if necessary. The x-rays came back negative, and the podiatrist informed me that my pain was caused by soft tissue irritation. She told me to take it easy, and it would resolve naturally with rest. When I told her of my plan to start running across America in a couple of days, the room went silent and her face became expressionless.

We headed south on I-25 to New Mexico. We intended to intersect my transcon route at Socorro, New Mexico and turn west. We drove the route backward for the first 750 miles or so. The plan was to scout out the running conditions and terrain, and understand what shoulders, if any, I would have to run on. The first night, we stopped in Socorro, New Mexico just before sunset. Socorro is a small town that must have blossomed due to being an intersection to two major highways that were trucking routes. The town is only a few miles from end to end. We found a motel, and told the night manager what we were up to. As soon as we told him I was setting out to run across America, he gave us a discount for our room. You could see the amazement in his face, and we presented him with a bright white USABA fitted baseball cap. The USABA had given me a bunch of hats to hand out along the way, and wear during media interviews. You would have thought we gave the night manager a million dollars. We had our first big fan, and it was apparent that what I was going to attempt was unique and definitely "not ordinary."

The next day we woke and headed west, backtracking through Quemado, New Mexico to Springerville, Arizona where we stopped for lunch at Booga Reds. It looked like a Mexican restaurant decorated with serapés and casual Mexican furniture. Our waitress came and took our order. I remember the chimichanga looked great, and I ordered one without sour cream. It was delicious. When we were paying our check, Mom told the waitress that I was going to run across America and we were driving to Los Angeles to start the run. It was obvious Mom was excited about the run, and proud of what I was setting out to do. The waitress's mouth dropped as she tried to process the words Mom had just spoken. I had small cards printed up that I could hand out to people who wanted to follow the journey, and possibly donate to the USABA. She took the card, we paid the bill, and left each other smiling and waving.

We continued on that evening to Wickenberg, Arizona and had entered the great Sonoran Desert that stretches from the eastern edge of Los Angeles far into Arizona. After another solid evening of sleep, we woke and headed west again, crossing into California where I realized that I would be starting with hundreds of miles of desert running. While we drove west, we passed three men who were walking with traffic, pushing shopping carts. They looked dirty, a little overweight, and tired, but far from being homeless. They looked as though they were on a mission of sorts. We kept driving west through the high desert of California and into the town of Twentynine Palms, we passed Joshua Tree National Park, then turned south and headed into the mass of humanity called Los Angeles. As soon as we left the high desert, the density of population and mass of highways and vehicles seemed to increase and crescendo the closer we got to the ocean.

Mom and I were very nervous about how I was going to run out of LA. My route had assumed I was going to run some parts on interstates, as I wasn't sure how safe I felt running through East Los Angeles, an area that had notoriously high crime and violence. We had a big problem, and neither one of us knew how we would overcome it. We had some connections in Los Angeles, knowing blind marathoner Adrian Broca and retina specialist Vince Hau, who were planning to run the first couple of days with me. Vince was scouting out a route for the first couple of days of my run to keep me on frontage roads that would parallel the six-lane Pomona Freeway (Highway 60) which was the route we intended to follow out of Los Angeles.

When Mom and I reached our accommodations in Santa Monica, we were relieved to be off the road after three days of driving. There was no time to relax, however. A film crew was meeting us at the room and planning to do an interview. I had grown accustomed to giving interviews to the media. It was weird to see myself on TV, in the newspaper, and in running magazines. Many of the questions were the same: "Why are you doing it? How many miles will you run each day? What will you eat? Is it safe for a blind person to be doing this?" The interview took the better part of two hours. Mom actually participated in the interview, and it was neat to see her excitement and energy for what we were about to do.

After the interview, we went to a hipster restaurant in Santa Monica. We tried to make small talk with each other. In each other's presence, we remained calm. As I started to overtalk and overthink what we were about to do, Mom just responded, "Jay, you're just going to have to do it." She tried to reassure me that I was capable of what was ahead of me. But the fact was, neither of us knew what was in our future. We both willingly stepped into an abyss of uncertainty, and we committed to not looking back until we reached the Atlantic Ocean.

I vividly remember feeling like I wanted to vomit many times the night before the run was supposed to start, and that nauseated feeling continued to grow through the night and into the morning. I was really scared, and didn't want to go through with the run. I felt like I had started something in motion that was much bigger than me, and I wouldn't be able to stop it. It was as if a boulder was rolling down a hill and picking up speed, and it was about to crash and explode into a million pieces with a thunderous explosion.

23

California—The Golden State

March 24, 2016, Santa Monica Pier

Before I knew it, we were driving right by the Santa Monica Pier sign I so vividly remember seeing in the move *Forrest Gump*. I was a bundle of nerves, and Mom was her usual self, trying to find the best parking spot at Santa Monica Pier. I never knew what her parameters were for finding the best spot, but I knew in her mind she was on a mission to do her best for me. I didn't know what to expect when we arrived. Would there be thousands of people, or nobody? I knew some people said they were meeting me there; however, I didn't know for sure who or how many might come out. There was some media exposure, and I didn't know if that would attract strangers. As it turned out, when we arrived at 9:00 a.m., only one other person was there, a representative from Delta Gamma—a sorority whose philanthropic mission is to serve the blind and visually impaired.

I was standing on the pier with all its tourist attractions, funnel cake, and souvenir stores. I wanted to get away from what was manmade. I could hear the ocean, and in the distance I could see where the color of sand met water. I needed to be there. Mom followed me as I stumbled my way down steps and around unfamiliar tripping obstacles like an uneven wood surface and waist-high poles that reminded me I was a man every time I walked directly into them. My tunnel vision didn't permit my eyes to perceive those poles unless I was looking directly at them.

I made it off the pier and into the sand. I wanted to take off my shoes and feel the sand on my feet but Mom cautioned against it. She seemed anxious, but was trying her hardest to remain calm. I didn't say anything and just walked across the sand with my cane to the ocean. I stood, and listened to the water lapping against the shore. I heard birds making the typical noises you would expect to hear at the ocean. I heard a family playing in the sand a fair distance up the beach. My eyes couldn't perceive them, but I could hear them laugh and yell with joy. I wanted to stay in that spot forever. I didn't want to leave. Suddenly, a wave of fear overcame me, like a tsunami. My legs shook and I was on the verge of crying. I was glad that nobody was near me. I didn't want anybody to know how scared I was. I didn't think anybody really understood why I was doing this run. Some probably thought it was insane. Others probably thought I was engaging in severe attention-seeking behavior, due to some unresolved childhood issues. Others may have thought it was about leaving a legacy and wanting fame.

I knew it was a true test of faith and a lesson in obedience. This run had absolutely nothing to do with Jason Romero. I wasn't the usual story of a person who overcame past transgressions of addiction with ultra-running. I was just a guy minding his own business, when suddenly I got a message from outside myself that I had to do something. I knew I would be ridiculed when, and if, I spoke of this experience. But that judgment and ridicule would come from humans; it wouldn't come from what had led me to this sandy beach in Los Angeles, California on this spring day. Whatever was happening to me, I was at a crossroads. I could live for myself, turn tail, quit and drive back to Colorado to live a comfortable life; or, I could choose to step into the unknown, go to a place of uncertainty where fear and pain were sure to lie in wait for me.

As all of this was going through my head, I made a choice. I told myself, I am going to be obedient. I am going to do what I believe I am supposed to do, regardless of how scared I am; regardless of how foolish others may think I am; regardless of whether I get hurt or die. I am going to fulfill what I have been Called to do. As adrenaline began coursing through my body, I bent down and saw a small sea shell. It was perfect in its imperfection. It was broken just like me, and I chose it to make the 3,000-mile journey to the Atlantic Ocean with me. My plan was to throw the sea shell into the Atlantic when I reached it. I stood back up with sea shell in hand, looked to the sea, and told myself, *Well, this is it . . . it's time do this!* I turned, and knew I couldn't look back. I had to keep moving and looking east, toward my goal.

Mom and I went back to the pier where a small group had formed. Adrian Broca, my friend and a hero of mine who is a blind marathoner, and his guide showed up to run with me the first day. More Delta Gammas from UCLA and USC had arrived. The President of the US Association of Blind Athletes had arrived to run the entire first day with me. A retina specialist from Kaiser Permanente arrived and planned to run the first two days with me. A friend from high school who lived in the LA area showed up. An attorney from LA who was soon to be married in Italy showed up. And, the girl I had moved to San Diego to marry over two decades before showed up with her family. We snapped some pictures, and at 10:00 a.m. Pacific Daylight Time, I started running east from the edge of Santa Monica Pier.

Picking up a sea shell from the Pacific Ocean

The day was supposed to be an easy seventeen-mile shakeout run. A normal shakeout run is a ten to twenty-minute easy jog the day before a 26.2 mile marathon. I had allotted four hours to complete the distance. I figured that would make it an easy trot and allow me to not break a sweat. I wanted to be totally fresh for the start of the "real run" from Los Angeles City Hall to New York City Hall. That was how Guinness judged the starting location, and in my head, that would be the measure for how my run would stack up against other transcon foot crossings of America. I would have the final four days and 200-mile jaunt from New York to Boston to perfect what I would say to my girlfriend when I saw her at the finish.

The day was beautiful with a blue sky and pockets of haze. Quickly, the temperatures were in the high 70s. It wasn't uncomfortable, but not an ideal fifty-degree running day. The miles passed quickly with good company. We laughed and joked, telling each other about our lives and why we liked running. Before we knew it, we had arrived at City Hall in about four hours. I learned that I had made a mistake in choosing some equipment for this run. My Smartwool socks that the Colorado Company had given me were drenched at the end of this run. I was always concerned about blisters on my feet, which wouldn't stop me from running but could make the experience very uncomfortable. My aunt Maxine, who is a nurse, taught me that friction and moisture are the main causes of blistering on runners' feet. My feet were gnarled with callused skin and regrown toenails, replacing toenails that had previously fallen off. The most painful blisters happened underneath callused skin and toenails. When this happened, I used to heat up a safety pin with a flame, then drill a hole through the toenail or callus to release a geyser of pus. Once the pressure is relieved, the pain subsides, and there is no more painful distraction from running. Without my pseudo-surgery, the blisters would just be a constant voice for the devil of doubt and would work hard to make me stop running.

Mark, the USABA President, suffered from the heat, went back to his hotel room and puked a couple of times. Most of the other runners seemed okay, although I think this shakeout run counted for their long run of the week. I did a couple of media interviews, then Mom and I headed back to our room in Santa Monica. We wanted to get a good night's sleep for the next day's run, the beginning of the real transcontinental run, which would start at 4:00 a.m. on March 25, 2016.

We chose a 4:00 a.m. start so we could get a decent distance out of LA before the Friday morning rush hour. City Hall was seventeen miles east of the ocean. I figured I could easily run ten-minute miles for three hours and be out of most of the "mess" of LA. Mom and I were already having minor altercations and arguments. Most were about small things, like which room I should sleep in, or whether I should be doing different types of recovery treatment. I'd learned that when Mom felt out of control, she became extremely nervous and anxious. I knew myself and our dance throughout our life. When either one of us projected our own anxiety onto the other, fireworks were sure to occur. We always talked things through and recovered, but the time to recover varied from minutes to days. I feared this when I asked my mom to crew me on the run across America. I even addressed it with a direct conversation, saying it wouldn't be okay for us to get into an argument, then not talk the rest of the day. I couldn't imagine what it would be like trying to put in fifty or more miles day after day, be in a disagreement with my mom, have tension between us, and no communication. I dreaded what it would feel like to be running mile after mile to catch up to the van, and have my only physical supporter not talk to me and be emotionally distant. Mom told me she wouldn't cut off communication, but I knew it would happen, and it was the best she would be able to give me during whatever situation we were confronting together. It would just have to be good enough. I was confident our relationship could withstand whatever we would encounter.

We got to bed by 8:00 p.m., and set alarms for 2:00 a.m. so I could start running by 4:00 a.m. I knew I was losing valuable recovery time by not sleeping longer; however, that was a consequence of being a bare-bones expedition with only one crew person and no RV. We would sacrifice sleep time to travel back and forth from motels to the daily starting and stopping points. My crossing would be different, and in some ways more difficult, than other transcontinental speed crossings, due to my one-person crew and need to find shelter at the end of every day; however, I chose my strategy, and I would just have to make it work.

On the morning of March 25, 2016, Mom and I woke and loaded up the van. Each one of us had a suitcase. We also needed to load all of the recovery equipment I was using, which was the equivalent of three small duffel bags. I had a backpack and Mom had a yellow duffle bag, each with our personal items we needed to feel "at home" wherever that might be. For Mom, that meant skin products, moisturizer, hair items, and toiletries. For me, that meant my headlamp, a digital audio recorder for journaling, a bottle of cologne (Happy by Clinique), a toothbrush, toothpaste, and deodorant—Secret. Scent is very important to me, and I think it may be heightened as a result of my deteriorating eyesight. I just love how Secret smells, so I use it. After all, the commercial says "Strong enough for a man . . ."

It was strange to think that was all I felt I needed to survive. My bare essentials were minimal enough to fit in a backpack. It took the two of us close to forty-five minutes to load and pack the van that morning. This caused me concern. Mom and I were fresh and we used forty-five minutes to load the van. Would this be our routine every day? I was willing to wing it, and not take so many supplies out of the van. Mom was much more conservative, and likes to bring everything and the kitchen sink, just in case we need it. Her strategy had paid off on multiple occasions when I was in multi-day races, or in Death Valley in 120° heat and when I ran for over fifty hours to cross Puerto Rico on foot. I had faith in my crew captain, but I knew we had to devise a quicker method of loading and unloading.

Mom drove us through the dark and desolate streets of Los Angeles into its heart at City Hall, where our starting point was located. Nobody was on the streets. A friend from college, Dave Pierce, who lived in LA was going to guide me in his car out of LA through the twists and turns of this mecca. After a couple of telephone calls, Dave and I located each other and he parked near our van. Dave and I had been in the same honors program in college. He nicknamed me Chip, and my fondest memory of him was when we were both sitting in class and he leaned over and whispered, "Chip, you're the missing link." For some reason, that was hilarious at the time, and we both burst out laughing. The professor didn't think so, and we both were reprimanded. Maybe Dave was right, though. Maybe, I wasn't normal, and some freak of nature. Maybe that was what I needed to be in order to take on what I was doing. Regardless of whether Dave's comment was prophecy or banter, one thing was certain—the people who cared about me were showing up to help me. My plan was to have Dave drive in the lead, I would run behind Dave's car, and Mom would follow me to block traffic. Because of the time of day, we didn't expect to obstruct traffic too much, as we hoped everybody was still in their slumber.

Dave lived in LA and we were relying on him to follow the route we had created to get us out of the city sprawl without getting lost and adding unnecessary miles.

Two more people met me at City Hall. The retina specialist, Vince, who ran with me the day before and my friend, Richard Hunter, who also has RP like me. Richard is a very special person and it meant a lot to me that he was there. This would be Richard's first fifty-mile run. It was a training run for him as he was planning to run a hundred-mile race at some point in the future. Richard had arranged his family vacation around this opportunity to run with me, and had his children and wife at a hotel somewhere in the city. He was planning to run fifty miles with me, then take his family to Disneyland. He is my kinda guy. More than that, Richard was integral to getting me to this point in my life. When I first heard Richard say, "Is that Jason?" as I walked toward him in the darkness with my bright headlamp blinding him, I thought of how we first met.

Two years prior, when I was in the very deep depression, I Googled "blind ultra-runners" and a link came up for a podcast about Richard Hunter. I listened to the podcast, and felt like I might have another person in the world who could understand me, and help me climb out of the depression I was in. In the podcast, Richard mentioned some things that became clues for how I could find him. I spent the next hour researching on the Internet and soon found an e-mail address. An e-mail led to a telephone call, and soon I found myself talking to Richard, who lives in Sacramento, California. He told me about his journey with RP. We were about the same age, although Richard's eyesight had deteriorated at a more aggressive rate than mine had. Richard used guides for running and his tunnel vision was closer to being like looking through straws. Richard was the first person I was able to talk to who I felt could understand what I was going through with my sight loss. He was gentle, an exceptional listener, and a very sensitive guy.

It's the polar opposite of what you would imagine when you looked at Richard, a handsome ex-marine, over six feet tall and a smidge over two hundred pounds. He is a mountain of a man, but that didn't come through over the phone. I only perceived a caring human on the other end of the phone—a person who loved running and has experienced what I have. Only, Richard was further along in the journey of sight loss than I was. And, he was doing okay. This man was going blind and he was okay. How could that be? Richard was my first and continues to be a very important role model and mentor for me as I become fully blind. In that first conversation, Richard invited me to participate in the US Blind Marathon Championships in 2014, which I ran and won. That win led to an invitation to join the US Paralympic Team and race at the World Marathon Championships in London in 2015.

I had almost reached Richard by the time I had finished my daydream. The retina specialist, Vince Hau, was going to guide Richard as we ran. Mark Lucas, USABA's president, and his brother had come back out to see us off that morning. After we took a couple of pictures on the steps of City Hall, we were off and running. Our small group moved well through the streets of LA. We talked about our families and told running stories. It was good to have the company, and I think it was a good buffer for Mom and me. Both of us were nervous, and when we were alone with each other, it was easy to clash.

Vince asked Richard about his "ghosts." I couldn't understand what they were talking about, and asked what he meant. Vince explained that, as the retina in the eye dies, a phenomenon happens. The affected person starts seeing flashes of light, almost like lightning strikes. Nobody knows why it occurs, but it is a symptom that people experience in late stages of retinal deterioration. I hadn't experienced this phenomenon yet, although my friend Richard had. I was worried and uneasy at the topic of conversation. I tried to change the subject, and not listen when the two spoke about going blind. It was too real. It was too big. I had to worry about running across America. I had no time to worry about going blind. As we moved to the outskirts of LA, we met some people from the local Empire Running Club, who were Vince's friends. As the day grew hotter and we got deeper into the miles, Richard began to suffer and needed to take longer breaks.

I was patient because I was fresh, but I sensed that I wouldn't be able to run and accommodate other people's running needs after this first day. Richard was the exception to this rule, and I was honored that he would even consider running his first fifty-mile run as part of my transcon. He was too important to me, and was one of several people who helped save me from a pit of despair as I came to grips with losing my eyesight. Eventually, we got to the end of the day, Richard had finished his first fifty-miler and Vince's two-day seventy-mile run was complete—it was also the farthest Vince had ever run.

My neighbor Lori had easily found us a motel that night since we were still in the outskirts of LA. The motel ended up being around $150. I was concerned, as my new and tighter budget only allocated $100 a night for motel accommodations. I couldn't afford to fund an overage of $50 per day for motels. I decided to just hope and pray that we would find cheaper accommodations as we crossed the country. Mom also discovered that the van consumes a lot of gas when moving at desperately slow speeds. A long slow day of driving fifty miles a day could consume an entire tank of gas. I had under-budgeted for this as well. I assumed my brother's van would get at least 250 miles to the tank. The journey was on, and whatever the cost was, I would just have to cover it with a credit card. I had received some donations through the website, but not nearly enough to cover the additional $20,000 or more that this expedition was going to cost. I didn't know how I would pay off the final bill, but I did know that I had credit cards with a total of $30,000 in credit limits, and it was looking like I would have to use every last penny of it while on this journey.

On the night of the second day, Mom and I again had tension between us. There was limited talking in our room, and it felt like the silence was deafening. Mom and I are very different in this way. I am an extrovert and she is an introvert. I always feel better talking, and she can become drained and irritable when she is forced to converse if she doesn't have the energy. I remember one time when we were sitting at a restaurant with each other, directly across from one another. We didn't say a word to each other for thirty minutes. I thought something was seriously wrong, and it was abnormal. Finally, I couldn't take it anymore and had to break the silence. When I asked my mom if she was mad at me or if I had done something to upset her, she said she wasn't upset and it was fine if we didn't talk, even though we were in such close proximity. We are obviously wired very differently, but that didn't change the fact that we loved each other and would die for one another without a second thought.

I knew this difference in communication and need for human interaction would come to haunt us during this expedition across America, and slowly chip away at me if I permitted it to affect me. After a full day of helping me, Richard, Vince, and members of the Empire Running Club, Mom just wanted to zone out and rest. I, on the other hand, wanted to recount the day, talk about our newfound friends, the new memories we had made, etc. Our differences would be our doom, or help us fulfill our destiny. It was our decision to make.

On the morning of the third day, I began running just outside of Chino, California. A couple of members from the Empire Running Club met me and ran with me through the sunrise to Riverside. I really enjoyed meeting new people, and the great conversations we had. Running was our commonality. It was something we could relate to. It was something that didn't need to be explained or understood. We just experienced life together, in the open air, propelling ourselves through whatever terrain we encountered, only needing water and some calories to keep moving forward. I believe we humans are in fact made to run. Chris McDougall's book, Born to Run, does a great job explaining the science behind how our bodies' cooling system, anatomical structures, and survival instincts are all specialized to enable humans to run great distances. In my experience, I have found that everything functions better when I run. My body and immune system are stronger, I am more alert, less prone to negative thoughts and depression, and am an all-around happier and more productive person when I am running regularly. My body is my Ferrari, and there can be nothing better than throwing on some shorts and shoes and taking it out for a spin. Running truly is a little slice of heaven on earth to me. Simple. Cheap. Fun.

The miles just seemed to climb throughout the day—ten, then twenty, then thirty, then forty. As Mom and I were ending the day, we realized we had a very large dilemma for the next day's run. We were approaching a section where I would be forced to run fifteen miles on the Pomona Freeway, which is a major interstate that feeds into Los Angeles and mushrooms into eight lanes of traffic in each direction. It was extremely dangerous as cars, motorcycles and semis were travelling at 75 mph and higher. I needed to connect into US Interstate 10 east, then catch Highway 62 and head north into the high desert toward Joshua Tree and Twentynine Palms. The ten-mile climb into the high desert on Highway 62 wasn't going to be easy either, as the road snaked through canyon-like terrain and there were no shoulders on the road or pull-off areas. Mom wouldn't be able to stop and support me, and the ten-mile climb from sea level to the high desert at 3,000 feet above sea level would make this a three-hour effort in the heat of the day.

Back in Denver, Carly was researching on Google Earth to see if there was a trail or some other way to get to the high desert and avoid Interstate 10. She found what appeared to be a Jeep road, although we had no idea if the van could handle the terrain. The trail would be a twenty-five-mile detour with only one direction to go. We had no idea how rough the trail was, or if it was still in existence. The images on Google Earth can be a couple of years old, depending on when the image was fed into the database. Mom and I decided to be conservative and stick to the paved roads. Our van was twelve years old, and we had the transmission worked on before we left. I didn't want our support vehicle to break down, as I would be left to run cross country pushing a stroller, trying to hit fifty miles per day. I braced myself for a painful next day as I finished off my miles of day three in Beaumont, California, when a stranger came running at me from across the road. The man seemed to appear from out of nowhere, like in a sci-fi movie. My tunnel vision had kept me from sensing his presence until I looked directly at him. People often suddenly "appear" in front of me. It can be very startling at times. The man was well-dressed in a button-down shirt, slacks, and dress shoes; he wore glasses, had silver hair, and was about my size. "Are you Jason Romero?" he asked. I stopped running. "Yes" came out of my mouth.

The man introduced himself as Robert Lasko. He, too, was a runner and had been following my run since it started a few days before. Robert asked what route we were taking to the high desert, and I shared our dilemma. Robert's eyes lit up, and he said he could help us avoid running on the interstate and the ten-mile segment of Highway 62 that had no shoulder or places for the van to stop so I could be supported. It was like a true-life miracle just happened. I had my back against the wall, and right before I was about to get squished like a bug, a side door opened and I was able to escape a dangerous and messy situation. I put Robert in touch with "home base"—Carly—and he arranged to meet us the next morning before sunrise on Easter Sunday.

Sure as clockwork, Robert was there waiting for us. I asked him how we were going to avoid running on I-10. He told me there were train tracks on the south side of I-10 that paralleled the interstate. His plan was for us to run on the train tracks so we didn't need to be on the highway. Mom would drive parallel to us on I-10 and get off at each exit and wait for us by the train tracks. It seemed like a workable plan, and we started running. In the dark of the morning, it was difficult for me to run on the tracks and not trip on the timbers. So we moved off the tracks and ran on crushed-gravel paths or access paths whenever possible. We were moving slow with all the adjustments we were having to make—almost fifteen-minute miles. As we ran, I asked why Robert had come out to find me and help me. What he told me was truly breathtaking.

Robert had been a runner since high school when he ran cross-country. He told me he had a love/hate relationship with running since the beginning. A few years before we met, Robert had been steadily increasing his training mileage, but began losing control of his bowels and losing weight. A visit to the doctor revealed that Robert had colon/rectal cancer. When the doctor told Robert it was Stage II cancer, Robert decided to celebrate not having Stage IV cancer (which is generally terminal) and run a 5K race where he placed third in his age group. As soon as Robert got to this part of the story, I was hooked and tingling.

Then, Robert went on to tell me that because his body was already so strong from running, the doctors chose to give him the maximum radiation and chemo treatments possible. After months of treatments and removal of a mass, the surgeon found no cancer, and only scar tissue. He had a 50 percent blockage of his colon from the cancerous mass when his treatment began. This was Robert's miracle, and although I couldn't see Robert's face light up as he told the story, I did hear his heart light up in his voice as he told the story. He said, "Running helped me survive and defeat colon/rectal cancer. I cannot and will not stop running."

I was truly blessed to have this man running with me, and guiding me in the dark. Robert said that he was drawn to help me, because when he was sick, he would always search out people who he felt were sicker and braver than he was to find inspiration to battle on. He felt I was in a much grimmer situation than he had ever faced, and so he chose to forsake his own wants and desires that Easter Sunday, and help me. It was ironic, because I felt he had it worse than me, and in fact, Robert gave me inspiration.

Regardless of our inspiration-fest for one another, we had to get moving faster. We found a trail that looked like it could get us off the train tracks and bypass the interstate. We ran it for about two miles before it dead-ended and was washed-out. The van couldn't pass the section, and if we continued on foot through the washed-out area, there was no telling when, or if, we would be able to reconnect with Mom in the support van. This was a big disadvantage of only having one support crew and one crew vehicle. There was no way to send another support car ahead of us to scout the route. All we had were Internet mapping sites to use on our phones, and Carly back in Denver to use Google Earth to try to zoom in as best as possible to help us route.

Robert and I had to backtrack a couple of miles and we continued on the train tracks. It wasn't easy for Robert, as the side-effects of radiation on that area of the body caused him to constantly duck behind bush after bush to take care of business. It didn't faze him, however. And I was accustomed to using bushes as cover for bio-breaks at that point in the run. I was forced to run a few miles on I-10 when the train tracks detoured to the south. Robert jumped in the van with my mom, I put the hammer down, and put in a few sub-eight-minute miles to cover about four miles on the shoulder of the interstate. Mom drove behind me in the break-down lane, and in no time we were off the interstate and exited onto Highway 62 heading north.

Robert had contacted a friend, Molly Thorpe, who had ran part of a transcon relay through this area to support the Boston Marathon bombing survivors. The relay went from LA to Boston, and people signed up to take part in the relay and hand off a baton after they completed their segment. As it turned out, Molly ran the exact section of the relay that went from the I-10 turn off up to the high desert. She ran a trail route to avoid the danger of running on Highway 62 which had no shoulders. It was the second miracle of the day. Molly was a school teacher who loved to run and was about to retire to become a full-time race director. One of her races bene-fitted an organization that trains guide dogs for the blind. It was absolutely uncanny how I was crossing paths with all these amazing people. She was blond and looked very fit, and about twenty years younger than her biological age. She was a patient runner and just trotted easily, chatting up a storm. As we covered the miles, she told me about a race she directed where the women were given tiaras and men were given T-shirts that looked like tuxedos and the finish line was a red carpet. As the runners finished, they were presented with a mini Oscar trophy. When Molly and I finished our miles together, she presented me with my own Oscar. I affixed "Oscar" to the dashboard of the Silver Bullet (our minivan) with duct tape. It's interesting how small thoughtful acts can be so large and meaning-ful. This was just the beginning of many amazing people I encoun-tered during this expedition across the home of the brave and land of the free.

Molly and I said our goodbyes in the parking lot of a gas station. Because it was a hot day, I had ice in my white hat (which had a neck drape to keep the sun off me) and I wore a Cool-Off bandana with ice in it. The bandana has chamois material sewn into it, and you are able to load ice into it. Once the ice was loaded, I wrapped it around my neck to keep my body cool. During my desert runs, I learned to manage my body heat by keeping ice near the carotid arteries on my neck. This helps keep my body temperature down by cooling the blood as it flows to my head. I also load ice into my hat to keep my head from overheating. With these two heat-manage-ment precautions, I have been able to keep my body from over-heating and am able to run hard in conditions where the temperature exceeds one hundred-degrees with no problem.

As you can probably imagine, as the ice melts, my clothes and entire body become saturated with run-off from the melted ice. I must have looked pretty bad at that gas station after being out in the sun for six hours, with dust and dirt from the trail and the smell of grime and highway pollution. Regardless, I needed to go to the bathroom, so I entered the gas station to ask to use their restroom. As soon as I walked in the door, I could feel all eyes move to me. It was like a movie scene where a person walked into a room and everything stopped and became immediately silent. I walked toward the counter and asked if I could use their restroom. The lady at the counter looked me up and down and said they didn't have a restroom. She wanted me out of her establishment, right away. I wouldn't be denied, and, with what I knew my body was about to expel, I had no choice but to persist. In my kindest, most under-standing voice, I admitted that I looked really bad and I explained that I was trying to run across America. As soon as I explained what I was doing, she permitted me to use her restroom. I was thankful, and I got her permission just in time.

As I was leaving the gas station, I noticed the music playing on the radio. It was a faith station and one of my favorite songs was playing. I asked her if she had the same faith as I. She said she did, and gave me a smile. I shared my story about feeling Called to run across America for a higher purpose. She then insisted on feeding me. The hot dogs that had been warmed and heated on the warming machine had caught the attention of my olfactory senses as soon as I entered the station. I asked if I could have a hot dog, and she insisted on giving me two. She even walked me over to the hot dog area and served me. She insisted on giving me a drink as well, and because I wouldn't take a soda, she gave me a bottle of water. I was dripping water all over her floor, and she didn't care at all. I thanked her for her hospitality, started chomping on my hot dogs, and walked out the door.

I learned a lot about life at that gas station in a short ten minutes. We make a lot of assumptions about other people without even getting to know them. I looked and smelled horrible. From a first impression, they wanted nothing to do with me. I was just an unkempt person trying to use the gas station for its bathroom services. At first, I felt really bad when I realized they didn't think I was good enough to even let me use their bathroom. There was a time in my life when I would have just turned around and walked out of the station, bitter and angry because I was rejected. But what good does that do?

I decided to not take their disgust with me personally and found my inner voice. I had to speak up for my own needs and try to connect with these people. I was vulnerable and when I explained my goal, that I was in a tough situation, I needed help and apologized for the state I was in, this simple act of humility was enough to diffuse the tension that probably had her thinking about pressing a virtual panic button. Then, when we realized we had something in common, the floodgates of hospitality opened up and we were the best of friends. This interaction challenged me to not take initial rejection personally, to speak up, to share about myself, and to ask for help. I hadn't always been good at handling this life lesson about working through rejection in relationships, competition, and work.

When I left the station, I continued running up into the high desert. The highway gained a shoulder large enough for Mom to drive the van behind me and block traffic. I ran uphill, steady and slowly at about a twelve-minute mile pace. I gained a couple of thousand feet of elevation through this stretch. Up until this point, it took me between ten and eleven hours each day to run fifty miles, including breaks and rest stops. I considered this to be a great pace, but probably too fast to sustain all the way across America.

At the end of the day, Mom and I did our usual routine. We drove to a gas station and grocery store to replenish supplies. I usually helped my mom pump gas and carry ice and groceries out of the store. We found a restaurant, bought dinner, and then headed to our motel accommodations for the night. Mom would usually check in while I sat in the van. Then, I would get a luggage dolly and we loaded up all our supplies which usually consisted of a suitcase, a small duffle bag, my HOKA backpack, a twenty-pound rechargeable battery for emergency power, a duffle-sized bag with my Normatec leg compression boots, a DonJoy Iceman unit, and a bag with more recovery equipment like foam rollers, an electrical stimulation unit, and an ultrasound unit. We also brought in a few plastic bins which had electronic equipment we needed to recharge, like my watch, phone, satellite music player, LED light vest, headlamp, and iPad. We brought a lot of equipment into the room, and I wasted a lot of recovery time by helping so much after running fifty miles for the day. I was very concerned about how much extra energy I was using with non-running activities. I didn't think I had much of a choice, as, in good conscience, I couldn't leave my seventy-year-old mom to do all of these extra crewing duties herself.

Once we replenished our supplies and got everything into the room, Mom usually had a glass of wine and I began my recovery work which lasted two hours. First, I took an Epsom salt bath and soaked my legs. I have read that Epsom salt baths help remove toxins from the body. I don't know if it was true or not, but they felt good and didn't hurt as near as I could tell. Every two or three days, I also took an ice bath right after the Epsom salt bath. I filled the tub up with half water and half ice, just so there was enough in the tub to cover my legs and family jewels. I always hated ice baths due to the shock that they gave my system, but the recovery effect was worth the shock and discomfort. Ice baths cause the vessels to constrict and this in turn forces the lymph system to flush waste out of the legs. This waste can cause the legs to feel heavy when running successive high-mileage days. The cold also helps reduce inflammation and encourage healing of micro-tears in the muscle that are caused during arduous exercise.

After the baths, I primped with lotion, deodorant, hair mousse, and cologne. Being clean just made me feel good. Next, I put my legs into the Normatec air compression boots. The boots inflated with air and squeezed my legs, presumably trying to perform a similar function as the ice bath to force waste buildup back into the torso for more efficient processing by my body. I used the Normatec boots in the morning, during a midday break, and at night. After using the boots for thirty minutes, I hooked myself up to an electrical stimulation unit to help my body repair any soft-tissue injuries. I also used the electrical unit proactively on my quadriceps, hamstrings, and calves. After that, I used a portable ultrasound unit on my feet and ankles to promote healing of damaged tissue. Then I was totally wiped out after running, getting supplies, and going through my recovery routine.

I felt upset as I did my recovery routine and watched Mom relax as she caught up on current events on her iPad and sipped a glass of wine. I was in conflict with myself. I didn't want Mom to suffer, and I wanted her to be able to relax. However, I felt like I was doing too much extra work. I only wanted to focus on running. I remembered watching *Running America*, and seeing Marshall Ulrich and Charlie Engle being massaged, fed, and cared for by multiple crew members during their transcon effort. Marshall and Lisa Batchen Smith had both warned me that I needed more crew members. They were right. Maybe in a hundred-miler or multi-day race, I could suffer and self-crew a bit; however, this expedition would strip me down and whittle away every spare bit of energy and enthusiasm I had.

For the time being, I was acting out my emotional issues by being snappy with my mom. I felt horrible about my behavior. I think she was also trying to get used to the concept of living out of motels, eating unhealthy food, driving five miles per hour for twelve hours a day and trying to contain her concern over my safety while running on highways. We both had a lot going on and the tension between us would ebb and flow, but it seemed to be growing. Sooner or later, I sensed it was going to burst.

The next morning, we got an early start at about 4:00 a.m. and I ran in the dark for a couple of hours before sunrise. It was magical to be in the desert near Joshua Tree at that time of day. I ran in front of the van on the shoulder of the road. Coyotes howled in the distance and the temperatures were chilly. I wore a GORE-TEX running coat and sweatpants over my normal shirt and shorts. The sunrise was quietly beautiful. I treasured that sunrise. It was like a rainbow was lighting up the horizon. There is something special about a sunrise in the desert.

As the sun rose, I saw nothing but a vast expanse of nothingness. There was sand and small shrubs for as far as the eye could see. In the distance, there appeared to be hills. Perhaps those are California's version of mountains. We lost cell phone service and I was unable to stream any music as I ran. I reverted to playlists of music that my children and I had created. The sky became blue and the temperature rose into the 90s. The semis blew by me at 75 mph on the two-lane highway. As we got farther east of Joshua Tree, the highway ceased to have a shoulder for my mom to drive on. She was forced to leapfrog me a couple of miles at a time until there was a street intersection or pull off onto a dirt road. I ran against traffic on the white line and tried to wave my arms as semis barreled at me. I routinely stepped off the white line into the sand to let semis have full access to the asphalt road. When a semi is going 75 mph on the highway, it is pushing an invisible wall of air ahead of it about ten feet in front of the semi. As I ran on the white line, I got walloped by the air wall, my hat and sunglasses flew off my head, and my body was pushed off the white line by the invisible force. Usually, this happened when I was within two feet of the passing monster of death. I learned to brace myself and put my head down so my belongings and I wouldn't be blown all over the place. If I successfully braced myself, I could maintain my position on the white line and keep running in an efficient forward motion.

Once the semi passed, however, there was a huge vacuum created behind it where air was displaced. I learned to lean away from the vacuum at just the right time to avoid being sucked into the road. If I leaned left, away from the semi, just as its rear wheels were passing me, I would have enough momentum so that the vacuum would only pull me back to an upright position and I could maintain my forward progress down the white line.

I had never run on a highway this close to cars, RVs, and semis. It was a new experience, but a challenge that I relished. There was something new to learn. I had always enjoyed improving processes and figuring out just the right way to do something. I love to study details and the minutiae until things are dialed in to perfection. Running on a highway with metal objects weighing several tons increased the stakes and helped me stay present and concentrate on something new for a while.

Avoiding death on the highway, however, became monotonous and boring after several days. I had figured out how to run on the highways and remain safe, at least for 99 percent of the time. The sun was blazing overhead. It was cooking my mom in the van, and me on the road. I think Mom and I were exhausted from the pace we were keeping. We were only on day five, but we were only getting four to six hours of good sleep per night, and we were physically exhausting ourselves. By mile twenty-five of day five, the steam valves needed to blow, and Mom and I lit into each other. It wasn't pretty, and I wish it hadn't happened, but it did. There was yelling, profanity, and stinging looks. All of the tension we were both experiencing was projected onto each other. I couldn't help but remember the cliché, "We hurt the ones we love the most." It was certainly true in this instance. By mile thirty-nine, Mom suggested that we just quit for the day. We had both been through a lot, and it seemed like a good idea to her.

I didn't even acknowledge her suggestion and I stubbornly kept running. I knew in my mind that if I willingly took a shorter day, I would break down mentally. I had to stick to what I had committed to—fifty miles a day or more. Anything less was failure in my mind, and it would be easier to make an excuse to not achieve the goal in the future. From an outsider's view, there probably wasn't much difference between a forty- mile day and a fifty-mile day—they are both extremely long distances.

But, from a transcontinental runner's point of view, there is a significant difference. A person can easily walk a twenty-six-mile marathon a day with no real injuries. They would have plenty of time to stop and eat, rest during the walk, and get plenty of sleep. An easy walking pace is three miles per hour. In order to walk a marathon, the person would be required to move for eight hours and forty minutes. Throw in a couple of hours of rest and bathroom breaks, and you have an eleven-hour day. If they increase their daily mileage to forty miles a day, they would be required to add an additional five hours of walking per day, which would make the day thirteen and half hours of moving time plus a couple of hours of rest and bathroom breaks. If they average forty miles a day, usually they would be jogging half of the time in order to decrease the amount of time they are on the road, and conversely increase the amount of time they have for rest and recuperation. When a transcon runner jumps to fifty miles per day, they are forced to run the majority of the day. In my case, I was running 95 percent of the time I was on my feet. I suppose that's why only six people in history had ever crossed at fifty miles a day or more, and this type of crossing has been called a world-class standard.

I wasn't so caught up in achieving a world-class standard as I was about keeping my word. I had said I would run fifty miles a day or more, and that is exactly what I was going to do. Pain and fear wouldn't deter me. Only a run-ending injury, like a broken bone in my lower extremity, would stop me from achieving that goal—or so I thought. I continued running and achieved fifty miles for the day. Over the last ten miles, I thought long and hard about my mom and what she must be going through. She kept saying that I didn't appreciate her, or what she was doing for me. She was probably right. How could anybody show adequate appreciation for another person giving up their life, becoming homeless, and taking on the discomfort and work she was enduring? In fact, I wasn't showing a bit of appreciation for her. I was so caught up in my own suffering and microcosm that I had taken her and her efforts for granted. We love each other dearly, and after a couple of apologies, a hug and reminding each other that we loved one another, we were back on good footing and headed for town and our motel.

As it turned out, we overshot our destination by fifteen miles. We had to turn around and backtrack to start our ritual of getting gas, groceries, unloading the van, and doing recovery. It seemed like everything that could go wrong, was going wrong. Mom and I saw the exhaustion in each other's faces. We agreed to sleep in the next day and get a fresh start. Things were just going downhill too fast.

The next day, we slept in until 6:00 a.m. By the time we had repacked, reloaded, eaten, and gotten back out to our start point, thirty-five miles from our motel, it was 8:00 a.m. This was a far cry from the 4:00 a.m. start we had previously been trying to achieve. Both Mom and I felt more rested and relaxed. I knew I could run fifty miles in twelve hours, and if I was focused, I thought I might be able to complete my miles in a little over ten hours. I needed to run focused and consistently so we could finish the day and still have enough time to rest. I was assuming the burden of running faster depending on how inefficient we were when I wasn't running.

This day was the capstone of our deterioration and desperation. The day seemed to start off well, and despite being in the middle of the Sonoran Desert east of Twentynine Palms in California, we seemed to be doing good. As we moved east, we passed the three men pushing shopping carts in the opposite direction again. The men were dirty, a little on the heavy side, and their skin was weathered and darkened from being in the sun for too long. As I ran in the opposite direction I yelled, "Hello!" to one of the men. He waved at me and shouted, "Hello!" over the noise of a semi careening down the road. I crossed the two-lane highway, introduced myself, and asked him what he was doing. He told me that he and his two friends were from Buffalo, New York, and they were walking across America. I was too awestruck to remember to ask my new friend his name. They had been walking for seven months and were heading for Santa Monica Pier, the place I had started less than a week before.

I asked him if he needed anything, and he asked for water. We walked to the van and filled his gallon water jug up with water. Another semi came careening by us on the side of the road, rustling our clothes with the air wall it was pushing. We decided we should part ways as stopping in this area on the side of this desert highway was too dangerous.

Mom was having trouble in this section of the desert trying to find safe sections to pull off. There were dirt roads every few miles that seemed to go off into the distance to nowhere. The only asphalt seemed to be the two-lane highway which boasted a white line signaling the edge of the road. The shoulder of the road consisted of one inch of asphalt and sand. Mom was worried that I was running too long without support in the desert—up to two and three miles at a time with no food, water, or supplies.

At around 11:00 a.m., I was running against traffic and I saw the van in the distance on the shoulder of the road. Mom was outside the van and waving her arm. As I got closer I heard her say, "Jay, keep running." I thought this was odd, and I ran over to see what was going on. She told me the van was stuck. She had tried to park it on the shoulder of the road where there was sand, and no asphalt. As it turned out, it was a soft shoulder and the front-wheel drive van became stuck, spinning its wheels as she pressed on the gas. We had a problem. Mom's plan was to call AAA, and get a tow. She wanted me to keep running so I didn't lose time trying to get my mileage. I knew that she and I couldn't separate. We had to stick together, regardless of what was happening.

She soon realized that there was no phone service in this area of the desert. After about thirty minutes and what seemed like an eternity, a Good Samaritan tow-truck driver passed us going the opposite direction. He stopped and connected his tow chain to the rear frame of the van and told my mom to put the van in reverse and accelerate when he started pulling. The plan was working well until the van reached the asphalt and Mom kept accelerating. She had the pedal to the metal in reverse and was about to crash into the back of the tow truck. I screamed, "*Stop!*" She slammed on the brakes, the tow truck driver kept accelerating, and the tow chain broke in half due to the tension.

Van stuck in desert outside of Twentynine Palms

Then, Mom continued going in reverse and ran over the broken tow chain. I immediately heard a hissing sound from the rear area of the vehicle. I suspected that the tire was going flat, and my hunch was correct. Immediately, I told Mom to drive to the nearest paved area where she could pull off to the side of the road and I would run up and meet her there to change the tire. The van needed to be on asphalt or a hard surface so the jack could lift the van. She sped off quickly, leaving me to thank the tow truck driver for his good deed. I ran a couple of miles up the highway where I found the van safely pulled off on a paved cutout on the side of the road. I was thankful she was safe and the van appeared to be in one piece. Our quick thinking had avoided the disaster of getting stuck out in the desert.

I had to unload the van and figure out where the spare tire was located. As luck would have it, the spare tire was in the main cabin of the van and we had to unload and disorganize all of our luggage, supplies, and equipment to access the spare tire and the jack. I put the jack under the van, and mumbled curse words under my breath.

I couldn't believe what had happened. We had gotten a late start and now we had a two-hour delay in my running day. How was I supposed to run fifty miles in eight hours? I couldn't do it without severe risk of significant injury. But I had to focus on one thing at a time. When I removed the tire, I immediately became speechless at what I saw. The tire had a twelve inch gash in it. Apparently, Mom had driven on the tire when it was completely flat and the tire was cut. We couldn't just repair the flattened tire; we had to replace it. The spare we had looked like a pathetic donut from the grocery store. It wasn't safe to drive on at high speeds or for long distances. To the east, we were eighty miles from the Arizona border, and to the west, we were fifty-some miles from Twentynine Palms, the town we had slept at the night before. It just didn't seem fair. Everything bad that could happen, was happening.

Mom and I were at each other again, and a torrent of misfortune after misfortune had befallen us. Twentynine Palms was the closest town we could attempt to seek refuge at and replace the tire. I had to make a decision then and there whether to keep running and try to achieve fifty miles for the day. It wasn't safe to keep running with the spare tire, knowing we needed to find a replacement tire as soon as possible. It was 1:00 p.m. and would be 2:00 p.m. by the time we returned to town to hunt for a replacement tire. Our day was done, and I was only sixteen miles into it. I felt totally defeated. Every effort I had made to keep us moving forward had been thwarted. It was as if some dark force was out there in the desert, trying hard to make me fail. It was trying hard to drive a wedge between Mom and me and create division. Mom and I both took a deep breath and just accepted the situation we were in.

We laughed on the way back to town. She said that she wanted to take a video of me cursing and throwing a temper tantrum while I attempted to change the tire. She was worried, however, that I might see her filming the incident and the situation would escalate into something even bigger. I laughed and I wished she had. I must have looked like a five-year-old who didn't get his way. But she was right about how I would have reacted if I saw her taping the tantrum. Bad things happened that day, just like they sometimes do in life. As Mom and I both practiced being patient and remaining calm, we were able to weather the storm, together. We also leaned on humor to get us through this difficult day. Our best weapon against the darkness that was attacking us was love, and we confirmed that "love never fails."

Our plan was to get a new tire, eat an early dinner, and drive out to where I stopped running at midnight. The plan was for me to start running by 1:00 a.m. and try to make up as much of the thirty-four miles that I missed on the flat-tire day. Our plan worked well and we found a garage that had the tire we needed. The charge was just a little over $100, and I felt a sting as it was an unplanned expenditure. I knew I'd just have to eat the cost, and I was sure there would be more where that came from. We got some food and cocooned up in our motel room while the sun was still burning the Sonoran Desert. Per our plan, we drove out to the starting point by midnight, and we had picked up some food and water to give to the three men who were walking from Buffalo to Santa Monica. We couldn't find them in the dark morning hours, so we left the food and water on the side of the road, hoping they would find it when they started walking the next day. They must have pulled their shopping carts over a berm of sand or back into the brush so they wouldn't be hit by passing vehicles. It was amazing how they just seemed to disappear. At 1:00 a.m., I ran in front of the van, trying to make up the miles I had missed the day before. We had our walkie-talkies and she would tell me when a car or truck was coming behind us. I would then run on the shoulder of the road to test the surface to see if it was safe for the van to follow me. For the most part, the shoulder was hard and the van was safe to pull off and let the overtaking vehicle pass us in the lane of traffic. On the rare occasion where the shoulder was soft, I would tell her to drive ahead until she got to a road where she could pull off and wait for me.

We didn't want the van to get stuck again, and we didn't want a drowsy driver to rear-end the van at high speeds. After all, who would expect a van to be following a runner at 5 mph in the middle of the desert at 1:00 a.m.? It was dangerous, but we made it work, and by sunrise I had somehow amassed twenty miles. For the rest of the day, we moved slow, and it felt very difficult to make any real progress. By 6:30 p.m., I was physically, mentally, and emotionally exhausted and needed to stop running. I had only chalked up fifty-five miles that day, despite giving myself an extra four hours on the road. The desert was turning out to be a daunting and formidable opponent.

There was too much work for my mom. She is comfortable being on her own, and I believe prefers it when crewing. But I knew I couldn't continue to help unload and load the van, pump gas, and help shop for groceries. The toll of running fifty-mile days back-to-back and overcoming countless unforeseen adversities every day was wearing on me. One day when I was talking with Carly about upcoming routing decisions, she made a joke about coming out to crew. She had never crewed a race and didn't know what was entailed. I just thought we needed more help and nobody else I knew could volunteer. I decided to take her up on her offer to come out and help crew. She asked how long, and my response was "As long as you can." She spoke with her employer and arranged to come out and help out for a smidge under three weeks. Her plan was to fly into Phoenix, and we would pick her up as we were passing through town; then, she would fly out of Wichita whenever we arrived. I believed that the extra set of hands would be invaluable.

Mom, on the other hand, wasn't so sure. She is accustomed to her privacy, and I was already stretching her comfort zone by forcing her to live out of motels and drive the van to support me. Now, I was forcing a roommate on her. A virtual stranger would be sharing a bed with Mom and travelling side-by-side with her during the day as I ran. I failed to understand the situation from my mom's perspective. She has a precise way that she likes to organize the van, prepare food and drink, maintain a schedule, and offer support so I can run with as little to think about as possible. All I could think was that we needed more help.

I didn't listen to her, or respect her needs when I made that decision. We should have had a two-way dialogue, and we should have talked through the situation more. I don't know if that would have changed the final outcome, but I do know that's what I should have done to make her feel better about adding a crew member at that stage of the run.

That night we finished just shy of the Arizona border. It took six days and 270 miles to cross the great state of California.

24

Arizona—The Grand Canyon State

Arizona state line

Early the next day on March 31, 2016, we crossed into Arizona. I carried a digital audio recorder to journal my thoughts. Attitude is everything, and I was reminded of this as I recorded my thoughts:

In one moment, you can be in a very tough situation, and then you see something and your perspective totally changes just because of one tiny little thing; in this case for me, it was the sign that I was in Arizona.

The power of positive thinking cannot be underestimated or overstated. Sometimes, like a light switch, I could turn a bad situation into a good situation. I have found that this is the secret of my unending and impenetrable resilience. I have developed an uncanny ability to see the silver lining in situations. Sometimes, I have been criticized and ridiculed for being an idealist and optimist. I believe attitude is a personal choice, and attitude is the ultimate arbiter. We choose how we will experience situations and life. Difficult and joyous situations alike can be fun or disastrous—the choice is ours. Sometimes when I tell people about the experience of running hundred-mile races and spraining ankles, puking, pooping in the woods, and helping other runners who are suffering, they grimace with discomfort and uneasiness. I, on the other hand, am smiling ear to ear, thinking how fun it was to be free, connected, and moving. Attitude isn't everything—it's the only thing.

On the day I crossed into Arizona, I shared the following thoughts in my journal, about what I learned.

Be thankful for everything you have. Don't focus on the things that go wrong, or a flat tire or losing time. You focus on the things you do have. I have my mom with me. And when I get mad at her, I'm reminded that she's the only one out here supporting me. I'm just thankful. It's been a great learning experience, and the desert has taught me a lot; although I don't want to go back there ever.

The desert in California emanated a dark presence and made me feel uncomfortable. I figured I was home free as soon as I got to Arizona, and that somehow as I crossed an imaginary line on a map, things would change for the better.

Well, I was wrong.

Within hours of crossing into Arizona, I found myself running against traffic on a good-sized shoulder of a highway toward a T-intersection. Thoughts of a different desert landscape careened through my head. The sand and soil seemed redder than the vanilla-colored sand of California. An RV was turning left at the intersection about a hundred feet ahead of me, and heading toward me. An impatient car wanted to overtake the RV and jockeyed for position. I couldn't really see what was happening, but I heard vehicles accelerating and engines revving. Before I knew it, I saw the car speeding head-on at me in the break-down lane. The RV was also speeding because it apparently didn't want the car to pass it. I stopped moving forward, flailed my arms, and then just froze, waiting for the impact of the car. All I thought was, *This is how it ends.*

The car passed and swerved in front of the RV, missing me by a couple of feet. My whole body shook and I felt adrenaline coursing through my veins. I just wanted to fall down and cry. Mom had driven up the road and didn't witness the event. When I was able to, I walked slowly, contemplating what had just happened, and what had almost happened. When I got to where the van was parked, I sat in the passenger seat with the door open and my feet dangling out the door. Mom urged me to get running so we could get to our stopping point for the night and get a good night's rest. I told her to hang on, and tried to explain what had just happened. She couldn't comprehend my brush with mortality and the emotions it had stirred up within me.

I sat in the van with my head in my hands. All I could think was that I had almost died. I almost lost the ability to ever see, touch, and talk to my kids again. I would never have seen my grandkids. I thought, "This is a stupid run. What's the point? Am I supposed to die out here because of some idiot driver?" I considered calling the entire thing off, and heading straight back to Colorado at that point. I was questioning whether the run was worth risking my life over. I have taken risks in my life, but they have always been calculated risks. Risks where I felt I had control and knew with my pre-planning, effort, and awareness I would be able to get through the adversity. This was wholly different. My life could be ended because of a bonehead choosing to drive recklessly. What a tragic end it would be.

But I honestly believed I had a Calling. I was doing this for something much bigger than me. It wasn't my personal desire to leave my kids, go into debt, injure my body, and risk my life. It was about having faith and being obedient to a Calling from something much larger than myself. If I truly believed I was Called to run across America and I quit because of a human trying to run me over in his car, what would that say about my faith? I really wouldn't have any. If I truly believed this was a Calling, however, the end of the run would be according to a larger plan. If I was killed by an errant driver, that would somehow be according to some larger plan that I was incapable of understanding. I had to choose to have faith or not. It was the hardest decision I have ever had to make. It was 100 percent an intellectual decision. I chose faith and to be obedient to another's will; and so I continued running. That afternoon when I recorded my audio journal, I had some very insightful thoughts about life and the first seven days of the run.

March 31, 2016
Audio Journal Recording

I've learned some lessons . . . like, when something bad happens to you, like when my mom drove into the ditch, lost a walkie-talkie, had a flat tire, or had to give up on a day of running, I could have sat there and been angry about all those things. I was angry, but that doesn't do anything good. It just lets others have power over you. Love and forgiveness can overcome this.

If I can just focus on the things I do have and the things I can do, like being able to run sixteen miles instead of focusing on not being able to run fifty miles, that's going to enable me to appreciate my life and take ownership of it.

Patience is another important thing the desert taught me. Instead of always trying to power through, and run hard and fast, I learned to just slow down and have patience. Things are going to work out. I don't need to go hard all the time. I don't need to be the first one, but I will get the job done. And, if it's about being the first one, why does it really matter if I am first? Who cares? What does it matter? Is it just about ego? Is it about saying I'm better than other people, so from a judgment perspective I can feel good about myself by downgrading others? What does it matter? It matters to always give my best. . . . Winning is not about beating others, it's about doing my best. And, it doesn't matter what place I come in, as long as I've given my best, I've won.

I've also learned about love. My mom and I started off this trip with some very bad nights—really bad arguments. There was even one time I was ready to take the baby stroller and just go at it alone. I don't know why I was so angry. I saw her as the problem, some external force. And, I came around and apologized. Maybe we both had a part in the disagreement, whatever it was, but the anger was all mine and that was my issue. Blaming things on my mom was my issue. So we got past that. And, she said some bad things to me and didn't apologize for them. And then I got angry about that, too. Well, she's just not going to apologize. And, I learned that the way to overcome anger and all of that is with love. Love conquers all and love never fails.

After I recorded that entry and finished my mileage for the day, we drove to the nearest motel in Salome, Arizona. That night when we arrived at the motel, Mom and I parted ways pretty quickly. I went directly to the room to begin doing recovery work, and she went to check us in. There was also a restaurant and bar near the main office. I soaked in the tub and did some social media posts to update folks on our daily mileage and the good lesson that I'd learned. I wanted the run to be uplifting and inspiring, so I didn't share all the drama that was happening behind the scenes. At the end of the day, I wanted the public to know the mileage for the day, and the life lesson I learned along the way. They didn't need to know about my internal strife.

I had spent a couple of hours doing recovery work and was resting in bed when Mom returned to the room. The people who owned the motel were from Colorado and it sounded like she had struck up a conversation with them. She had also sat at the bar and had a couple of drinks to relax. I took issue with her going off the clock, checking out and not helping me as I worked into the night to do recovery and the entire nighttime routine independently. There was an inherent conflict with this situation, because I needed her to have rest and be able to blow off steam, but I also I needed her to be all-in all the time. At that moment, I was glad another person would be coming to help us in a few days. At the rate we were going, maybe Mom and I would get across the country, but would it cost us our relationship? Emotions were very high and unpredictable.

I lay in bed, thinking about others' attempts. It seemed as if whenever somebody opened their mouth and said out loud that they were going to break the transcon record, they ended up failing. I thought the best approach was to just run and let my actions do the talking. My goal wasn't to break the transcon record, but I did want to establish a new Guinness World Record for Fastest Transcontinental Crossing on Foot by a Blind Person; there was already a transcon record category for a man (46 days, 8 hours, 36 minutes) and a woman (69 days, 2 hours, 40 minutes). Unfortunately, Guinness opted not to accept my application for a new record category for the blind. They did, however, tell me that they would recognize a new record if my run surpassed the men's record. I knew this was out of the question. In the back of my mind, I toyed with the idea of what it would take to break the existing record. I also reasoned that if I went after the record, my run would become self-centered and ego-motivated. My run was a Calling, about something much larger than any world record. It was beyond my understanding, and regardless of whether the Guinness company recognized the record or not, it would be a record for the blind and visually impaired if in fact I could make it all the way to the Atlantic Ocean.

I was feeling very isolated from the world, cut off, and as if I was the last person on earth. My day consisted of three major activities —running, taking in nourishment, and sleeping. Nowhere in those three things was an outlet for my extroverted personality. I derive energy and thrive on human interaction. With the next sunrise came a special day, because Bacho Vega and his family were coming out to support me. I had met Bacho a little over a year earlier when I ran across Puerto Rico. Bacho is a very accomplished ultra-runner who doesn't DNF and has tackled some very tough races. I always admired him for his mental strength and mental game. He came in third in the Puerto Rico crossing, and I came in fourth. I knew Bacho would be able to run with me, as many miles as I could do.

He told me that he is always looking for ways to teach his children life lessons. Apparently, my run was an example of a few such lessons, like friendship, service, desire, doing hard things, not giving up, and creating a plan and following through on that plan. Bacho told me that he brought his family out to support me to get a first-hand look at these principles in action. Per Bacho, "You can talk and preach and read about things all you want, but having firsthand experience is the best way to teach."

Bacho's thoughts hit me hard, and I felt the largeness of the run. On a daily basis, I received messages from people all around the world via social media, Strava (a website that connects athletes) and e-mail. I wanted to be normal, but the task I was undertaking was making me far from normal. I was an anomaly, and I wasn't sure how I felt about that. I didn't have much time to think, because I had to keep on eating, drinking, sleeping, and putting one foot in front of the other. My mom also had deep respect for Bacho, and his family's presence helped us reset our perspective on the daily quarrels we were having.

It seemed like the miles just passed as easily as breathing when I was in Bacho's presence. Bacho had literally come out and saved me when I was running the last thirty miles of the Badwater Ultramarathon in Death Valley in July, in temperatures that reached 120°. I just couldn't get moving, and then Bacho began running with me. Somehow, he was able to get me to eat, drink, and eventually run. I don't think it was any special advice Bacho gave me; I think just being in his presence gives me strength. I'm sure it is something larger that neither of us can understand, but regardless of the underlying reason, I have found that I am able to run comfortably whenever this friend is near me.

I had two more friends, Christy Daniher and her father, meet us when we were approaching Phoenix; only these friends had driven about eight hundred miles to reach us. Christy was a special friend who I had met in Washington Park in Denver a couple of years before. I was out for a normal run around the two-and-a-half-mile loop of the park when I saw a canopy tent with a bunch of gear that looked like an aid station. This was out of place, as this park was a picnic and jogging haven, and no races were scheduled to go through the park on this day. I went to the makeshift aid station and asked what was going on. A pretty blond lady explained that her friend was running for twenty-four hours in Washington Park in order to raise money for a young man who had suffered a neurological injury.

The blonde turned out to be Christy and she seemed exhausted. I asked what I could do to help, and she said I could relieve her and crew the runner. Apparently, Christy had been supporting this runner for over fifteen hours and needed a hand-off. I told Christy I'd be back as soon as I could run to my mom's house and take a shower. I recruited Mom and nephew, Rocket, and we supported the runner for the remainder of his run, giving Christy a much-needed break. Christy and I became friends on social media, but never really knew one another as true friends. I learned on Facebook that Christy was an endurance athlete herself and a multiple-time IronMan finisher. When I was getting ready for Badwater, I had an opening for a crew position and Christy volunteered to fill the position on a moment's notice. She also volunteered her dad to fill the position if she couldn't get the time off work. All I could think was, *Who is this person?* As I got to know Christy a little bit better, she told me that she really supports people who get outside of their comfort zone and push themselves. Christy was definitely this kind of person. My original Badwater crew person eventually was able to make the trip, and Christy gracefully bowed out.

My next major encounter with this amazing woman happened when I humbled myself to start fundraising to support the run. She was the person who pledged $1,000 immediately after I began begging for funds on social media. Christy's message was, "I'm giving you $1,000 to support your run." I didn't know how I felt about that. It was too much money. I didn't even really know her. I wasn't sure I could accept that much money from anybody. I texted her back, and admitted my feelings of uneasiness. She responded saying, "You need to accept it. And, you need to accept all help that people will offer you."

When Christy and her dad showed up and found me running on

the highway in Arizona, it was amazing. All I could think was, "There are really good people in this world." Christy and her dad drove twelve hours on a Friday, met us Friday evening, paid for our lodging, cooked us dinner, crewed, and ran with us Saturday, and drove another eight hundred miles back home on Sunday. Oh yeah, and Christy gave me the only foot rub I had during the entire run. Where do people like Christy and Mr. Daniher come from? When I asked Christy why she came to help me, she said that what I was doing was something "epic" and it might be the only time in her and her father's life that they would get an opportunity to participate in something of that magnitude. I didn't understand her perspective, but I sure did appreciate all the love, caring, and warmth her family had shown me.

Carly joined our crew as we were passing through Phoenix. Somehow, someway, Mom and I were getting things done, but I was heading into a deficit of exhaustion, and even if Mom didn't feel like she needed more help, I did. Carly was in her late twenties, and arrived all smiles and bubbly-eyed. That soon changed. Carly jumped into the passenger seat of the van and we continued our daily routine. Mom took the lead and demonstrated what we were doing—I ran one mile, then a crew member gave me food and drink, and I continued running. In the van, a lot of things were happening that I was oblivious to. Mom was trying to keep records of how much nutrition and hydration I was taking in to make sure I didn't go into a deficit. She was also trying to navigate our route, and ensure that when we stopped on highways, they were safe locations. In addition, she had to prep the food. She had to make sandwiches and cut them into small pieces, and bag them, plus peel and cut vegetables and fruits, cool drinks, top off water, and monitor and restock ice. Then, she needed to access the supplies in the van.

On foul-weather days, I might change into and out of rain gear multiple times a day. In addition, depending on sweat rate and temperature, I might require multiple sock and shoe changes and re-lubing of areas that consistently chafe—butt cheeks, thighs, nipples, underarms, and areas where my pack rubbed my shoulders and back. During my daily rest period, roughly after I ran my first marathon distance, we would need to partially unload the interior of the van so I could have a place to lay down. After my break, nap, and lunch, the van needed to be reloaded and reorganized again so we could quickly access necessary supplies. At the end of the day when we arrived at the motel, we needed to unload all of my recovery equipment and clothes. The wet clothes needed to be dried so we could re-use them the next day without laundering them, assuming they were still somewhat clean. The dirty, stinky clothes were bagged and awaited laundering which happened every five or six days.

Carly jumped right in and started volunteering to do whatever needed to be done. For me, an additional crew member was perfect because it got me out of having to load and unload the van at the end of the evening. I also was able to get dropped off at the motel right after my running day was over and didn't need to go with the crew to get gas for the next day and restock supplies. But for Mom, an additional crew member was additional complexity. She had developed a routine, organized supplies, and had an extremely efficient process for how she was able to do all of the duties that were required to support me. Now, I was forcing her to re-engineer all of the processes she had perfected in order to incorporate an additional crew member. It must have been total chaos for her, and I don't know how she ever let me bring in a brand-new crew member for almost three weeks. She later told me that she thought the additional crew member helped get me through the run, but wasn't necessarily a lot of help to her.

The first night Carly was there, she volunteered to take the van to get gas, restock ice, buy food for the coming day, and get food while Mom and I started our nighttime routines at the motel. We gladly accepted her offer. After about an hour and a half, we were wondering where Carly was, and whether she had gotten lost. Within a couple of minutes of entertaining that thought, she came through the door. We were relieved to see her and have dinner; however, something was wrong with her. She is usually all smiles, but this time she wasn't smiling and had her head down. She looked like she was ashamed for some reason. I asked her what was wrong. She replied,

"You're probably going to fire me on my first day."

She went on to explain that the van was stuck at the gas station. She hadn't seen a curb and accidentally ran over it and the van got stuck. She had walked back to the motel from the gas station. Mom and I almost immediately said, "let's call Triple-A." Mom was already dressed since most nights she slept in the clothes she was going to wear the next day in order to be more efficient. Within thirty minutes, the pair were back from the gas station with the van safe and sound. Although Carly didn't show it, the incident had shaken her a bit. We had only really known each other for six months and at best were arm's length friends. She didn't know me or how I would react, or how my mom would react to a letdown or a mistake. To an extent, we were strangers to one another.

Later in the trip, Carly told me she expected Mom and I would be very upset with her for getting the van stuck. What happened was totally different—nobody got upset and we all worked together to solve the problem. No fingers were pointed and nobody was made to feel guilty. We were a team, and if one team member was stuck, we all jumped in to help them get unstuck.

As we left Phoenix, Arizona and headed east toward Payson and Heber, we climbed higher and higher into the mountains. I never knew Arizona had such high mountains. One day, it seemed like I was climbing for thirty miles up twisting, winding roads with no shoulders and blind corners. It was normal for me to have a semi passing me with about a foot between us. Because of the curvy roads, the semis were only going about 50 mph, but it was still very unnerving. We also had 5 mile segments where I would have to wait to be crewed because there were no safe pull-offs for Mom to park the van. My nutrition was off, and I was bonking trying to climb the mountains and stay safe.

Ultimately, I made it up the mountain and it took me an extra hour and a half to complete my fifty miles for the day. On very difficult days like this, I chose not to run one more "make-up mile" to offset lost mileage when we flatted out in the desert and only achieved sixteen miles for the day. The mountains in Arizona played with my mind for the next two days, rolling up and down. They topped out at just under 9,000 feet above sea level; it would be the highest point of my transcontinental run. Although I had purposefully avoided routing through Colorado because of the elevation and possibility of snow, the altitude of the Arizona mountains was having a draining effect on my body. The smell of pine trees and crisp mornings reminded me of the Rocky Mountains back home in Colorado. There is peace in the mountains, and this section of the run had the same effect on me and lifted my spirits.

As I cleared the mountains and descended toward the New Mexico state line, I encountered headwinds. They lasted for eight straight hours on this particular day. I burned up a lot of energy, but chose to run into the wind and hope gravity would offset some of the effort. On a daily basis, I gave myself an assignment to finish running fifty miles within twelve hours or less. If I could accomplish this, then my crew and I would have enough time to do our night-time routine, and I could get at least six or seven hours of sleeping recovery per night. When it was a tough running day with mountains, headwinds, storms, etc. I slowed down, my running time increased, and my recovery time decreased. I also lost an hour of recovery time every time I crossed a time zone. On days when I was going to cross a time zone, I made special preparations to be extra efficient so I could finish fifty miles in eleven hours, to protect my sleep time. Sleep, in my opinion, is the most important recovery method for any runner. The body heals itself when we sleep. The more sleep I was able to get, the more my body could repair the damage I was doing to it.

As I finished my fifty miles on my last day in Arizona, we were approaching Springerville, Arizona. As I jogged down the shoulder of the highway toward my invisible finish line for the day, I saw a couple of people ahead in the distance. They were waving their arms. I couldn't make out what was going on and didn't know if they needed help, or what they were doing. Sometimes, people would randomly drive up and offer me a ride, and ask where my car had broken down. I would tell these good people that I was okay and just running. Many times they would ask where I was running to. When I answered that I was running to the Atlantic Ocean; their faces would become stone and there would be a very long silence. The reaction was always the same—there was a pause while their minds tried to process my words. When the drivers processed what I had just told them, there would be different reactions. Some people's faces would light up and they would say encouraging things like, "No way! Don't stop, man!" Or they would offer to get me a meal and bring it back to me. Or, one guy made me come over to his car and he gave me all the cash in his wallet which was $100. His parting words as he drove off were, "Don't stop!" I was always inspired by the goodness of the people I encountered as I ran.

As I got closer to the two people waving their arms, I thought I heard my name being yelled. *I must be hallucinating,* I said to myself. Then, as I came even closer, I realized that the figures weren't apparitions; they were real, and, they were in fact yelling my name. Two females were on the shoulder of the road in the middle of nowhere waiting for me. *Who are these people?* I wondered.

One looked taller than the other and appeared to be holding something white. I needed to get very close to visually make out who they were. When I was within about five feet, I recognized that one of their voices was familiar. I must have looked like I didn't recognize them, because all of a sudden, one of them said, "Jason, it's Destiny."

Destiny was the waitress who waited on us at the restaurant in Springerville where Mom and I had stopped for lunch some three weeks prior. Apparently, Destiny had been tracking my progress. On the day we left her, she told me she would bring me something to eat if we saw her again. Sure enough, she brought me a chimichanga with no sour cream, the exact thing I had ordered from her three weeks prior. Destiny also brought out her daughter Kinley to meet me.

My emptiness and melancholy was neutralized by these two angels who had somehow appeared at exactly the right moment when I needed to know that I wasn't alone, abandoned, and forsaken. I was reminded how powerful and important human connection is. A very simple random act of kindness changed my entire world to be right-side up, when it was upside down.

A couple of years prior, I had begun cutting the toe box off my shoes with a straight razor blade. This was a trick I had learned from Uncle Ted. When a person stands on his feet for a long period of time, gravity causes fluid to build up in the feet, and swelling occurs. Usually, in multi-day (one, two, three, six, and ten day) racing, it is common for runners to bring multiple pairs of shoes to wear as their feet swell and grow. I found that if I sized up a half size, cut the toe box off my shoes, and lay on my back and elevated my feet throughout the day, I was able to prevent my feet from swelling two and three additional shoe sizes. Also, I didn't have any blisters on my toes after cutting off the toe box and I never had another bout of dreaded "black toe." Black toe happens where a blister forms under the toenail, causing the toenail to die, turn black, and eventually fall off. As far as I was concerned, I had just liberated my feet from enduring unnecessary suffering. When some people saw my shoes, they affectionately called them Sandal-OKAs. They looked like sandals and I tied them so loosely I was able to slip them on and off without lacing or unlacing them. I only ran in one brand of shoes—HOKA ONE ONE—the best ultra-running shoes as far as I was concerned. HOKAs have an enormous amount of cushioning, and for me, they were the perfect complement to help my foot adapt to paved roads and concrete sidewalks and paths.

When I ran with the toe box cut off on gravel roads and shoulders of highways, it was common for me to get pebbles and gravel in my shoes. I rarely stopped to get rocks out of my shoes as it was fairly common for it to work its way into and out of my shoes every mile. As quick as they entered the shoe, they exited. The particular pebble that had taken a ride with me the entire day a few days prior had stayed with me for the last twenty miles of the day. I knew I should have stopped and taken it out, but my stubbornness and desire to finish early that day prevented me from a thirty-second pit stop to remove the shoe and rock, and continue on. The rock must have caused a blister to form on the outside of my foot, then the next day it must have popped and I was running on raw flesh. I never inspected my foot, as I had more pressing injuries, and was trying hard to deal with my emotions. On this particular morning, I didn't feel like I could put pressure on the foot to stand. If I couldn't stand on the foot, how on earth was I going to run?

After three days, and the injury continuing to get worse, I figured I had better inspect my foot and see what was going on. When I pulled it close enough to see it, I realized that the pain wasn't from blistering. I had bumps on my foot where the pain was originating from, but they weren't pus-filled nodules like normal blisters. They were red, inflamed, and the entire foot was swollen around and underneath the bumps. It only took me a few seconds to figure out what had happened—I had been bitten or stung. A spider, ant, or scorpion must have gotten into my shoe, and stung or bit me a few days prior. The untreated area had just became more and more inflamed with the constant pounding, and the hot, moist environment was ripe for bacteria to jump in and cause some extra irritation.

I cleaned the area as best I could with alcohol to try to stave off infection. Mom got the largest pair of shoes I had for the trip. Somehow, I had to try to shove the swollen appendage into a shoe so I would be able to run for the day. My foot was throbbing. The shoe was more than long enough, but it wasn't wide enough to accommodate the inflamed foot. I had to think quickly as I only had about thirty minutes until I needed to be on the road running. I decided to get a razor and cut the shoe where the foot was inflamed. Perhaps if I removed the area on the upper of the shoe that was causing pressure on the inflamed area, the pain would decrease. My mom watched as I carefully drew an outline with a Sharpie on the shoe to mark the area I was planning to surgically remove. After about two minutes of careful cutting, I slipped my foot into the shoe. *It worked!* I trimmed the shoe a little more to remove even more material, but luckily I was going to be able to run that day and put pressure on the foot. It took about a week for the bite or sting to resolve completely. I learned a valuable lesson from that experience, one that ultra-runners are keen to respect. When running extreme distances, a crack can turn into a crevasse if left unattended. I gambled on this one, and lost. However, with innovation, I eventually overcame this obstacle but with endurance of much unnecessary suffering.

Sandal-OKAs cut to accommodate toes and insect bite

After 381 miles and a little under eight days of running through desert and over mountains, it was finally time to bid adieu to Arizona, The Grand Canyon State, and cross over into New Mexico.

25

New Mexico—The Land of Enchantment

New Mexico state line

It was rainy and dreary when I crossed into New Mexico at 9:00 a.m. on April 8, 2016, after running 704 miles across California and Arizona. I was still following Highway 60 eastbound, and found that it was a common trucking route. It seemed like wherever I went, the semis were sure to be waiting for me. On any given day, over a hundred semis would go flying by me at fifty to eighty miles per hour. By this time, I had grown accustomed to being pelted by wind bursts and gravel, having water puddles sprayed on me, and losing any loose-fitting clothes, sunglasses, or hats when the semis buzzed me. Once in a while, Carly would run a few miles with me, and it was apparent that she wasn't comfortable being that close to the metal boxes of death. I always had her run behind me or off on the shoulder of the road so I would be the first one to get hit, if such an accident were to happen.

The weather was just ugly that day. A large storm system seemed to be following us like a drone. Whichever way the road bent, the storm seemed to shift and follow us. The sky was dark, and the smell of rain and humidity was in the air. It reminded me of the movie *Twister* where storm chasers drove directly into these types of storm cells, hoping to have a close encounter with a tornado. I, on the other hand, wanted nothing to do with a tornado, or wind, or rain. Adverse weather played constant tricks on my mind and enabled doubt to sit on my shoulder and whisper "It's okay to quit" into my ear. After six hours of having the storm chase me, I had achieved thirty miles and it was time for my daily break. We were in the middle of nowhere, and the sky just seemed to be getting darker and darker. I told my mom that I thought we should forego the break and just keep moving forward. If the storm caught me and overtook me, it would be miserable to run in wind, rain, and hail. She agreed, I guzzled a Starbuck's frappuccino, and grabbed a sandwich and kept running. I needed to keep my calories up to keep moving at the pace I was keeping. By forty-five miles, I knew the storm wasn't going to overtake me, and it had finally stopped its eastward march and blown south. After nine hours and twenty minutes of running, I had somehow completed fifty-one miles. It was mind boggling that I was able to run that distance at that pace after having run for fourteen days straight, averaging just under fifty miles per day.

When I first contemplated running across America, I spoke with a couple of people who had crossed at fifty or more miles per day— Marshall Ulrich and Perry Newburn. Both of them warned me of a break-in period my body would go through as I began the run. The body is just not used to doing that high a mileage on a daily basis, and there was no way to simulate it in training without risking severe injury. Both men told me that my body would, in effect, revolt against what I was putting it through. My body would think that I was trying to kill it; hence, it would send pain signals to my brain in an effort to get me to stop torturing it. Meanwhile, it would actually be strengthening areas of weakness, rebuilding muscle, and making the cardiovascular and pulmonary systems as efficient as they could be. My body had to build itself into a machine that could withstand the torture of fifty plus miles a day on the feet day after day. The break-in period was really about a consistent build-up of physical pain, and learning to become accustomed to running in pain.

As part of that, I experienced a strange phenomenon. At night when I slept, I would sweat profusely. Each night I would wake up twice and would move to different parts of the bed because my clothes and sheets were soaked with sweat. I started on the left side, woke, then moved to the middle of the bed, woke, then moved to the right side of the bed, then woke up for the day. Nobody ever told me this would happen, but in speaking with other runners who have run consistent ultras day after day, they reported similar night sweats. My assumption was that the body was working hard repairing itself while I slept, and the heat created from the repair work resulted in a high sweat rate.

I also experienced another strange phenomenon. My hair and nails stopped growing at the same rate as before. I didn't shave often, and didn't need to. It took me about thirty days to grow the same length of beard as it normally took me to grow in one week. My assumption is that my body directed itself to use protein to repair muscle structures as a priority, and hair and nail growth was a much lower priority. Hence, I realized that I wouldn't look like Forrest Gump at the end of my run if I had chosen to let my beard grow. I didn't really care for beards much, even though it had become quite trendy in the ultra-running world to grow one. I had decided to let my feet define my running, not a beard or some other fad.

After I crossed into New Mexico, I figured I had emerged from the break-in period and my body understood what I was asking of it. After all, I just ran my fastest day of the entire expedition, and wasn't any worse as a result. I ended with the same injuries that I had when I started the day—Achilles tendonitis, IT band syndrome, sprained ankles from falls I had sustained in Arizona, and the residual inflammation from the bug bite/sting on my foot. I was in pretty good shape, relatively speaking.

While running across America, I also learned that many small towns have rich histories and fame for which they are never fully given credit. One of those towns was Pie Town, New Mexico. I actually learned about Pie Town after I had already run through it and was lying on the highway. I would have Mom stretch me on the side of the road in the break-down lane about three hours after starting running in the morning. I was lying down and Mom was stretching me as my chiropractor had taught us some two months prior. She was straining with her petite frame to stretch my leg which was exceptionally tight. The sight must have looked extremely unusual to passersby, but that was normal for us at this point. On this particular day, a truck pulled over to see what was wrong. The driver and his wife exited the truck and walked toward us as we were doing the stretching routine. Their names were Tony and Shannon, and they were proud Pie Town residents. They asked if we were okay. My Mom explained that I was running across America, and they immediately responded, "Oh no! We'll call an ambulance!"

I chuckled and reported that I was okay and that my mom was just stretching out my legs so I could continue running for the day. Our routine was so foreign to normal everyday life, that Mom and I had become accustomed to such reactions when we explained what we were doing. After we calmed Tony and Shannon, they asked if we had a slice of pie in Pie Town. I sorrowfully admitted that I hadn't, and they told me what a shame that was. Their town had the best pie in "all of the US." They also told me they had a hostel right on the Continental Divide Trail which runs from Mexico to Canada. They explained that through-hikers regularly sought refuge there and feasted on pies while recharging their energy stores to continue on their trek.

It felt good to know that there were other souls out there some-where doing epic long-distance treks. I knew that I was joining a club of people who just unplugged from life, and set out to pursue something huge regardless of how long it took. Somehow, I would be changed as a result of what I was experiencing. Maybe it wouldn't be apparent immediately, but inside, I knew that I would never be the same person I was before I had started running from Santa Monica.

The day was fairly uneventful and we finished outside of Magdalena, at the Very Large Array (VLA) of radio telescopes. We were in the middle of nowhere, and there were twenty-seven satellite dishes eighty-two feet in diameter which were situated in a Y shape. Each satellite dish weighs 209 metric tons, and they are on railroad tracks so they can be moved to create an expanded or compact Y. I had first seen these telescopes in the movie *Contact* with Jodie Foster, when I was young. The telescopes are used to research black holes and cosmic anomalies. In the mid-90s, the VLA was used to follow up on the "Wow! Signal"—a seventy-two-second transmission that was received some three decades earlier by the Search for Extraterrestrial Intelligence (SETI). Regardless of what these things were being used for, their sheer size and presence was impressive. Little did I know this would only be the beginning of strange occurrences for us in the Land of Enchantment.

Very Large Array of radio telescopes outside of Magdalena, New Mexico

That night, I sat in the bathtub soaking in hot water laced with Epsom salts, trying to soothe my aching legs and feet. As per my usual routine, I took this time to upload some pictures from the day's run, report daily mileage, and share a lesson I had learned during the day. Up to that point, everything was pretty normal. Then I noticed I had a message from my girlfriend. She told me she was hurting, in too much pain, and she was "letting go." I couldn't breathe. It felt like I was suffocating.

She and I had our ups and downs in our relationship in the prior four years, and we had gone through some tough patches where we had hurt one another. However, we also had made many more amazing moments together, and had shared ourselves with one another more deeply than either of us had with any other person. I didn't understand what was happening. I didn't understand why she was breaking up with me. I knew her, however, and whatever she was feeling was very real to her; in her mind and heart, her actions were necessary and justified and she was beyond being able to cope with the pain that she was experiencing. I ached for her suffering.

All I could think of at the time, however, was myself. My aching and suffering. My plight. My pain. My reaction wasn't compassionate or understanding. I was hurt and angry and felt abandoned. The person I loved didn't love me. I was losing her. What would happen when I reached Boston? She was the underlying reason for me choosing a finish in that city. Would I finish this run without being able to land in the arms of the person I loved most? I wouldn't see her beautiful face or feel her warm embrace if I were able to drag my battered body clear across America. My fairytale ending just evaporated. I was empty and I cried.

The next morning, I had no desire to run. When Mom dropped me off at my starting point, I just sat in the van. She could tell I had no desire to move, but she didn't know why. Finally, I got out of the van and started walking and crying uncontrollably. All I could think of was my girlfriend, our first kiss, how I held her hand, our bouts of laughter, all of the things we had told each other. I fell to the ground, screaming and pounding the ground yelling *"No!"* The sight must have looked extremely strange—a man on the side of the highway, punching the ground and screaming at 6:30 a.m. I didn't want her to leave me. I was so hurt. It was like I had just gotten run over by a semi. All of my motivation had been immediately sapped from me.

I desperately wanted to call her, but I feared the conversation would end with her confirming her intent to end the relationship. I couldn't bring myself to do it. I could barely walk. I wanted to quit the run right then and there.

I had five people in my life who were part of my inner circle—people I trusted with everything. She was one of them. I wanted to spend the rest of my life with her. As the hours passed and I walked lethargically, my crying and sadness turned to anger. I chose to just cut her out of my life, at least for the rest of the run. I convinced myself that if I gave energy to her and tried to talk her back into a relationship with me, I wouldn't be able to complete my mileage or the run. I was having a mental and emotional meltdown, and somehow I had to stop it or I wouldn't be able to continue. I felt completely abandoned, but, by choosing to not talk to her, I made a huge mistake.

I loved this woman, and wanted her for the rest of my life. When things got really tough, I turned away from her instead of turning toward her. It was one of the most cowardly things I have ever done in my life. Regardless of how depleted I felt. Regardless of whether her actions were warranted or not. Regardless of any other factor, if I truly loved this woman, I should have stayed the course and endured, because one thing is certain—*love never fails*.

Instead, I chose a cowardly path of what I believed was self-preservation. I closed down, blocked her calls, unfriended her on social media, and tried to prevent any further contact from her. I thought I had to insulate myself from her, and I didn't feel like I could handle the pain of more breaking up in my current state. I didn't know if I could go on. I knew I didn't want to go on. However, I also knew that I had started this run not because of my own desires, but because it was something I was supposed to do. Something larger was Calling me to cross America on foot. I wished so hard that my relationship with my girlfriend was different. I hated that day, and as I write this, I can feel all those emotions of emptiness, loss, and love for her all over again. Somehow, I needed to just keep moving forward, despite my overwhelming desire to pack up, go home, and curl up in a ball and cry. That day was the worst day of the entire run.

I knew I had to complete fifty miles to keep moving across America and not put us further behind schedule, so I just kept putting one foot in front of the other. It was at that point I realized that my biggest obstacle in running across America wouldn't be the physical challenge . . . the mental challenge would be the toughest part of the run. I would be constantly challenged with deteriorating relationships, emotions that were stirred up when cars drove at me at highway speeds and forced me off the road, fear of animals chasing me, emotions in response to relentless headwinds and ominous storms, my mental reactions to physical pain, and feelings of isolation that were stirred up from lack of contact with people who cared about me. My psychological reactions to these constant adversities were the real threats to me completing the run. Every day I wanted to quit, multiple times most days. Most days it was overwhelming to think about how far I had to go, and if I gave myself a pat on the back and thought about how far I had come, my mind would immediately do the math and I would be shocked with the distance yet to be covered. I refused to even look at a map to evaluate distance when we were in New Mexico. My heart ached. My body ached. I just felt an indescribable amount of pain.

Fifty miles came and went, and we drove to a cozy bed and breakfast just outside of Mountain Air, New Mexico. I remembered how cool it looked from the outside, and as I entered the building, it was even more interesting. The building felt like I was in the nineteenth century, the floors creaked when I walked, the lighting was soft, and the rooms were spacious and unique. I had my own bed, and as usual, Mom and Carly shared the other bed in the room. I slept hard, but I did remember dreaming this particular night because it was in vivid color. Usually, I don't dream in color or see faces, but I experienced both during that night's slumber.

For some reason, Mom seemed unusually tired the next morning. I figured it was just the exhaustion of what we were doing that was taking a toll on her. I knew she would make a comeback, however. We had to drive twenty-two miles west of the bed and breakfast to get to my start point for the day. As I ran east, we decided to have lunch and take my midday break in the town we had stayed at that previous night. Linda was the owner of the bed and breakfast and she was waiting for us with lunch when we arrived at Mountain Air. She provided a delicious lunch and we sat near the van in some shade and visited with her. The conversation eventually came around to whether we had rested well the prior night. I said that I was exhausted and slept like a rock. She seemed relieved for some reason.

I asked Linda why she had asked that question. Linda said that they had some people visiting their bed and breakfast that night and she wanted to make sure they didn't disturb us.

"What were they doing?" I inquired.

"They set up some equipment to record paranormal activity."

"Like Ghostbusters?" I asked.

Linda told us that her bed and breakfast was haunted by a fourteen-year-old girl who had died there. She said that the investigators had recorded lights and sounds on the video and audio equipment the night we had stayed there. I remember Carly, Mom, and I exchanging glances with one another in puzzled bewilderment. The conversation quickly ended and we were soon on our way. About an hour after we had left Linda, I was at a refueling stop when Mom told me something that brought me to a standstill.

Mom hadn't slept well at Linda's bed and breakfast. She had woken up in the middle of the night and saw a light floating beside her, about two feet in diameter. She said it was by the lamp, but the lamp wasn't turned on. She recalled looking at it for about fifteen seconds, then closed her eyes and tried to sleep. She wasn't scared, but felt very uneasy. She tried to go back to sleep, but was unable to, and that was why she seemed exhausted in the morning. Mom swears she doesn't believe in ghosts, but she was also certain about what she saw that night, and that it wasn't a dream. None of us tried to reconcile what had transpired; we all just seemed to want to collectively forget about what had happened and move forward, not dwelling in the past.

The next day, we Intersected Highway 54 east of the town of Socorro, bid farewell to Highway 60, and began moving northeast across America. This highway would cross six states in our transcontinental journey. The less turns we had to contend with, the better. Mom and I had extremely high anxiety when we crossed through major cities or had to worry about navigating to stay on course. I was a stickler about not running an additional unnecessary step. Getting lost was simply not an option. When we strayed off course, I lost my cool and had a temper tantrum. I don't know how Mom put up with me and my tantrums.

About midway through New Mexico, I reached the thousand-mile mark. It was a huge accomplishment, and I wanted to have a huge celebration. I was secretly hoping that my crew would surprise me at that mile marker with a cake, or a dance party, or something. It wasn't to be, however. There was no enthusiasm for the milestone, except for what I brought to the event. I wrote "1000" on my left arm with a Sharpie and asked Mom to take a picture so I could post it on Facebook that evening. She snapped the picture, and that was it. No party. No hugs. No telephone calls. No nothing. I felt like the run didn't matter to anybody, and I was deflated.

That night when I checked Facebook, my spirits were raised. A class of elementary school children in Wisconsin, Ms. Kinnamon's class, had been following my run and they had made signs congratulating me on reaching a thousand miles. Their signs read "WOO HOO!", "#1 RUNNER", "1000 MILES!!!", "ONWARD JASON!" and that picture lifted my spirits. We were a third of the way across America, but it seemed like we had been on the road forever. Mom was exhausted, Carly was exhausted, and I was exhausted, but I wanted a distraction from the torture I had experienced thus far. I later termed the first thousand miles of the run—PAIN. The second thousand miles I termed SETTLING IN, and I began to really enjoy being out there running day after day, despite the usual setbacks and adversities we had to overcome.

1,000 miles completed

Some days, the most difficult thing I had to figure out was how to maintain some sense of dignity when Mother Nature called. Because I'm a guy, a quick stop for number one was pretty easy. I just faced the opposite direction of traffic and did my business. Once in a while, traffic would be coming from both directions and I'd get a toot of a horn. I always took that to be as encouraging as possible and considered it a compliment for my manliness.

Taking care of number two however, was a whole different matter. My original plan was to take my Uncle Chris's advice —"Never pass up the opportunity to visit a bathroom." If I was running by a gas station or restaurant in a town, I should have stopped in to sit on their commode and try to do my business. Without fail, whenever I passed on such an opportunity, I inevitably had to defecate within a couple of miles. My back-up plan was to use a five-gallon Home Depot bucket that we had outfitted with a toilet seat. The plan was to line the bucket with a bag, poop in the bag, then tie it up and put it in the next trash receptacle we came across. Mom wasn't too fond of driving in the van with poop in a bag, and my body was very active, given that I was consuming up to 10,000 calories a day in order to sustain my energy levels. Also, the van and bucket weren't always near me when duty called. I learned to always carry small amounts of toilet paper with me—enough for two calls from Mother Nature. I learned to lean against trees and carefully keep my socks and shorts out of harm's way. I learned how to position myself behind bushes to give me cover. I learned how to position my body so not to cause my legs to cramp, but to enable me to relax enough be able to "do my duty." It wasn't pretty, and it seemed never-ending.

Mother Nature bucket

I made a game of it, and tried to figure out ways to get my business done as comfortably as possible, with as much privacy as possible. The game came to a screeching halt in New Mexico one afternoon. I had a call from nature and was in the process of using my bucket. Mom had positioned the van so as to shield me from the road, and we opened the passenger car door to give me more privacy from oncoming traffic. I was in the middle of a "relaxation break" when lo and behold, I heard a car driving up behind us. It stopped two feet in front of me as I sat on my throne with my back to the van and my shorts around my ankles. The driver's side window rolled down, and my mind spun. I felt embarrassed, ashamed, mad, violated, and humiliated all at once. As the window rolled down, I noticed that the vehicle was black and white and had blue and red lights on the roof. A police officer had just intercepted me taking a deuce on the side of the road. All I could think was that I was going to get a ticket for indecent exposure. As the window rolled down I heard,

"Is everything okay?"

"Officer, I am legally blind and I'm running across America. I'm so sorry. I was running and I just had to go. There was no bathroom around, sir. I just had to go." I heard the words come from my mouth as if I was a third person witnessing this bizarre interaction.

"You just had to go?" he said.

"Yes, sir. I just had to go."

"I just wanted to make sure everything was okay and that you weren't broken down."

That seemed like enough for the officer, and he was ready to get on his way. As soon as I realized that I wasn't getting a ticket, and that the officer was only checking to make sure we were alright, I suddenly felt like chatting him up. He politely declined, rolled up his window, and drove off, leaving me alone on my throne once again. I settled in on a mentality that if animals can do their business in the wild, so could I. I always took care to bury my souvenirs so as to leave no trace.

I was putting up fifty-one-mile days at this point with relative ease. We had our routine, and I knew when to push and when to be patient. Our goal was to finish the day not feeling depleted. Things seemed to be on the upswing. I had experienced something curious with my shoes, however. I noticed that they wore out after only two or three days. As I ran against traffic on sloped roads, my right shoe became shaved, and the outsole became nonexistent after about a hundred miles. The left shoe showed signs of wear, but still could handle several more days of use. When I tried to walk on a flat surface with the shaved right shoe, I felt my ankle bend outward due to the wear on the shoe. The only way I could make the shoes work an extra day was if I ran on the opposite side of the road with traffic and had my mom drive behind me to block an errant vehicle from running me down from behind. The highways didn't always have shoulders that allowed for this, and most of the time the shoulders would allow for this scenario only ten miles at a time.

I had a problem—a very big problem. HOKA had agreed to be a product sponsor and give me free shoes for training and the run. They had originally given me twelve pairs of shoes. By the time the run came around, I only had eight pairs and guessed that I'd need another twelve to make it all the way across America. I have a wide foot, and only one model of shoe fits my foot without causing pain —the Bondi Wide (2E). As it turned out, this was a hot-selling shoe and HOKA couldn't keep the shoe in stock. Before I left for the run in March, the HOKA rep had promised to send me twelve more pairs of shoes for my transcon. She said that they would be in on April 1st, and she would send them immediately. I was concerned because I didn't know how we would receive them as the run was taking place, but I figured we could work it out. Also, I didn't see another option as the shoes were sold out.

When April 1st came, I started contacting the HOKA rep about the shoes. They couldn't confirm a certain date for me to receive the shoes. After a couple weeks, I was down to my last pair of shoes and the issue had reached a breaking point. Either I needed to get the shoes ASAP from HOKA, or I would have to stop running. I wasn't okay stopping—I had used these same shoes for the past two years, and any time I tried another brand or model of shoe, I experienced foot pain.

When I finally pinned down the HOKA rep and asked for the shoes that were promised back in March, she told me the shoes shouldn't wear out as quickly as I was reporting. Their product development team disagreed with what I was experiencing. She then went on to tell me that she hadn't held my twelve pairs of shoes when the April 1st shipment had come in, and that all the shoes had been sold off to retailers. The only option I was given was to wait until the May 1st shipment of shoes came in.

I was going to be out of shoes at twelve hundred miles. I still had over eighteen hundred miles to go. What was I going to do? Mom, Carly, and I sat in a motel room pondering our fate, and the fate of the run. Would we give up, or could we somehow pull another rabbit out of our hat? We had a clue from the story we had been told by the HOKA rep. The shoes were available, only they were in the retail market and they would cost full price—at $160 a pair, they weren't cheap. Carly was great on the computer, and I asked her to scour the retail market and see how many Bondi Wide (2E) shoes in my size she could find that were available. Within a half an hour, she had found twenty-two pairs. We bought all of the Bondi wides in my size that were available on the retail internet market. The cost exceeded $3,000, but that was nothing when compared to the prospect of having to stop the run due to running out of shoes.

Over the next few weeks, we had shoes overnighted to our motels at the cost of $80 per shipment. The retailers weren't used to receiving such large orders, and we had to work with their distribution centers over the next few weeks until we received all the shoes we had ordered. It was just more unplanned expense that I didn't know how I would pay back; however, I planned to deal with that problem after I reached the Atlantic Ocean. The crisis was averted, and I started running that day at 6:45 a.m., only fifteen minutes later than planned. We were becoming experts at overcoming adversity, or so we thought.

On the eighth day in New Mexico, I had enough of the desolate landscape that had plagued my visual sensation since the beginning of the run. Basically, I had been running through deserts up to that point—some had small shrubs and tumbleweeds, and some had nothing in them. The exceptions to the desert were a few days of mountains and the large cities we had passed through. I grew to appreciate the desert and its beauty, but it was time for a change.

This would be my last day in New Mexico. I dedicated my miles that day to a man named Paul Scott Favro, a twenty-six-year-old who has autism and was riding his bike from Brampton, Ontario in

Canada to San Jose, California in the US to spread the message to follow your own path. Since my son Sage has autism and loves to ride his bike, I daydreamed that one day maybe Sage would want to do the ride that Paul was undertaking and that I could crew him like my mom was doing for me. The fantasy wasn't based in reality, and I would never push Sage to embark on such an extreme undertaking. However, if he did on his own volition, I would be there to support him, or any of my children.

Paul was a huge inspiration. I knew firsthand what he was encountering with foul weather and travelling on highways. What I couldn't understand was how these external stimuli were triggering his autism and the daily struggles he was having to overcome in order to not quit. Paul was my inspiration for my eighth and final day in the Land of Enchantment, completing 405 miles across the state.

26

Texas—The Lone Star State

Texas state line

As I ran a northeasterly route on Highway 54, I was about to clip the northwest corners of Texas and Oklahoma. Although I was in these lands for only a few days, I learned a lot. When we found the state line sign for Texas, I thought there would be a big old star on it, or a gun, or something tough. My assumptions were incorrect, again. The sign read "Welcome to Texas: Drive friendly —the Texas way." I wanted to take that sign with me and engrain it in the hearts of everyone behind the wheel on the highways. Most people were courteous, but the ones who weren't courteous risked the safety of my crew and me.

We crossed into Texas and finished a few miles east of the state line. We had to drive twenty or so miles to our motel in Dalhart, Texas. I quickly learned that we were in cattle country. As we drove from our stopping point to Dalhart, I sensed the odiferous musings of cows. I know the smell of methane well from my family's roots in Greeley, Colorado. The scent soon became overpowering, and we had to roll up all the windows in the van and I raised my shirt to breathe through it in an effort to stave off nausea from the choking smell. It became stronger still.

On the horizon, I saw a thin black line, with green below it and blue above it. I knew the green must be a field or grass and the blue must be the sky. I didn't know, however, what the black line was. It seemed to stretch as far as the eye could see. As we drove closer and closer, Mom said, "They are cows!"

We were in cattle country, and cows were everywhere. Only, these cows weren't frolicking in the fields and running about munching grass and sipping from streams—they were in fenced holding pens. The square structures were maybe 75 feet x 75 feet. There appeared to be at least fifty heads of cattle in each pen— crowded. Most of them had their heads sticking out of the pens into feeding and drinking troughs. Their backsides were facing the center of the structure, where other cows were standing or pushing their way to the fence in order to feed. They were standing in their own feces and urine; hence, the choking smell. I didn't know how people could survive with that smell. In fact, I didn't see any people out and about. I guessed that whoever tended these cows would need to wear gas masks in order to survive.

What does it profit a person who gains the world and loses his soul? was all I could think.

Whether it's a publicly traded company or a cattle ranch in Texas, the lesson is still the same—we must always do the right thing, even if that means we will make less money. Money is just a means to an end, it is not an end in itself. As I thought about the business implications of what I was experiencing, I came back to reality and identified a very real problem I was going to be faced with the next day when I tried to run past the twenty miles of methane-choked cattle farms. How would I breathe? Would I pass out from the smell? It couldn't be good for me, and I didn't see any people out in the cattle farming operation. But the cows survived somehow, and I was thinking I could as well. Maybe I would just have to endure vomiting from the smell.

Mom suggested I wear a handkerchief around my face to help "strain" the air. I played with the suggestion, but soon realized it only heated the air. I could still smell the methane as well as my own noxious breath, and a simple layer of cotton did nothing to prevent the methane from coming into my lungs. I opted to not use the handkerchief. I was hoping for the best the next day, and included a request for help in my prayers that night.

The next morning as we drove out to the starting point, the weather was foul. It was absolutely freezing—I put on three layers of coats, including a down coat. Usually, my legs don't get cold, but I had to put on two pairs of sweat pants, gloves, and a hat to keep warm. The wind whipped me nonstop. I tried running, but the effort was futile. I was running directly into a fierce headwind that was blowing the methane toward me. The strength of the wind, however, was diffusing the methane and making it possible for me to pass by the cattle farms without getting sick. I walked for seven hours into the wind, only covering twenty miles. I wanted to quit and was absolutely demoralized. It seemed like it was going to be a thirty-mile day at best. I did some quick calculations in my head, and realized that if I could run ten-minute miles for the next five hours straight, I would be able to make fifty miles for the day.

The wind had died down to just an annoying headwind. I stubbornly lowered my head and locked the time into my watch, to ensure that I was averaging ten-minute miles. After five hours, I looked at the distance on my watch and it had buzzed for the fiftieth time that day, marking fifty miles. As I looked back at my day, I realized that my prayers had in fact been answered. I had received a windstorm that blew away choking fumes and made it possible for me to travel twenty miles by cattle farms. The wind also forced me to walk and conserve energy so I would be able to run once I had safely passed the cattle. While I was experiencing the day, I didn't understand it and was frustrated; however, once the day was done I was able to look back and understand that it had worked out perfectly in the long run—just like life always does.

After a day and a half battling the weather and fumes in Texas, I crossed into Oklahoma at 1,131 miles into my transcontinental run.

27

Oklahoma—The Sooner State

Oklahoma state line

Although my time was short in Oklahoma, I had at least two great lessons while in this state.

The first great lesson I had was when I was on the road running and listening to my headphones as I had for the last twenty-six days.

I played music I had arranged into my favorite playlists according to my moods. I had bought audiobooks in eclectic genres and listened to countless books like *Eat & Run* by Scott Jurek, *Ultramarathon Man* by Dean Karnazas, *Born to Run* by Chris McDougal, *It's Not About the Bike* by Lance Armstrong, *Iron War* by Matt Fitzgerald, *The Road Less Travelled* by Robert Peck, *Mere Christianity* by CS Lewis, *God's Story, Your Story* by Max Lucado, *I'm Here to Win* by Chris McCormack, and I even tried listening to *Fifty Shades of Grey* by EL James at one point, but it wasn't doing it for me.

I also had subscribed to SiriusXM and found some channels with cool entertainment. One of my favorite channels had recordings of old radio shows from before the time when TV was invented. I could see the scene in my mind, a family huddled around their radio listening to a story coming from their sound box.

Every day, I wore headphones and purposefully put noise into my head for entertainment and distraction. But in Oklahoma, I reached a breaking point. The noise became too much. Even at its lowest volume, I just couldn't take it anymore. Why was I trying to drown out what I was doing? I was using noise to distract me from my day that I had considered boring, monotonous, and torturous most of the time. I could no longer distract myself, and the noise was only making things worse. The next time Mom crewed me on the road, I gave her my backpack which I used to carry my phone and headphones. She asked if my phone needed charging. "I can't take it. I can't take the noise," I responded.

I kept running and I *listened*. I heard the sounds of birds, but there were no trees. They must have been nested in the tall grasses. I discovered that different cars, trucks, and semis have different sounds. I heard the wind. I heard the sound of tractors and farm equipment in the far-off distance—too far for my eyes to perceive, but not too far for my ears. The chaos of filling my ears and mind with noise wasn't canceling out pain or fear or foul weather or hopelessness. Meeting chaos with chaos only created more chaos. I broke through and learned that meeting chaos with peace will result in peace. My mind went blank. I was "in the zone". I just ran, and ran.

I didn't feel pain, anxiety, fear, elation, or joy, I just was. I was just a running machine.

Peace for me was coming from within, not from without. For much of my life, I thought more money or possessions would make life easier and somehow I would be happier. Wrong. I thought if a woman loved me and wanted me, somehow I wouldn't feel lonely. Wrong. I thought if I did something truly exceptional, my father would teach me how to be the man I wanted to be. Wrong. On that highway in Oklahoma, it became crystal clear to me that the peace I was looking for in my life could never be found outside of my being. I was at the precipice. I had to look deep within myself, and stop making excuses for why things had happened. I had to accept myself for the person I was, and wasn't.

It was at that point that I really began to grow as a person. There were four themes that began to emerge in my heart, mind, and experiences:

- Faith and Hope—being able to believe in something for which there is no evidence, regardless of whether you are a minority of one. Hanging onto and chasing dreams until they are fulfilled;
- Patience—being able to remain calm in the face of adversity and waiting out the storms of life until clearer skies present themselves;
- Consistency—being able to stubbornly make relentless forward progress toward a goal on a daily basis regardless of whether you feel like doing the work; and
- Forgiveness—being able to release the pain and burden of anger and hurt in order to lighten the load on my heart, body, and spirit.

These were the "secrets" of maintaining my mental strength that I discovered on this run. The themes were clear, but the experiences I had on a daily basis which gave texture and detail, and filled out these concepts were far from over.

The other great thing I learned in Oklahoma wasn't so esoteric or deep in personal and spiritual growth. This lesson was about failure. I had woken up at a Comfort Inn in Guymon, Oklahoma to the sound of rain on our motel window which was backed by the darkness of the pre-dawn. It was raining hard; harder than we had experienced on the run to date. I knew that if I stepped outside, I would be instantly drenched. My mom turned on the TV and flipped to a news channel. The weatherperson confirmed what we were experiencing—a storm system was upon this part of Oklahoma and torrential rain and thunderstorms were to be expected all day long.

Mom was eating up the news and seemed riveted by what she was hearing. I snapped at her and said, "Turn it off!" I didn't need more people to confirm that I was in a crappy situation. I thought about the pros and cons of running in this type of weather. I knew the temperature would be cold in the morning, but would be manageable by the afternoon. I had the proper clothing to manage hypothermia, so I didn't see that as a problem. I had also successfully used trash bags in the past as ponchos to stay relatively dry in marathons and hundred-mile races. And, after all, my skin is waterproof and I knew I wouldn't melt if I got wet. I did have a problem with my shoes, however. I had cut off the toes, and my socks and feet were sure to get soaked. Twelve hours of running on wet feet would result in blistering, loss of skin, and possible infection. An injury of this type would increase physical pain significantly and potentially hamper my ability to attain fifty miles per day on future days.

I discussed the problem with Mom. Her initial suggestion was that we could take the day off as a rest day, or just wait until the rain subsided to a manageable level. I wanted to agree with her and take the day off, but I knew I couldn't let that thought out of my mouth. "That is not an option!" erupted from me. I knew that if I stopped running every time the weather got bad, I would never make it to the Atlantic Ocean. Taking the day off was like quitting in my mind. If I didn't get out there and run that day, it would be really easy to quit again the next time the weather looked bad or some other adversity was upon us. I had to go headfirst into that storm, regardless of how much I didn't want to.

Mom also knew the risks of me running for a full day on wet feet. She suggested tying plastic grocery bags around my feet and duct-taping them around my ankles to create a moisture barrier. I liked the concept, but identified some flaws with the idea. First, I was concerned that I could easily slip on a wet, oil-slicked road when the bottom of my shoe was covered by plastic with no gripping surface. Next, I knew how quickly my shoes wore down from scraping the road. A plastic grocery bag would only last a few steps before the bottom ripped and water entered the structure from the bottom of my shoe. The strategy couldn't keep my feet from getting wet. I settled on the fact that we would just need to do as many sock and shoe changes as possible. I had about eighteen pairs of shoes in the van with me at that time. I had no idea how we would dry them out after that day, or what problems we were creating; however, it was the only solution I could see for how I could run in those conditions and prevent injury to my feet.

I wanted to check the nearest Walmart to see if there was anything that could help us contend with the weather. I remembered seeing some heavy-duty ponchos in the camping section when I was at my local Walmart back in Denver. We were well past our 6:30 a.m. start time by the time we even got to the store. I was lethargic and making every mental excuse I could to postpone running in the storm. We went directly to the camping section and found the ponchos. We also saw some rain suits that looked cool. They were hooded jackets and pants that were supposedly waterproof. We opened up a set and I tried it on. My spirits were immediately lifted. This might make running in this weather bearable. I could keep my body dry and warm, although I would still have to contend with wet feet. We put a couple of rain suits in our shopping cart.

Mom just couldn't stop suggesting the plastic bag duct-taped around my shoe to keep it dry. Thankfully, I was listening to her and hadn't gotten grumpy or adversarial. She was making sense, and she knew what she was talking about. She is probably the best crew captain on earth and she knew that if my feet became injured, the trajectory for the rest of the run could be changed.

She suggested creating a cover for the shoe, since she understood that the bag would be ripped if it was wrapped around the bottom. Before I knew it, we had gallon Ziploc bags, a fresh roll of duct tape, a staple gun, and staples in our cart to create "shoe covers" for my Sandal-OKAs. We paid for our things and sat inside the Walmart as I created the shoe covers. I cut a U in one side of the gallon plastic bag, reinforced it with duct tape, then put the U over my shoe and stapled the invention into the soft midsole. The staples were parallel to how my foot would sit in the shoe so there was no risk of me impaling my foot on a staple as I ran. Three-fourths of the shoe was covered from the front to my ankle. The rain suit was baggy, and the pants seemed to provide some extra coverage over the back of the shoe. *This just might work!*

Homemade waterproof shoe cover

It was 8:30 a.m. by the time I got to my start point. It was still raining cats and dogs. I got out of the van and started running. The rain suit and shoe covers worked. I couldn't believe it. Then, I discovered a shortcoming of the waterproof innovations we had created. A semi passed me, driving through a trough of water on the road and sprayed a wall of water on me. My body and feet were dry, but my face was soaked. The water dripped from my face down into my suit and was making my body wet. I flagged down the Silver Bullet and asked for a visor. The rain coat had a hood, but the skin on my face was exposed. I figured that if I wore a visor, it would keep my face dry and prevent water from seeping inside my suit. The strategy appeared to be working, but after a mile, the visor was sopping wet and my hair was getting wet and cold.

I asked the crew to make a waterproof visor from a baseball cap I had brought. They cut the top of the hat off and duct taped some plastic bags over the visor of the cap to make it waterproof. It wasn't pretty to look at, but it looked like it just might do the job. I put on the visor, and tightened the hood of the jacket around my head. I was waterproof except for my skin. Now, I just needed to do a field test of our final fabrication. I needed a semi to spray me with water at high speed. Luckily, I didn't have to wait long. A semi was on its way at me. I lowered my head so the visor would protect my face. *Zoom! Splash!*

Running in Guymon, Oklahoma with rain gear

Water drenched me just like we've seen in the movies. However, I was dry. *It actually worked!* My crew and I all celebrated our crazy invention. I was going to be able to run in the rain. But Mom noted that I wasn't that visible with the rain so I donned a flashing vest and a clear plastic poncho to try to protect the electrical circuitry of the flashing vest. Off I went, running in the rain, chopping down the miles. It was scary. It was miserable. It was cold. But I was still running and I hadn't quit. That alone was enough to keep my spirits high enough to continue making forward progress.

After about eight hours of nonstop rain, the skies finally began clearing. Not long after that, I stripped off the rain gear and was back in shorts, shirt, and shoes (without rain covers). I was moving good and feeling strong. Mom and I had an agreement that I wouldn't run in the dark after sunset. We had agreed to a zero tolerance rule here for safety reasons due to my eyesight and night blindness. So I was pushing seven-minute miles as sunset approached. When the sun finally dipped below the horizon, I stopped running and looked at my watch. It read forty-eight miles. It was the second day I failed to achieve my goal—the other time was when our van sustained a cut tire in the desert four weeks prior in California.

My update on Facebook that evening read:

Day 27—48 miles completed. Lesson for today—sometimes you give it all you had and you still fail to meet your goal . . . and failure is OK. Out of 26 days of trying to hit 50 miles, we succeeded 24 times. We made It to Kansas today . . . ONWARD!!!!!

A lot of people responded to that post, encouraging me, and telling me that I hadn't failed. They pointed out that I had run almost halfway across America. They noted that I hadn't taken one rest day. They reasoned that forty-eight easily rounds up to fifty. I appreciated the sentiments and positive thoughts; however, the fact was, I failed that day. I also openly admitted it and made no excuses for missing that goal. It was a stark reminder that in life we all fail. And, for all of our successes, we fail many more times than we succeed. The strange phenomenon is that we as a society don't embrace failure and seem to relish only celebrating success. In running, as in life, I have learned that I learn much more from my failures than I do from my successes. It is humbling to fail. At times, it seems heroic and unusual for a person to admit failure. To me, it is just part of living and doesn't speak to my character or who I am as a person. It is only a snapshot in time of where I'm at in life— succeeding, failing, or swinging for the fences, and always giving my all. If there was a success that particular day, it was that I never stopped trying to achieve my goal despite the crappy weather and desire to not run in those conditions. The success was judged by the journey, and not by the end result.

I spent less than a day in Oklahoma and travelled thirty-six miles through the panhandle of the Sooner State.

28

Kansas—The Sunflower State

Kansas state line

K ansas shaped up to be a lot more than I expected. I knew it would be windy and there would be plenty of cornfields— Kansas didn't disappoint on either of those two fronts.

We had become seasoned expeditioners, accepting challenges

283

and obstacles head-on, solving them, and moving forward. It really didn't matter what was thrown at us, and it didn't seem like anything was going to halt our forward progress. This became crystal-clear in Kansas when I ran up to the van for a midday break after completing twenty-seven miles. I heard a hissing sound and suspected that we had a tire going flat. I checked the tire and, sure enough, we had a slow leak. We had a portable battery unit with an air compressor so I topped off the tire with air. I grabbed a back-pack and loaded it with food, and grabbed two handheld water bottles. I told Mom to drive to the next town wherever that might be, find a place that could fix the tire, then come back and meet me. I had enough nutrition and hydration to go another twenty-three miles. We only had one crew vehicle, and we didn't want to waste precious sleeping time messing around getting our tire fixed after I finished running for the day. If we had more crew who could run with me, or more vehicles, I would never have been left alone to run by myself. We were low on resources, so we just became extremely resourceful and got the job done.

Early on in the transcon, this predicament would have probably caused us a lot of anxiety and we would have overthought how to handle it. At this stage of the game, it was just another situation we had to overcome in order to keep making progress toward the Atlantic Ocean. Within no time, Mom had the tire fixed and found me on the highway running toward our evening stopping point.

I ran those first two days in Kansas for my two eldest children— Sierra and Sage (I had already dedicated a day to my youngest daughter, Sofia). I was missing my kids terribly by this point. We kept in contact by calling, texting, and FaceTiming daily. However, there just is no substitute for being able to hold your child and touch the people you love. My kids' lives had endured a lot by this time of the trip. There were car accidents, sad times, friendship woes, school meetings I had missed, and so much more. I was trying to be a long-distance parent. When I got a call where one of my children needed me, I stopped running and found a place to sit on the side of the road. I gave them my full attention and tried to help them work through whatever situation they were experiencing. I would be a good dad to them, even if I felt like I had abandoned them to do this run. I felt like a bad father many times during the run. But then, my kids would tell me stories about how they made a presentation to their class about me being on the road and running across America. They were proud of me, and what I was trying to do. It was just hard for all of us to be apart.

On the third day in Kansas, it felt like the bottom fell out for me, again. I had five people who I relied on in life, to help me keep it together and stay strong: my ex-girlfriend, three children, and my mom. One by one, I felt like I lost the support of all these people. My ex-girlfriend was experiencing pain and let go. My three kids had lives of their own, and were trying to manage life with an absent father. Mom had been homeless for a month, was trying to survive running across highways, and had to deal with me having emotional peaks and valleys. I found myself spiraling into a depression on this day. I felt like I was the only person on earth. I was all alone; totally isolated. And I was sinking into more and more isolation.

"Why am I doing this?" came out of my mouth as I shuffled down the highway. "Because I'm supposed to do this," I responded back to myself.

At that moment, I was overcome with a feeling of energy and revitalization. My stride stretched and the sound of my feet striking the ground quickened. The slouch of my shoulders disappeared and my back straightened. I felt like Ussain Bolt running a hundred meters in perfect form. Then, I felt overwhelming love and peace. I don't know how to explain it, except to say that I knew I wasn't alone. Something much greater than me was trying to let me know that I would never be alone, and that this world is temporary. I didn't hear voices or have a dream and see angels, but I definitely felt something. That evening, I videotaped myself on my GoPro and recounted the day's events. I was at fifty-two miles for the day and looking fresh as I ran down the highway. I wasn't panting, and had a huge smile on my face as I described what I had felt. It took me thirty days of nonstop running and almost 1,500 miles to learn and truly believe that I'm not alone, and I will never be alone. I felt like I was truly loved, and it filled me with an insurgence of energy that fueled my forward progress. I didn't feel lonely for the rest of my run. A huge piece of my mental struggle had just been lifted, and I felt a release of anxiety and nervousness. A feeling of love snuffed out the voice of doubt.

At the end of the day's run, we drove to our lodging for the night in Kingman, Kansas. We should have known something was awry when the sign outside the motel advertised its best features as "touch tone phones" and "cable color TV."

There was a horse show in town, and the motel had the last available room. The next closest town was thirty miles away, and we had already driven twenty-five minutes from our stopping point to get to Kingman. I was exhausted, and just needed to rest and start my recovery routine. I didn't care what the room looked like as long as it had a bed and a shower. Mom had a bad feeling about this place, and her instincts were spot-on throughout this trip and my life. As I entered the lobby, I saw a sign on the door that said, "Absolutely no discharging of firearms allowed." That should have been another hint, but I wasn't paying attention. I was still feeling optimistic from the day's events. The room was $50. *What a steal!* I thought to myself.

Then, the clerk told me they were going to discount the room another $5. I couldn't believe my ears. It was like a gift from heaven. Then, I asked why they were giving me an extra discount. "The room doesn't have running water," the clerk responded.

My heavenly gift just vaporized. I took the key, and Mom, Carly, and I walked hesitantly toward the room, not sure what we were going to find when the door opened. The motel had only one level, and the rooms were side by side, like a strip mall. I took the key and opened the door, trying to be optimistic and have enthusiasm. As soon as I opened the door, I smelled stank, smoke, and must. The room had two beds and was just plain nasty. Carly started laughing. Mom shot me a look as if to say, "I'm not sleeping in there." I tried to hide my disgust and shot a smile at both of them.

"Let's see if this place has water," I joked. I tried the shower and the water worked. I shouted, "The room has water!" trying to let them know it was going to be okay. They were still standing at the door, not wanting to enter the pit. Next, I went to check the sink and, as I turned on the faucet, clear liquid came pouring out, hot and cold. I didn't see any problem with the water, and again found myself shouting that things were okay. Then, I felt something on my feet. They were wet. The water filling the sink was going down the drain and emptying onto the floor and my feet. I quickly turned it off. By this time, Carly had entered the room, laughing at me with the GoPro turned on. She didn't want to miss capturing this unbelievable situation. I inspected the sink and saw that the P-trap was broken—that's why the water was spilling out onto the floor. I knew how to fix this problem.

"Get some duct tape!" I instructed. Almost instantaneously, a roll of duct tape was in my hand, and I had an assistant cutting strips of tape. I created an extension for the cracked P-trap and repaired it. I tried the faucet again, and voila! The water wasn't spilling out onto the ground. I yelled to my mom that the sink was working. She was nowhere to be found. She had left this pitiful situation in disgust and was busy re-gassing the vehicle, restocking ice and supplies, and finding some food for us to eat for dinner.

This would have been the best *Punk'd* episode ever, except Ashton Kutcher was nowhere to be found. I had to shower to feel a little better. Carly had left the room as she couldn't stand the smell of the smoke, was a germophobe, and swore bed bugs were all around us. The water in the shower was warm and it rinsed away the blood, grime, and sweat that I was used to accumulating during a day of running on America's highways. The room only came with one bar of hand soap, but that was okay. I washed my hair with it and it did the job of cleaning my body. I was satisfied and felt better.

I scanned the shower area for a towel. There were no neatly folded white bath towels with accompanying hand towels and washcloths. There was one towel that was about 18 inches x 24 inches. It was a shade darker than sky blue, and even my eyesight could make out that the towel was stained. It was well-worn, and had strings hanging off of the edges. I could hear the horror music from *Psycho* in my mind as I glanced between the towel and the dirty clothes I had just taken off, which I was sure had food and my excrement on them. It really was a coin flip which to use to dry off—my dirty running clothes or this stained towel.

I reached for the towel and hoped for the best. As I used it to pat dry my body from my legs up, I smelled smoke, and I could have sworn I felt a burly trucker hugging me as I put the towel around my shoulders to dry my back. The towel smelled as disgusting as the clothes I had just shed. I screamed and threw the towel, which appropriately landed in the trash can. I put on some clean clothes to sleep in, doused myself in cologne, and sat on the toilet with the lid down, waiting for my crew to return. I felt violated.

When they came back, I heard them laughing as they entered the room. They came in with trash bags and plastic tablecloths. They covered the beds with the plastic tablecloths, then put trash bags over the pillows. Next, they sprayed Lysol and Febreze all over the room and opened windows. The strategy was to not have us touch the beds in case there were bed bugs. Also, we didn't bring luggage into the room so things wouldn't be contaminated if there were creatures among us. I was exhausted and fell asleep quickly as Mom and Carly cracked up at the environment we had devolved to.

When I woke in the morning, I didn't see anybody in the room. Their bed and pillows were all wrapped in plastic, but they weren't in the room with me. In a short amount of time, the door opened, and in walked my trusty crew. I asked where they'd been.

"We slept in the van," I heard their tired voices say in unison. Apparently, they had tried sleeping on the plastic, but the side of their bodies that was touching the plastic began to sweat, and the stench of the smoke, stank, and must prevented them from being able to get to sleep. To top it off, it got really cold in the room because we left the windows open in an effort to diffuse the pungent odor. They were exhausted, and I was too, but I didn't care. I had to start running by 6:30 a.m., and we had to figure out how to get down the road another fifty miles regardless of our exhaustion. We left the motel vowing to never return.

We loaded the van and drove back toward our starting point. After about forty-five minutes, we still hadn't reached the place we had stopped the day before. Because we didn't have phone service at that location, we were forced to manually mark the ground and tie flashing to brush. I knew we hadn't passed the flashing and circles on the ground, as all three of us were looking intently. However, we had been driving too long, and the highway was wrong. There was a grassy median on this highway. The place where I stopped the day before was a two-lane highway with no median. Suddenly, I feared that we were lost and on the wrong road. Mom was driving on autopilot, as she'd only gotten about two hours of sleep. I looked at the atlas, and realized that we were probably on the wrong road. We must have missed a turn.

I snapped at my mom and blamed her for us getting lost. It was nobody's fault, but this detour meant that my start time would be delayed over an hour, and I would be forced to run harder to make up the time, or forego a midday break so I could achieve my goal that day. The alternatives just weren't acceptable to me: either I didn't achieve fifty or more miles, or had to extend the day and run into the night. I felt like I was already performing as good as I could. This mishap was going to make this day very painful. It was additional pain that I didn't need to endure, except we made a mistake.

The van was silent. I know Mom and Carly both felt bad for us getting lost, and the blind guy had to look at the atlas to get us back on track. We were all just exhausted and worn out. We needed to be patient, give each other grace and forgive instantly. If there is one thing my mom can do, it is drive fast. She was able to make it so I was only an hour off of our projected start time. When we saw the flashing, she flipped a U-turn and dropped me off. I untied the flashing, threw it in the van so we wouldn't leave a trace, then I began running.

I knew negative thoughts could overtake me and I could remain bitter for the rest of the day, but what good would that do? I had already learned this lesson about letting go of bitterness when cars drove at me in the break-down lane, forcing me to jump off the highway and tumble into ditches. On ten occasions, cars intentionally drove directly at me in the break-down lane and swerved to miss me at the last minute or forced me to jump off the road.

In order to stay focused on the task at hand, I had to monitor and maintain a positive attitude. I have often said that attitude is everything. I have also been criticized for being optimistic and an idealist. My response has always been, "Consider the alternative." In life, we can choose to sit with our lemons and be bitter, or we can add some sweetness and make lemonade. I have always tried to be the guy who makes lemonade. On this particular day, I decided to put my fitness to the test, and increase my pace by one minute per mile. That meant I would be running between nine- and eleven-minute miles, depending on terrain, headwinds, etc. I had specific pace goals for myself, depending on what the environment had in store for me. If it was a big uphill, I aimed for no slower than sixteen minutes per mile. For a gradual uphill, I aimed for twelve minutes per mile. For a moderate downhill section or wind at my back, I could be in the nine to ten minute per mile range. For torrential rain when it was hot, I aimed for sixteen-minute miles—if I went any faster I would sweat out the inside of the suit and over-heat. For torrential rain when it was cool, I aimed for thirteen-minute miles. For headwinds that were runnable, I aimed for twelve-minute miles. For headwinds that weren't, I aimed for sixteen-minute miles. When I was just exhausted and mentally destroyed, I had a walking pace of twenty minutes per mile, and that signaled I needed a break to reset myself physically and mentally. I ran over 95 percent of the miles across America.

As I ran on this two-lane highway in Kansas, I clipped off the miles at a ten-minute pace. I was feeling good, not breathing hard, and was accommodating several injuries by adjusting my stride. I learned early on that if I played with my foot strike, stride, cadence, and upper body movement, I could take tension off of whatever injury I had and let it heal. Of course, as one injury healed, another one presented itself. It was a constant game of healing injuries and managing new ones.

I was moving good, and so were the semis. There was no shoulder, only a white line and a drop-off that was about five feet into an irrigation ditch. Mom drove up a few miles to find a street that intersected the highway so she would have a safe place to wait for me. I was used to being crewed every mile or so, but I would just have to go longer this time, as we had no choice. Up ahead, I saw a semi plowing down the highway at me. I was running against traffic, and I had no choice but to run on the line. I waved my hands so he would see me, and I prepared for the wind burst that I knew was coming before the truck would pass me. The semi saw me and swerved a bit into the oncoming lane to give me safe passage, and I was thankful. As the semi moved, I noticed that a second semi was tailgating the first one with about fifteen feet between the two monsters. The second semi couldn't see me, but it must have cued off the first semi and assumed something was in the road, because it moved into the oncoming lane as well.

I was relieved because I didn't know what I would have done if it hadn't moved. I would have literally been inches from the semi and trailer. My ears sensed more vehicles. There was a third semi tailgating the second semi, but it didn't have time to react, and it was holding its course with a wheel on the white line at this point. I dove, and tumbled down the embankment just in time as the third semi passed me on the white line where I had been running. The sound was so loud. There was also a fourth semi tailgating the third one and it drove down the white line as well.

I was a little bruised up and sore, but at least I was alive. I laughed. I'm not sure why. After I found a place to climb back up to the highway, I dusted myself off and started running again. I had to run even faster as I had to make up for the time that I was in the ditch. When I reached the van, I told my crew about what had happened. They laughed and said when they saw the four semis pass, they knew either I would get out of the way, or we were going to be dealing with a whole different situation. We carried on, and I just kept running, feeling grateful that I had survived yet another near-fatal encounter. I began to feel like nothing was capable of stopping us. We had something protecting us or we just happened to be the luckiest people on earth. Either way, I was still running and wasn't in a hospital bed or worse.

That night, our goal was to reach Wichita. A nonprofit that supports blind and visually impaired people, Envision, had contacted me and wanted to meet me as I ran into town. They also comp'd me a room at the super swanky Ambassador Hotel in downtown Wichita. By the time I got to the outskirts of Wichita, I needed a rest. I had been running ridiculously faster than what I was accustomed to, but I still felt good. We found a Sonic drive-through restaurant, and I lay down and elevated my feet while I munched on a burger, fries, and a large banana shake. At this point, I could eat anything and my body would just incinerate it for fuel. I was still losing weight and was about 135 pounds at this point, down from the 145 pounds that I had started at. I considered this a huge success, as I didn't know if I could continually power-eat 10,000 calories day after day. I felt like I was starving all the time. I ate from the moment I woke until I fell asleep.

After Sonic, I kept on running to meet up with my new friends from Envision. I ran through a neighborhood and there were a couple of guys on a golf cart who offered me a bottle of water. They asked where I was running to, and I told them the Atlantic Ocean. Their jaws dropped and one of the guys dropped the beer he was drinking. It took them a little bit to process what they had just heard. Then they asked, "Do you want a beer?" We laughed, gave each other high fives, and I felt their immediate respect for what I was attempting to do as I continued running. As I came out of the residential area, I was approaching an intersection with a couple of gas stations. On one corner, there was a throng of people.

"There they are!" Mom yelled out the window as she drove by me to meet up with the people from Envision and the Kansas School for the Blind.

The two organizations had brought out staff members, their blind and visually impaired clients, and their children. We stopped and talked and hugged. This was a big part of the reason I believed that I was Called to run across America. I was supposed to demonstrate that the blind and visually impaired community is capable of anything and everything. As I spoke with staff members, they told me amazing stories of blind people finding employment, living independently and finding love. Many aren't so fortunate, so, it was Envision's mission to positively impact the lives of the blind and visually impaired in Wichita. I was humbled to have this organization support me. A small organization like Envision proactively sought me out, comp'd me a room, and gave me one of my largest donations to help cover my expenses for the run.

I shared time with all these people who had waited for me for over an hour on a hot street corner in Wichita. When it was time to leave, a blind man—Cloe—and his daughter wanted to run with me for a while. I gladly accepted their company. His daughter was sprinting ahead of us. I couldn't keep up with her as she was just too fast. I held Cloe's hand as he had no light perception. We ran on the sidewalk and he was curious about how to qualify to be on the US Paralympic Team. I shared my experience with him, and we had a great conversation with a lot of laughs. At one point, a boy on a bike road up behind us and yelled, "Get out of the way!" He must have been ten years old.

I became upset and stopped. His tire hit my Achilles tendon. I turned to face him and said, "We are blind. You can see. Do you see our canes? Please go around us." He peddled right through the middle of our group on the sidewalk, bumping a couple of my newfound friends. Cloe and his daughter didn't think twice about the incident. This wasn't the first time somebody had been rude to them. After about a mile, a car met us and picked up Cloe and his daughter. We hugged, parted ways, and I kept running to the Ambassador Hotel in downtown Wichita.

I was still pretty upset with the kid on the bike. Cloe and his daughter modeled forgiveness for me, and I remember how they gave immediate grace to this child. I am a better person for that one mile that I ran with Cloe and his daughter.

As our van rolled up to the Ambassador Hotel, it was clear that we were out of place. There were nice sports cars, limos, and Mercedes in the parking lot. Our van was packed to the hilt, making strange noises, and Mom had banged up the front fenders quite a few times. As the side door slid open, I was exposed to an older couple as I only had my running shorts on at that point. The bell-hops were cracking up at the contradiction of our motley crew and the regular customers. I made it up to my room, and it was like a penthouse suite. Just twenty-four hours before, I was molested by a nasty towel in a room where I had to use duct tape to give us running water in our sink, and now, I felt like a king in a fancy room with tons of space and the most comfortable bed I had ever slept on to date. My Facebook post that day was:

50 miles complete. Today's learning: what a difference a day makes.

And, how true is that simple saying that Mom had drilled into my head. Her mother had drilled it into my her head as well. Both of them always said, things will always look different, and better, in the morning. Usually, a good night's sleep will make any dismal situation seem better. It was true, and it was a lesson to have patience when things got tough. This night would be Carly's last night on the road with us. She was scheduled to catch a flight first thing the next morning. She had been with us for five states and almost nine hundred miles. There were no sad sappy good-byes; only a quick pat on the back and a heartfelt "thanks!" Nothing else needed to be said, and in the morning she took an Uber car to the airport while Mom and I resumed our regular routine of making relentless forward progress toward the Atlantic Ocean.

The miles just seemed to pass leaving Wichita. We passed through just in time, as a couple of days later, a series of tornadoes ravaged the Wichita area. By that time, however, we were far from Wichita. As I approached Eureka, Kansas I encountered another person on the side of the road screaming my name. It had been quite a few states since I'd experienced that phenomenon, and I was wondering who it was this time. It turned out to be Ryan Ortiz, second in charge at the US Association of Blind Athletes—my biggest supporter of VISIONRUNUSA. He was in Kansas for another event, extended his trip, and drove over two hours to find me on some desolate highway to say hi. What a great guy! He also decided to run a half marathon with me, and we chatted and laughed. I told him stories about my run, and he told me stories about his family and life back home in Colorado.

I felt so removed from my life back home in Colorado. It was as if I had just checked out, and life went on without me. What was interesting was that most of the updates I got on life back home were mundane, routine, and more of the same. People lived life with a status quo existence. I didn't hear any stories about people being chased by wild animals, diving off highways to save their lives, or duct taping P-traps so they could brush their teeth at night. Life back home was pretty comfortable. The wild expedition my mom and I were on was totally foreign to people back home. We both knew that nobody could ever understand what we were going through. Only another runner and their crew could begin to understand our adventure. Mom and I were crossing America, and that had been done before, but we didn't know of anybody who had crossed at the speed we were crossing with such limited crew and resources.

It was turning out to be a true exercise in pioneering, and discovering just how much resolve and resilience Mom and I had. The time spent running and hamming it up with Ryan was great. And it was wonderful to know that USABA was still strongly supporting me. The run wasn't bringing in hundreds of thousands of dollars for USABA, but they were getting thousands of hits on social media and click-throughs due to the media visibility of VISIONRUNUSA. I was doing my part during media interviews, giving props to USABA, and I felt good that this organization which had taken a chance on me and the run was benefitting from the run.

During our final day in Kansas, a police officer pulled us over and asked what was going on. I went through my normal explanation and when I finished my canned speech, the police officer told me about his father—Larry Buck. Larry had a degenerative eye condition and had gone totally blind. When Larry was diagnosed, the doctors told him to figure out how to do something that he could do with no sight. Larry decided to become a chiropractor. By being blind, Larry has been able to develop some innovative chiropractic techniques and he is a regular speaker at chiropractic conferences. The police officer was so proud of his father. I daydreamed that one day my kids would tell a similar story about me. In my heart of hearts, I hoped that my life would somehow positively impact others in a positive manner. I also realized that Larry's blindness made him stand out in a world of sighted people. His gift of blindness enabled him to discover and create new things that perhaps he would never have discovered had he retained his sight.

Blindness doesn't have to be a curse. Blindness can be a blessing.

I was too late to catch Larry for a chiropractic appointment that afternoon. And the next day, he was travelling to another office for appointments in a different small town in Kansas. I never personally met Larry, but I know his story, and it inspires me regularly.

As I continued northeast through Kansas toward Missouri, I found some ranches with cattle. These cattle were running and trotting through green fields of grass and grazing. There were no holding pens here like I had witnessed in Texas. Sometimes I talked to the cows and exchanged moos. It can get really boring running down a highway by yourself for twelve hours a day, and being a cow whisperer is kinda cool. But there was something else I discovered that must be a cow thing. As I ran by, they all ran in a pack toward the fence where I was running, then they ran with me for a while (sometimes a minute, sometimes five), then they ran away from me back into the field and would come to a complete stop. This same phenomenon always happened when I ran by free-range cows fenced along the highway. I was thankful for the company, and it was important to me that they ran with me. Somehow, there was a connection and, however silly it was, it was a constant reminder that I wasn't alone.

Eight days and 422 miles later, I was more than halfway across America and had finished my sixth state. Next up, Missouri.

29

Missouri—The Show Me State

Missouri state line

On my thirty-fourth day, I crossed the state line and entered into Missouri. I noticed something changing about the landscape I encountered as I ran. When I started on the West Coast, I crossed deserts and very dry and arid environments. As I travelled east, there was a lot more vegetation and my surroundings seemed to be a lot greener. The different hues of green were really amazing. It was the first time my eyes had ever been treated to so many shades of my favorite color. I also noticed that the homes had huge grassy lawns on over an acre of land backing up against wooded forests. I wondered how they could keep their lawns so green and manicured. Then it occurred to me that I never noticed any sprinkler systems in Missouri. Why didn't they need sprinkler systems?

I soon had the answer. In Missouri and the eastern US, it rains *a lot* in the spring! The rain wasn't torrential, but it was constant and enough to make me need to constantly change clothes, shoes, and socks to stay dry. I was back to wearing waterproof gear. A bad case of chafing could cause my skin to be rubbed raw, and make running very uncomfortable. I used a lot of anti-chafing products and found that different types worked better in different climates. My preferred anti-chafing lubes are Aquaphor (a Vaseline-like jelly), Blister Shield (a roll-on lube that can last all day), and Glide (a specialty lube that works good for a few hours but tends to break down on very long runs). As I ran east and the environments became more humid, I experimented with using powder to prevent chafing. I was surprised to learn that it actually worked. I regularly used Gold Bond in the most private of areas and it kept things sliding, dry, and provided a little minty stimulus to keep things interesting. I also began using Gold Bond on my feet to keep my toes dry. The plastic bag shoe covers kept the rain off my socks and feet, but the heat given off by my feet made the humid air condense on the inside of the shoe covers. The net result was that my socks and feet were constantly wet. I knew this was significantly increasing the risk of blistering. Hence, I changed socks and foot beds in the shoes often.

I am a huge fan of socks made of Merino wool. For this run, Smartwool had given me a boatload of socks to use. I was grateful, as I believe socks are as important as shoes for running. The right socks and shoes can make running effortless. And the wrong socks and shoes can make running a real chore sometimes. The Merino wool material had always worked great for me in the dry Colorado environment where I lived. The socks seemed to keep my feet warm in the winter and cool in the summer. They also always dried quickly from sweat or after running through puddles or streams. They just worked well in a dry climate. As I ran east into more humid climates, they didn't work as well. They weren't able to dry out as thoroughly or quickly. I experimented with socks made from synthetic material (polyester) and found that they wicked moisture away from my feet more efficiently in high humidity environments. When I coupled the socks with Gold Bond powder, and regular sock and foot-bed changes, I solved my blister concerns.

I didn't figure this out all by myself or overnight. Mom was constantly coming up with ideas about how we could do things better, prevent problems proactively, and be more efficient. She had been my crew chief for all my races, and as far as I was concerned, she is one of the best in the world. Although she had never run farther than a half marathon, she was a voracious learner. She observed what other crews were doing in different races like the Leadville 100, Badwater, multi-day racing, and the self-supported trans-island crossing of Puerto Rico; and she adopted other crews' best practices. She learned by talking to other runners and their crews. In a sport where everybody does things differently, and there is no right or wrong, she relentlessly tried to figure out what could work for me—her runner.

Whenever she was with me for a race, I knew all I had to worry about was running. She took care of everything else, like keeping us organized, reminding me to eat, take salt, and drink, she ensured I checked the color of my urine to ensure my kidneys were functioning properly and that I was hydrated. She knew when I needed sunglasses to be able to see, or a headlamp for impending darkness, or trekking poles for a technical section of a run, or gloves to protect my hands when I fell, or to treat an injury early before it became a race-ender, etc. She simply is the best I've ever seen and experienced. There can only be a handful of people on Earth who could crew a transcon runner single-handedly moving fifty miles a day for two months straight. I was blessed to have her crewing me, and, more importantly, I have been blessed to have her as my mom.

We felt the hospitality of Missouri just a few short miles into the state. I was met by a group of three people standing on the shoulder of the road as I ran into El Dorado Springs. Beth, Jim, and Elaine were residents of the town and had been following my run since I began in California. They were kind, peaceful spirits, just like I had known people from the Midwest to be. I was always interested to learn why people were interested in the run, so I asked the group. Elaine explained that she was from the local Lions Club and that it was important for me to continue running because it was a great demonstration of what blind and visually impaired people are capable of doing. The Lions Club is a service organization founded in 1917 and there are currently over 46,000 chapters around the world. A large part of the Lions Club's focus is a program called SightFirst. The program focuses on providing services and opportunities for the blind and visually impaired. Elaine told me that Helen Keller challenged the Lions to support the blind in 1925, and they responded to that challenge and has been working to help the blind ever since. Elaine gave me a contribution to my run on behalf of her chapter.

I felt humbled, and part of me didn't feel worthy of the donation. I thought about Helen Keller who neither had sight nor hearing. She went on to literally change our world for the better. She established a legacy by sharing the wisdom she had gleaned from her life's experiences. I don't think she ever got any free rides because of her challenges in life. And, she didn't use her challenges as excuses to not live life.

At that moment, I felt weird because I was being embraced as a blind person by the Lion's Club; however, there were other organizations supporting the blind that didn't accept me because I still had light perception. With the help of my mom, I came to realize that I just needed to be me and didn't need to be accepted into a group. I also struggle daily with the fact that during daylight hours I feel like a sighted person because I can move around independently without the aid of a cane. However, when the sun sets, I see nothing. On a daily basis for my entire life, I go between being sighted and being totally blind. Thus far, every morning when I have woken up, I have been able to see something; however, I know the day is coming when that won't be the case. And, slowly over time, I have had to struggle with the fact that I see less and less during the day. Although I seem to function well during the daylight and have a jovial spirit, I know that I am still in a grieving process and probably will be until I have no light perception and I have to deal with seeing nothing.

A lot of my friends who have degenerative eye conditions have told me that I am in the toughest part of the process right now. I still have some sight, but it is constantly deteriorating. As this happens, I am forced to constantly adapt in order to sustain the same quality of life as my eyesight deteriorates. Just when I figure out how to do something and create an accommodation, my sight gets worse and I need to figure out another accommodation. It has been a lifetime of this incessant work of adapting to figure out how to get through college and law school, be successful in the professional world, travel independently, be social and maintain friendships, parent my children, and be a competitive runner. Every person is dealing with some type of adversity, and these adversities are meant to teach us exactly how incredible we can be. Without these adversities, we wouldn't be challenged to change and be the best that we can be. Adversity gives us a chance to amaze ourselves on a daily basis. Just when it seems likes something is impossible, we figure out a way to make it possible. Once we've done this enough times, we begin to really believe that everything is possible. Perhaps that is why I was given my eye disease. Perhaps I was destined to run across America. Perhaps, without having the challenge of constantly adapting to adversity, I wouldn't have had the mindset or willpower to do what I was doing at exactly that moment. Perhaps, having a positive perspective on an adversity can transform it from a liability to an asset.

The gift from the Lions Club, and being reminded that this run was important to complete strangers, lifted me up and renewed my strength. For my midday break that day, I was craving a hamburger with french fries. Mom had found a rest area on the side of the road with covered picnic tables. She fixed me a place to rest on the ground with blankets to pad my back from the concrete and a pillow to rest my head. I took off my shoes and put my feet on the picnic bench to elevate them while I snoozed. I nodded off, and thirty minutes later, she woke me up. I was amazed at how I could fall asleep on the ground on a dime during the transcon. Before the run, it would take me about an hour to fall asleep.

Midday sleep breaks under a cabana, in a yard, and on the highway shoulder

After my nap, I was ready to dig into my hamburger and fries. I took a big bite into the burger and sensed something hard. I figured somehow a rock must have found its way into the burger. I swished my tongue around, trying to isolate the hard object so I could expel and not swallow it. I found it and worked it to the front of my mouth so I could grab it with my fingers. Sure enough, it didn't belong in the hamburger and appeared to be white in color.

Maybe it was a bone and not a rock, I thought.

My tongue brushed across my teeth and I noticed something was different. There was a gap between my two front teeth. I looked closer at the bone and realized it wasn't a bone from the hamburger. *It was part of my two front teeth!*

I panicked. My first thought was how much time am I going to lose trying to get my teeth fixed? I had almost made up enough miles to get to a fifty mile per day average after having had the cut tire in the desert four weeks prior. I surely wasn't going to waste another day finding a dentist, filling out paperwork, sitting in an office waiting my turn, then having a dentist visit with me with no sense of urgency to get me back on the road. At best, I figured I would waste four hours getting the tooth fixed. At worst, it would be a full day. If I lost that amount of time, I feared that I wouldn't be able to make up the mileage to average fifty miles per day. That was the goal I had set for myself, and I was going to achieve that goal. I had to figure out a way to solve this problem.

I called to my mom so she could inspect my teeth and see what exactly had happened and how bad it was. My tongue sensed that it was huge, but Mom didn't seem that concerned, although she did say, "We have to get that fixed." I took a selfie with my phone to see what the damage was. Sure enough, I was missing half of each of my two front teeth. I had cracked my teeth as a child, and had fillings in that area. My guess was that the fillings had come out and what was left was a void. I called my dentist back in Denver who I trusted. When I got on the phone with her, she started hamming it up about my run. It turned out that the local radio, newspaper, and television had been keeping Denver up to date on my run from time to time. We exchanged pleasantries, then I let her know what had happened and how I didn't want to waste the time to go to a dentist. She asked me to send her a picture. I did, then we got back on the phone. She told me I could wait until I got back to get it fixed, unless I started having pain in the area. She gave me strict instructions to brush three or more times a day and rinse with a fluoride mouthwash in order to protect the exposed area of the teeth. With all the sugar I was ingesting in the form of Mountain Dew and frappuccinos, the area was very susceptible to decay. All I needed was for her to tell me I could chance it, and my anxiety subsided.

I made a goal at that point to learn how to whistle out of the gap between the middle of my teeth and spit water out of the gap. I'd seen both of these in movies and figured I had a lot of time to learn to do each. What could have been disaster was just transformed into hours upon hours of entertainment as I ran across America's roads.

I finished eating my burger and fries and quickly learned that I would need to find a different strategy for eating. I couldn't bite directly into food to rip it apart. It would have to be in pieces that could fit into my mouth so I could let my molars grind down the food. I adapted my eating style, just like I adapted my running stride and gait when a new injury presented itself. Nothing was going to stop me, or so I hoped.

Highway 54 mushroomed from a small two-lane road into what seemed like a massive interstate with four lanes in each direction and a large grassy divide. The highway also had a wide shoulder. When our route gave us this type of road, I chose to run with traffic and have Mom follow close behind me, blocking traffic. It must have been horrible for her as she was driving 5 mph for twelve hours a day. I can't imagine what that must have been like for her. We were en route to pass right by the Lake of the Ozarks. I had always heard about the Ozarks and how beautiful they were. Everything was green, temperatures were good, and the rain was just a drizzle that didn't require too much in the form of clothing changes. It was a great place and day to be running. We saw houseboats and houses with boat docks, and at one point I had to stop and snap a couple of pictures. I learned why people coveted this area, and I wanted to bring my kids back to this spot to experience this American treasure.

On my thirty-seventh day of running, I encountered the Missouri River which extends from the Rocky Mountains in Montana to the Mississippi River in St. Louis. It was massive. I had never seen a river that big and far across. The color was brown and the vegetation was green. It was magnificent, and I felt the excitement of a child who was seeing something for the very first time. While crossing the river on a small steel bridge, I captured the experience with photos and video. For me, it signaled a big accomplishment. The end of that day marked an even bigger accomplishment. I had run over fifty miles that day, and my daily running average had eclipsed fifty miles per day, again. I was officially in what I dubbed "the fifty-a-day club". Only six people in the history of the world (that would be six in 107 billion) had ever crossed America on foot at that pace. I now had a shot at being the seventh person in that club, if I could hold the pace for four more weeks. I knew I could be knocked out of the club, and potentially not even finish the run, in an instant. However, for this brief moment, I thought about how neat it might feel to be part of such a group of people who had accomplished such an inconceivable feat. In the next moment, I realized that, regardless of what happened, I just had to do my best and that this wasn't about my own personal pride. This run wasn't a "Jason thing." This was a Calling, and I wasn't doing this for what it could do for me, but for what it could do for others. I was out here on these highways as an act of service and humility. Why else was I apart from my children, charging expenses on my credit card, and risking my life on a daily basis?

I had been giving interviews to local newspapers and radio stations since the run began many weeks prior. The US Association of Blind Athletes had been arranging the interviews in an effort to publicize the run and help fundraise. Sometimes I took a phone call and was on a live morning show where the television audience saw pictures of me running and my voice was streamed live as I was interviewed by the hosts. Sometimes they were remote radio interviews. Sometimes a reporter would meet me and ask questions. The interviews were great as I was able to challenge society and employers to rethink the capabilities of the blind and visually impaired. They were also becoming a distraction from the run, as I would need to go back and forth with the USABA to coordinate the interview, then I would need to take time and do the interview. I also needed to be cordial and mask the mental and physical pain I was experiencing so I could deliver a strong message. It wouldn't be good if I met a reporter and spent the whole time crying because of everything I was trying to hold together. The headlines would read "cross-country runner falling apart." This, however, was the reality. The miles had taken their toll on me, and my stubborn strength was beginning to crack and show signs of vulnerability. It was getting harder and harder to finish fifty miles every day. My body was aching in all areas at all times. Doubt had perched its Lazy Boy recliner on my shoulder and sweetly sang, "This can all be over now if you just quit."

On my second to last day in Missouri, I had agreed to give two interviews in the same day. The first one was a phone interview and it was first thing in the morning. For the first hour of my day, I struggled to even walk. Every step was excruciating. After an hour, I loosened up a little, but more importantly, my body remembered how to tolerate the physical pain I was experiencing. The interview was going to take place while I was going through this morning ritual of embracing the pain. I had to stop several times to just listen to what the reporter was asking me. My concentration wasn't on the question coming from the other side of the phone, it was on making my body move forward despite the pain signals that were lighting up my cerebral cortex. When the interview was over, I was relieved. My pace was slow, and I only covered half the distance as I usually did during this time of the day. During my midday break, I had another interview scheduled.

When I could stop and rest for a break, I always took a thirty-minute nap, then massaged my legs and ate for thirty minutes. For this break, it took thirty minutes for the reporter to find us, and I didn't sleep because I was waiting for him. When he arrived, we made small talk as he didn't want to just dive into the interview. Then we did the interview, then he wanted to take some pictures. By the time the interview was done, an hour and a half had been spent, and I hadn't eaten or slept. I would have to run really hard for the second half of the day to make up for the lost time so I could achieve my goal for the day by a reasonable time so Mom and I would have enough time to sleep.

My right knee, hip, and back were the worst of my injuries at this point. When my knee bent too far, it caused a lot of pain. So my run looked like a stiff-legged shuffle. That new stride wreaked havoc on my hip and lower back because the impact of the stride was no longer being absorbed evenly by my foot, ankle, knee, hip, and back as nature had intended. I had changed the mechanics of my running to lessen pain, and that caused other injuries. Most of the time, this is how running injuries arise. During the run, I learned that whenever I had an injury on the right side of my body, I needed to treat the entire right side as that injury would creep into other areas. For instance, pain in my right foot could easily create a strained hamstring, Achilles tendonitis, ITB syndrome, and a tight back. I treated everything proactively on the right side of my body from back to toe whenever I had an injury. This was in addition to the two-hour proactive recovery and injury prevention work I did every night since day one of the run.

It occurred to me that other transcontinental runners who did speed crossings weren't doing live interviews. They had PR people to do that. They also weren't posting on a daily basis to Facebook, giving personal updates on their mileage and experiences. Heck, speed crossers had a team of people doing things for them, and they definitely weren't loading and unloading their supplies every night into a motel room. They had RVs that were their moving hotel rooms and kitchens along their route. I was envious of those resources and support, but my reality was different. My Mom and I didn't have the luxury of a team to do this manual labor so we just did it ourselves. But that also meant I didn't have as much energy or time to be doing other things. I realized that the interviews were a good thing for the USABA, but they had become a real liability for my chances of making it to the Atlantic Ocean. I called Mark Lucas, the President of the USABA, and explained the situation. I felt bad, because if I stopped the interviews, the run might not raise as much money as it could have if I continued the interviews. On the other hand, the time required to complete the interviews was jeopardizing the run as well. "Do whatever you need to do, Jason. I support you and the USABA supports you," was Mark's response.

30

Illinois—The Prairie State

Illinois state line

The Mississippi River was big in my mind's eye, and even bigger when I was able to take it in. It is massive. Nothing stood in the path of this mighty waterway, and if it did, it would surely be swept away. Again, a steel bridge permitted us passage over the river. I took my GoPro with me as I crossed the bridge. There were no shoulders and two cars could barely pass one another in opposite directions at the same time. I was waving cars by me as there was no room for my body width and a car to share a lane. I walked most of the bridge, wanting to remember what the

Mississippi River looked like. I closed my eyes to pretend like I had no light perception and practiced remembering what the river looked like. I did this several times until I could see the river with my eyes closed. I wanted to keep this image with me even when I was a thousand miles away back home in Colorado, even when my eyes could no longer see.

Not long after crossing the Mighty Miss, I found myself on a two-lane highway in the green backwoods of Illinois. There were a lot of mosquitoes and gnats flying around me. For some reason, they really liked my hair and face. I put on a hat with a neck drape and sunglasses. They were everywhere—in my mouth, nose, and eyes. I sprayed bug spray all over me, but that did nothing to deter them. I swatted at them, but the swarm only seemed to grow. I noticed that when they landed on me, if their wings became wet, they could no longer move. I doused my hat and clothes with water so I was a sloppy, wet mess. As soon as the bugs touched my clothes, they were stuck like a fly to fly paper and they eventually met their demise. I hated to be a bug killer, but it sure beat flailing my arms and choking on the bugs in my throat and picking them out of my eyes.

When I met my mom, she quickly gave me food and drink from inside the van, as we didn't want these things to infiltrate its climate-controlled interior. My hat and shirt were white; however, by my midday break, there were dead bugs all over me and my clothes. I stripped down except for my shorts and quickly jumped in the van to take a break and find refuge from the swarm. Mom was holed up in the van as well, and we heard and felt some flying insects once in a while inside the van, but it was tolerable. After an hour break in the van, I donned my bug suit, doused it with water, and reapplied bug spray.

As I continued down the highway that day, I noticed a guy walking in the other direction on the opposite side of the road. He was wearing a hat with a drape, long sleeves, and pants. He was carrying a pack on his back and plastic bags were criss-crossed on his front side. This man was clearly out of place, as was I. We were tens of miles between towns on a desolate road. *What is he doing out here?* I thought to myself. Before I could answer myself, I was running across the highway to him, yelling, "Hey!" I introduced myself and asked him his name. With the hint of a smile, he said his name was Mike. I asked if he was okay and what he was doing out on this highway.

"I'm walking from the Atlantic Ocean to the Pacific Ocean," Mike said nonchalantly.

"My name is Jason. I'm running from the Pacific Ocean to the Atlantic Ocean," I responded.

We were both stunned, and had a brief pause of silence. Mike was a small business owner who had decided it was his time to cross America on foot. He had started at Coney Island in New York, gone down the Eastern Seaboard, and was now heading west. He was averaging around thirty miles a day and was self supported, meaning he was all by himself. Some days he would go longer than thirty miles and some days less, depending on where motels were located. His daily distance was dictated more by lodging than by any numerical goal. He had already travelled about 1,400 miles on his journey. I knew I had a little over 1,000 miles until I would reach New York. His path wasn't as efficient as it could have been, but his journey wasn't about speed or precision. From the tone of his voice and the ease of his presence, I could tell that his journey thus far had done him well.

Mike asked about my journey, and wondered if the van was with me. He had seen the signs that said "Blind Runner." I confirmed that I was this runner, and my goal was to go fifty miles a day. I also told Mike that my starting point was Santa Monica Pier, and that was to be Mike's ending point. We took a couple of blurry selfies and exchanged numbers. We both appreciated bumping into one another and sharing stories, but it went without saying that each of us still had a lot of work to do before our day was done. And, as quickly as we met, we parted ways, Mike heading west to the Pacific Ocean, and me heading east to the Atlantic Ocean.

As I ran on that day, I kept thinking *What are the chances that I would meet another person out here doing the same thing as me?* At the beginning of the trip, I had bumped into three guys from Buffalo in the California desert who crossed America on foot. Their crossing was eight months in duration. Mike would eventually reach Santa Monica Pier after four months on his feet. I was on target for a two-month crossing. Was it coincidence that we all crossed paths, or was it part of a larger plan? Regardless of how one chooses to answer that question, one thing was for sure—I knew I wasn't alone.

Exhaustion had returned to plant its flag on Mom and me. We weren't talking much, and there was a lot of silence. I interpreted the silence as something negative. I think Mom interpreted it as peaceful and restful. Oftentimes, I would try to add energy to the morning and make jokes as we drove out to our starting point. Mom drank her coffee, seeming slightly annoyed at my words and energy, constantly reminding me, "I'm not a morning person."

I was coming up on 2,000 miles on this particular day. I remembered back to my first 1,000 miles. I was celebrating and taking pictures to memorialize the moment. In the movie *Running America*, I remembered Marshall Ulrich's crew holding a ribbon banner and surprising him with a cake to celebrate his accomplishment of 2,000 miles. I had hoped long and hard for some type of recognition like that. It was not to be, however. On that day, when my watch buzzed, I was all alone on a highway. I screamed with joy and congratulated myself—"Jason, you've doing something really big!" I walked off the paved shoulder to the gravel alongside the shoulder. With my right index finger, I wrote "2000."

2000 miles completed

Then I snapped a picture. I had to reconcile not having anybody to celebrate with and the hurt feelings that accompanied it, with the fact that I knew I was loved by many. It seemed like a contradiction in concepts. How could I feel so alone and abandoned by so many, but know at the same time that these same people did in fact love and cherish me? I had felt this way many times before in my life, but this situation seemed to put an exclamation point on it. I carried on running to finish the day. That night, Mom snapped at me and said she didn't even know we had crossed the 2,000 mile mark, and was surprised to learn about it from my Facebook post that evening. I was angry for how alone I had felt, but used discretion when answering my mom. I just said, "Yeah, it was about midway through the day." During this trip, I had learned a very important life lesson.

A gentle answer deflects anger, but harsh words make tempers flare.

I have generally been good in my professional life in putting this principle into practice. However, in my personal life and when I am in a stressed environment, I have been less than perfect in practicing this principle. On this occasion, however, I did okay.

I had to ask Mom for a favor that evening as well. I had a nasty case of plantar fasciitis developing in both feet. The previous morning, I had used RockTape to provide support and lessen pain while I ran on the foot. Basically, I applied a strip of stretchy tape to the affected area in a prescribed way, and it acted like an ACE bandage did for support, and increased blood flow and natural healing by the body. Some people question whether it works; however, I can attest that it does, and at times I had almost the entirety of both legs taped due to injuries. As the injuries healed, I removed the tape, then as they occurred again, I would re-tape the injured area. The previous morning, I was rushed and cut the strip of tape too long for my right plantar. As a result, when I placed the tape on my plantar and perpendicular to my foot, the tape rode up high and onto my ankle. I didn't realize this at the time, but it would cause me a big problem. When a person runs, the ankle structure compresses and rebounds with each step. When I accidently stretched the tape too much from the foot over the ankle, I impaired my ankle's ability to rebound after each step. The result was that my right ankle was locked into a permanently compressed state, and all the muscles around the joint were in a contracted state. After a full day of running on this, it had become very painful to put any weight on the foot. My chiropractor, Dr. Brendan, back in Denver was on call and was supporting us remotely. He diagnosed that the ankle needed to be *distracted* as I wasn't able to rotate it or move it. Basically, the ankle was fixed to my leg in one position. Distraction meant that the ankle had to be yanked in a certain way and direction in order for it to release and become mobile again. As I explained the situation to my mom, we both knew that she was going to have to yank my ankle. She had some arthritis in her hands and wasn't sure if she would be strong enough to pull it. I explained our trepidation to Dr. B, and he sent us a short videotape of himself yanking his son's ankle.

Mom saw the video and became more frightened. She kept saying, "What if I do it wrong?" My only response was, "Well, if you don't do it, I know that I can't run fifty miles tomorrow." She assumed the position and grabbed my ankle as instructed. I grabbed a pillow and covered my face as I expected to feel intense pain when she pulled, and I figured I would scream into the pillow. Without warning, she yanked the ankle and we both heard some things pop, and I felt bones sliding in my ankle. I told her to do it again, and I thought it was working. She yanked it a couple of more times until we heard no more popping and I didn't feel anything else sliding back into place in my ankle. I tried rotating it, and magically I had full range of motion again. It was a miracle. Mom and I laughed at what had just happened. There was nothing we felt we couldn't overcome. We called Dr. B and celebrated the distraction, laughing the entire time at how insane this adventure had become.

The next morning, my ankle was good as new, excepting a little soreness. I took off running in the morning and made good progress that day. While I was running, I had heard a bunch of sheep making noises and *bahhh'ing*. They were penned up in a fence about fifty yards away from the road. Naturally, I was bored and prone to speaking to animals at this point in their native tongue, so I, too, began *bahhh'ing*. Then, they would *bahh* and I would *bahh* back, and, so on. After about a minute of this and being mildly amused and entertained, I heard something other than the sheep—a bark. It wasn't a normal bark like you hear while walking through a neighborhood. It was a bark that sounded like, "You'd better get out of here or I'm going to eat you." In my mind, I saw Cujo, a rabid St. Bernard on the other end of that bark. What I saw running at me was about the same size, although it was gray and white. A sheepdog was barreling toward me, and I sprinted as fast as I could. By the time the dog got to the road, I was about thirty yards ahead of it and running scared as fast as I could. The dog didn't give chase —it knew it had done its job to scare me off. The dog must have weighed over a hundred pounds, and I could only imagine what would have happened if it had gotten hold of me.

That incident really got me thinking. My kids were on my mind more than ever. My two youngest children had continuation ceremonies from elementary and middle school on June 1st. At the pace I was running, I could reach Boston and then take three days for my mom to drive back and reach Denver on June 5th, and miss the continuation ceremonies. Or, I could stop my run in New York City and make it back to Denver just in time for the ceremonies. At this point, there would be no girlfriend waiting for me in Boston, and I was hoping the organization I was going to meet in Boston could understand me choosing family first. Finally, my real run all along was from LA City Hall to NY City Hall. I broke the news to Mom that I was only going to New York, and it didn't seem to faze her. She comfortingly said, "That's far enough, Jay."

I felt her approval, and in my thoughts I heard her say, "What you have already done has been enough. It's more than I ever imagined was possible." She didn't let me hear those words, however. Our job wasn't done. We still had a thousand miles to go. At this point however, we permitted ourselves to look at a map and see how far we had travelled. I had run two-thirds of the way across America. When we looked at the map, it looked like an inconceivable distance. Neither one of us could believe that I had actually travelled that far on foot. Except for the fact that we lived it, I'm not sure either of us believed it was possible. Then, we looked at the distance yet to be travelled. It was only about three to four inches on the map we were looking at; however, those few inches would drive us both to our knees.

The last thousand miles I called HANGING ON. In my life, it has always seemed like when I got closer to finishing something, the effort required to complete the task became exponentially more. It took herculean efforts to get up in the morning, to do laundry at the same frequency as before, to eat as frequently as was required, to keep up with social media . . . whatever it was it just became more difficult. Mom and I just wanted it to be done. We still had three weeks left, and had to find a way to gut it out.

The next day was perfect weather. The day had started slow as usual, but after three hours of running, I was hitting my stride and running fairly well. On this particular day, I was running down a two-lane highway lined by tall green trees. It was picturesque and peaceful. There were no shoulders to speak of, and a guardrail was where the white line on the road should have been. Mom had driven up to find a place to pull off the road so she could crew me. I saw a blue truck in the distance. As I normally did whenever I saw a vehicle coming at me, I waved my right hand to ensure they saw me. The truck just kept accelerating and coming at me, not changing its course. It was hugging the edge of the highway where I was running. I waved both hands frantically, and yelled so the driver would notice me. The truck just kept accelerating and wouldn't change its course. I turned sideways and leaned backward over the guardrail. I felt the tires of the truck just missing my toes, felt the wind of the speeding vehicle pelting me, and heard a loud *crack!* I had closed my eyes because I didn't want to see what I feared was going to happen.

My arm whipped around my back and spun me in a circle. Suddenly, my right hand throbbed then went numb. The side mirror of the truck had struck my hand as the truck sped by me, accelerating all the time. I thought for sure my hand was broken and I screamed in pain in the middle of the road, holding my hand that was dangling from my wrist. It seemed lifeless, and when I tried to close or extend my fingers, nothing happened. I looked toward the truck and I saw its brake lights flash for five seconds, then it accelerated and sped off. There were no other cars on this highway, and the truck could have easily given me more room.

I knew I could continue the run with a broken hand, so I wasn't scared that the run would be over. I was however, seriously PO'd at what the driver of that truck had done. It was wrong on so many levels. It was a reminder that what I was doing was extremely dangerous. Even with all the close calls I had experienced up to that point, I never felt as victimized on the run as I did at that point.

When I caught up to where Mom was parked, I recounted what had happened and asked her to inspect the hand. By this time, I was able to make my fingers move a little, but the entire appendage was still numb. I was able to run with it, so we agreed to just keep moving forward and stop in at an urgent care if we found one. We iced it to minimize inflammation. After about an hour, the numbness ended and I regained feeling in my hand—throbbing pain. Slowly, the fingers began working again and I didn't think anything major had been broken.

Anti-vehicle stick

And, that is when I stopped having close calls with vehicles that drove by me. I ran with a stick after that. If a vehicle was coming too close to me, I extended my arm with the stick, and invariably cars would swerve so their vehicle wouldn't be scratched. Most of the time, the driver honked at me, yelling obscenities, and sometimes flying "the bird" at me. The upside was that, after I began running with my stick, I wasn't hit by another vehicle.

Illinois had left a bitter taste in my mouth and I was happy to put it behind me. This was a good test of forgiveness. I know the driver went on about his life and had forgotten about me. If I chose to hold onto the anger I felt that day, my entire being could be consumed about this one time a total stranger just about killed me. It isn't for me to ensure justice is enacted on that driver—that is up to a higher order. My work is to forgive the driver, let go of my negativity, and move on with my life to do good things. Forgiving this driver would be easy compared to forgiving my father. But it was becoming clear to me that forgiving my father was part of the work I was supposed to do as part of this run.

I was in Illinois for roughly five days and covered a total of 271 miles in the state.

31

Indiana—The Hoosier State

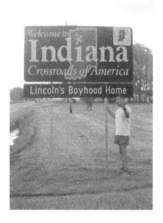

Indiana state line

M om and I made it a customary practice to stop at each state line sign and snap a photo. They were milestones for us, and I think they served as mini goals to celebrate running across another state. At least it kept our mind off of the hundreds of miles still to be covered. I had used this strategy in my business career and other areas of my life. When I sat down to "eat an elephant," I just focused on taking one bite at a time. It was hard work, but I always tried to keep my mind from wandering into the future about all those other bites. All I could focus on was taking my current bite, and that next step which would bring me closer to New York City, and eventually my children.

As we were snapping a photo with the sign, a man (Mr. Trimble) walked toward us from his house. He had seen our van and the "Blind Runner" sign caught his interest. I went through the story of how I was running across America, but that wasn't the part of the story Mr. Trimble was interested in. He asked, "Who is blind?" I explained that I was, and shared the details of my eye condition with him. A big smile erupted from Mr. Trimble's face. He told me that he was legally blind in one eye. We compared stories of what we could perceive visually, then we each told some stories of funny situations we had been in as a result of our deficient eyesight. We laughed and had an instant connection. I told Mr. Trimble that I was going to dedicate all my fifty miles to him that day. He gave me a big ol' Midwest hug and told me to keep running.

I was amazed at how many blind people I had come into contact with on this run. We were everywhere, but I hadn't met so many until I ran across America with the word "BLIND" emblazoned on our van.

It was inspiring for me to run for people on a daily basis. It made the run more personal, and meaningful for me. And when I really hurt, all I did was think about whomever I was running for that day, and I didn't want to let them down. Deep in my heart and soul, however, I was running for something much larger than a person. It was overwhelming to contemplate and try to digest.

I dreamt that as soon as I entered Indiana, I would see kids playing basketball and shooting hoops. Maybe I would bump into Bobby Knight along the route. This dream had no basis in reality, and most of what I saw was farmlands. I couldn't discern the crops, but I could see fields neatly planted and hear the sound of farming equipment. Some machinery must have been twenty feet tall with tires that were over ten feet in diameter. They were painted green like all John Deere equipment. I couldn't fathom what it was used for, and all vehicles just moved aside as these things would truck down the highway from farm to farm. Once in a while, I toyed with the idea of running right between the wheels and letting the thing drive right over me. There was no risk of injury as long as the driver kept a straight path. The only concern was if the driver tried to swerve to not let me pass between his tires—and that was likely if I attempted the stunt. I just pulled off to the side of the shoulder, stopped, and marveled at the behemoth as it passed me by.

There were plenty of other *big* things out on America's highways. There must have been some super secret things trucked from one destination to the next. From time to time, I'd see multiple police cars and blocking vehicles with flashing lights on the highway, followed by a semi pulling an open-bed trailer of forty feet in length with a huge object tied to it. The object was covered by a tarp to protect it or to hide what it was. The things were huge and would easily take up two lanes and the shoulder of the road, where I was running. The first time I encountered one of these wide loads, the lead vehicles honked at me. I thought they were just saying hi and cheering me on. I waved to them. Little did I know that their honk meant "Get out of the way, you dummy!"

The next thing I knew, a big metal thing came right at me in the breakdown lane. The trailer carrying it was in the highway, but the cargo was so behemoth that it extended off the trailer. I dropped to the ground, and the thing went right over me. It was a close call. It didn't seem sharp, so I don't think I would have been cut in half, but it probably would have knocked me out and possibly broken some bones. From then on, whenever I saw lead vehicles with flashing lights, I stopped running and stepped as far off the shoulder as I could and looked for the wide load I knew was soon to come.

The next day, May 8th, was Mother's Day. I dedicated all the miles I ran that day to my mom. It wasn't enough. I started the day by telling her "Happy Mother's Day" and joking that she deserved only the best—I had made her homeless, she was in the middle of nowhere, and she could feast on as many peanut butter and jelly sandwiches as she wanted. We laughed. As I ran mile after mile that day, I replayed how my mom had raised me from birth. I had countless memories of great times and times of struggle. One thing was certain however, she really loved me. I couldn't fathom how she was out here to support something I believed in. I think she even really questioned whether I in fact had a Calling or whether this was just some stunt to try to fill a void in my life.

Regardless of what it actually was, she was going to support me —her child. She risked her life on a daily basis. She went well past the point of exhaustion and depletion. But she never quit on me— on the run or in life. I only hoped I could love my children as much as she had loved me. We laughed and joked that day. With just about two weeks to go, we were both getting antsy and excited to have the run over. We looked at the map every day, sometimes more than once. At a half inch per day, we were moving closer and closer to New York City.

My brother was tracking our progress from back in Denver. His advice was "Just tell Jay to keep on going." He was scared something was going to happen and I wouldn't make it. Mom and I were already contending with this fear multiple times a day. It actually wasn't even a fear of something that could happen in the future anymore. Mom and I knew a multitude of things were still ahead of us and we would have to overcome them if we wanted to get to NYC. Any of the adversities could stop us at any point. And heck, who would blame us if we stopped? We had gone so far. We had suffered so much. We had done more than anybody thought we could. But, Mom and I still had more to do.

I remember getting a communication from a good friend telling me, "Jason, you should take a day off. You're absolutely killing it. Give yourself a rest." My immediate response was something along the lines of, "Hell, *no!* The only way I am stopping is if some EMT is loading my dead body into an ambulance. They will have to bury me before I will stop!"

My friend's response was, "Right on! Onward, Jason!"

That devil of doubt was screaming loud into both of my ears to quit. Everywhere I turned, there was another good excuse to just pack it up. I reached out to Marshall Ulrich at this point, as I had done at different points of the run when I was struggling. Regardless what time of day I texted him, or where he was at on his world travels, he responded to me almost immediately. This time, my communication was along the lines of, "Marsh, I'm suffering bad. How do I hang on and not quit?"

The response I received was, "Jason, you're doing great. I am real proud of you and you should be very proud of what you've accomplished so far. I remember this part of the run. It was really hard for me too. You can do it. Hang in there. Marsh."

He couldn't give me a magic pill or secret advice. His message was simple: "Don't quit." He was only one of six other people who had done what I was doing, who could understand what I was experiencing at that moment—the depression, the anxiety, the agony, and the pain. My mom had a front-row seat to watch my suffering, but she was going through her own intense suffering on top of watching her child cry for mercy.

We had visitors that day, including a couple (Frank and Melissa) who were pregnant. They had driven two hours to find us and bring us supplies, and were friends of the retina specialist who had run with me in California six weeks prior. I felt bad as I didn't thank them for their efforts nearly enough. A mother and her daughter (Shelly and Julia) drove an hour each way to find me, say hi, and run with me. Shelly is a guide for visually impaired runners at the Boston Marathon and had her "Team with a Vision" shirt on. I felt bad because I had changed my finishing location from Boston to New York. I forgave myself and replayed the words my mom had told me: "Jay, you've run far enough." A couple of faculty members from Ball State University also found me and ran some miles with me that day.

The weather in Indiana was unpleasant. It rained often, and it was hot. It made it hard for me to use my rain gear, as I would just sweat it out from the inside. It was better to just wear a light breathable jacket, get soaked, and then change clothes and powder up where I was chafing. The roads were relatively flat, as they had been for the previous 1,200 miles since leaving Arizona. I was quickly approaching Eastern Ohio, and I knew from that point on, I would be confronted with seven or eight days of rolling hills. It would be an epic finish if I could keep pace at fifty miles a day through those hills.

That night, Mom and I ended up at another nasty motel. I was exhausted and stubbornly said we were staying the night there. It was raining very hard. Mom left me at the room, as usual, and went off to do her post-run chores—refuel, restock supplies, laundry, and have a drink so she could deal with me. Before she returned, I called her and told her we had to find another motel. Our room had been remodeled and it stunk of paint. The air conditioning smelled of must, and only cooled to 78°. The water from the sink came out a rust color before becoming clear after a minute or so. The comforter on the beds were old and worn. When I lay on the sheets, I swore I felt things moving on my legs. I don't know if it was real or not, but I wasn't making the same mistake as we did at the motel in Kansas.

I had friends who were coming to meet us that evening, driving five hours from Kentucky to run with me for a couple of days. They found a Holiday Inn forty-five minutes away from where we were and texted me the address. I called Mom and let her know the good and bad news—we were going to sleep at a Holiday Inn that night, but that meant we would have to sleep one hour away from our stop/start point. She didn't care, and supported me in the decision I made. I knew I just signed up to run harder the following day because we would use two hours to drive to and from my stop/start point.

With just twelve more days to go, I had two friends from Kentucky join me—Will Rivera and Jeff Proctor. Mom and I had met Will and Jeff at a race in Puerto Rico. Will is retired from the military, owns a running store in Etown (Elizabethtown), Kentucky (Running Soles), was an accomplished runner and started his ultra-running career off with a bang by clocking a sub-seventeen-hour finish in his debut hundred-miler. Jeff is a regular on Will's crew and loves running himself. Both guys were extremely positive and came at exactly the right time. Mom and I were wearing out, and we could no longer feed off each other's energy. Neither of us had any.

Will told me he was going to run with me for two days. I was so excited. Jeff would crew Will as Mom crewed me. Our day started out fun. We talked and laughed. Will can tell stories and kept me well entertained. But the weather couldn't figure out what it wanted to do. It would rain, then clear up, then rain, then clear up. I had grown accustomed to adapting to the weather every mile or so. I'm not sure I needed to take the time to change clothes so frequently, but it did offer me a chance to rest, eat, and check on how my mom was doing. By the time we had reached our midday break time, I thought for sure we had gone over thirty miles. In fact, we had only gone twenty-six miles. I was devastated. How could this be?

I had memorized what level of effort was required to go twenty-six miles or eclipse thirty miles before the break. I had exerted a lot of effort the first half of that day. However, my effort wasn't focused on running. I was focused on talking with Will. I was experiencing gut-wrenching laughter and talking at an elevated and excited volume. Often, I would turn to face Will so I could see him as we spoke. All of these little things made my running extremely inefficient. I had burned a bunch of extra "matchsticks" (energy) by hamming it up with my buddy. I only had a finite amount of matchsticks each day to use, so I knew I had to be careful about how I used my energy for the remainder of the day. We were able to get to fifty-two miles that day, and I called it a great success, given our late start, our low mileage morning, and the weather.

I felt great. Will looked beat up. Will wasn't accustomed to running so slow, and definitely not on sloped roads like we were on. We all retired to our rooms that night, and Mom and I did our usual routine. The next morning came with the snap of a finger, and Mom and I were excited to have Will and Jeff with us again. I was full of energy and cracking jokes before we drove out to the start point.

That day brought us all a real treat. A visually impaired runner from Ohio, Dee Char, came out to run with me. She had found someone to drive her a couple of hours to find me, then she ran with Will and me as we guided her. Then, her ride gave her a lift back home. I was so humbled by this new friend I had made. Dee and I had met each other via social media. She is very much a go-getter in the visually impaired athletic community, and has inspired

32

Ohio–The Buckeye State

Ohio state line

We only had four states left—the equivalent of the combined distance of the Badwater Ultramarathon, the Spartathlon, the trans-island crossing of Puerto Rico, the Leadville 100 and the Javelina 100 that I had participated in. Basically, I had a little under two weeks to run the same distance as all of these races added up, back to back to back. And, I had to do this after already having run 2,400 miles over the last six plus weeks. It was absolutely mind-numbing to even consider.

I knew Ohio was going to start like a lamb and end like a bear. I had been warned about the rolling hills of Eastern Ohio by many people. It really didn't matter, and I didn't care because they were just one more obstacle between me and my goal of reaching NYC. Whatever tried to get in the way, would simply be overcome. The commentators were welcome to pontificate and speculate about adversity, but I didn't need to listen to it. I had one job at this point— run.

I received some heart-breaking news while I first started crossing Ohio. My Uncle Ted Epstein, who had been my inspiration to explore extreme athletics, had passed away. He was one person I wanted to tell about the run. That conversation would never happen in this lifetime. All I could think was that I hoped Uncle Ted would have been proud of me, and the distance I was covering. Mom told me that his wife, Vivian, had called her and offered to give us Ted's speaker system that he used when he was biking across America. Apparently, he had mounted it on their support vehicle and blared music so that he would be energized when approaching his van. I had mixed feelings about my Uncle Ted passing. I knew his suffering from Alzheimer's Disease was finally over and he was in a better place, but I was also very sad that this pioneer of extreme adventuring had been taken from this earth.

The days seemed to pass with ease in Western Ohio. The weather was good and the roads were flat. My body was beat up, and my mind was scrambled, but it felt like I was being pulled to New York, like metal to a magnet. At times, running felt effortless, as if I was having an out-of-body experience. My arms and legs churned and propelled my torso forward, my eyes saw the movement and the ground passing underneath my feet, but I wasn't sensing breathing, or my heart pounding, or anything else. It wasn't a near-death experience. I think I was just so exhausted, my mind was shutting down certain sensations to let my body do what it had been programmed to do for so long.

Ohio was beautiful, and Mom described it as the state she liked the best. Everything was green. The people were nice. Drivers were courteous, and the food was good. As we passed central Ohio, we entered Amish Country. I had heard of Amish people, but never really understood the culture or religion. The first thing I noticed when we approached the town of Berlin were horse-and-buggy carriages. There were a lot of horse-drawn carriages on the highway and on the shoulder where I was running. I also noticed that many of the men had beards. In the village, there seemed to be a lot of little shops and a lot of tourists. It seemed that Amish living was a tourist attraction. I'm sure that was good for the local economy. The shops seemed to focus on furniture, textiles (quilts and clothing), and food. It looked like a culture clash of twenty-first-century Americans in shorts, flip-flops, and baseball caps mixing with what appeared to be more of what I envisioned pilgrim and early settler living. Everybody was respectful, and I didn't sense any animosity from either culture. They seemed to be mutually symbiotic and able to co-exist.

As I passed through Berlin on the way to Sugar Creek, where our lodging was that night, I was intercepted by a man who wanted to run with me—Robert. Robert was polite and asked if I wouldn't mind company while I ran. I was more than happy to make a new friend, and I was feeling good and running strong. Robert and I got to know each other and talked about things like family and running. I asked him about the Amish way of life. He explained to me that there was really a spectrum that went from traditional Amish living to Mennonite living, and that the life was based in faith and a belief in Jesus Christ. From there, different people chose different paths depending on a variety of factors.

I didn't fully grasp all of what Robert had explained, but I did know he was a kind man. He exuded goodness, and I was thankful I met him and could call him my first Amish friend. Robert told me that his buddy, Freddy, had intended to meet us that afternoon, but he had to work late. Because of this, Freddy had made plans to meet me the next morning for some miles. Robert ran me to the highway exit for our lodging that night at the Carlisle Inn. Then, one of

Robert's family members picked him up and he was gone as quickly as he had appeared.

Mom and I had agreed to splurge at the Carlisle Inn and pay $160 that night for our room. We were trying to keep our nightly lodging expense to $50-$75 per night but we were both beat, and I decided I would just have to bite the bullet and figure out how to pay for it when I got back to Denver. As we drove up to the inn, Mom and I were thoroughly impressed. The grounds were immaculate, with rolling green hills everywhere. The inn was an architectural masterpiece and exuded charm and coziness. As I entered to check in, the lady at the front desk was exceptionally nice. She was expecting us and was aware that I was running across America. She didn't bat an eye at my disheveled, dirty, and aromatic first impression. Her smile seemed to say, "I'm glad you have arrived."

I checked in and went back to the van and told Mom she was going to love it. The room was like a suite, and we had a sitting area off French doors on one side of our room. It was like we had arrived in our own little heaven on earth after battling through hellacious highways. The phone rang, and a woman's voice on the other end said,

"Mr. Romero?"

"Yes, this is Jason."

"Mr. Romero, we understand that you are running across America, and we understand that you are doing this because of a Calling, sir. We aren't going to charge you for your room or anything else. Tonight is on us. And, if you don't mind, sir, we would like to have our manager take a picture with you if that is okay with you?"

I'm not sure what came out of my mouth, but in my mind I was thinking, *no way!* In the next instant, I found myself at the front desk, then taking the picture with the manager, then sitting in a hot tub with a glass ceiling marveling at a beautiful sunset in Amish country. Mom was sitting outside our room, taking in the beauty of Ohio and having a glass of wine and room service. From out of nowhere, the kindness of complete strangers had come to our rescue in a moment of need, again.

After a great night's sleep, Mom and I woke to torrential rain.

We had to leave our pampered cocoon and get back on the highways and get to New York City. I had to get there so I could get back to Denver by June 1st for continuation ceremonies. As we dollied our luggage to the lobby and loaded it into our van, Mom and I noticed a man standing in the lobby. It was 6:00 a.m. and pouring rain. It was Freddy, Robert's friend. We shook hands and introduced ourselves. He had a light windbreaker and his running gear. I had my rain suit on—a waterproof jacket and pants. The clouds were dark outside and it was raining hard. I told Freddy he could ride shotgun in the van until it cleared up, then he could run with me.

"No. I'm going to run with you now." That made me look at Freddy with an "Are you nuts?" look. His face was blank, and my facial expression didn't draw a response. I figured if this guy wanted to get soaked, that was his decision. The fact that he was going to run with me in the rain made me instantly like him. As we drove out to our start point, Freddy hopped in the van with us. The only place for him to sit was on top of my poop bucket. I told him what he was sitting on. He didn't care. *I really like this guy!* I thought to myself.

We got out of the car and started running against traffic. It was raining cats and dogs, and Freddy was instantly soaked. I could hear Freddy's socks and shoes making a *squish* sound with each step. Then, it happened. A semi passed us and sprayed a wall of water over us. I ducked my head in time and my rain gear protected me. Freddy got soaked and looked like a wet poodle. He just kept running and talking with me.

Who is this guy? Is he a real-life guardian angel? I wondered.

The rain let up to a drizzle after about an hour. Freddy ran with me for another hour in the drizzling rain and was intent on taking me to a market where his mother worked. Freddy told me they made the best cinnamon rolls ever. I was always up for dessert, so it sounded perfect to me. When we arrived at the market, Mom and I took time to go in and meet Freddy's mother and everybody who worked at the market. Everybody was so kind. Freddy's father had met him there to pick him up and give him a ride back home. I think Freddy was close to my age and it was so neat to see a family so close-knit. Mom and I tried to pay for the cinnamon rolls, but they had none of it. They asked me what else they could do for me. My response was simply, "Please pray for me."

With that, Freddy's father said, "Okay," and grabbed me by the shoulder. Before I knew it, Freddy's family and coworkers were circled with Mom and me, and Freddy's father was asking God to watch over me and grant me safe passage to New York. I was really humbled and grateful as I left that market and continued running.

As amazing as that morning was, the day turned sour and Mom and I didn't even realize it. We immediately got lost and added a few miles to our journey. The sting of getting lost and adding miles to the run had become more tolerable. The first few times it happened, I attacked my mom. I yelled at her, saying, "I just want to run. I don't want to be responsible for anything else." She responded with silence, or let me know in no uncertain terms that she was doing the best she could and she was overloaded as well. I felt horrible for how I had yelled at her. She had forgiven me before I even had to ask. What an amazing person she is and what amazing love she gave me.

The last two days of Ohio were the beginning of the final torture. I was running hills non-stop. They were just steep enough to make me want to walk, but not long enough to justify wimping out to walk them. I learned to run hills in Eastern Ohio. I was constantly climbing or descending. The scenery was beautiful, but the constant elevation change was torturing my already fatigued legs. Everything below my waist was injured at this point—hips, IT bands, quads, hamstrings, knees, Achilles tendons, and ankles, and plantar fasciitis had sunk its fangs into both my feet. I didn't know how I was moving every day, but somehow, I was getting closer and closer to my final destination.

It took me five days and 257 miles to cross the Buckeye State from west to east.

33

Pennsylvania–The Keystone State

Pennsylvania state line

From this point to City Hall, I would be calling on Carly back in Denver multiple times a day to help us navigate. There simply was no direct path through the remaining three states I had to cross. We had two GPS tracking systems she was able to access via an Internet connection. Sometimes both would work, sometimes one wouldn't work, sometimes neither would work. I carried my phone with me nonstop from this point forward. Mom and I also used walkie-talkies regularly to keep in communication. On our first day in Pennsylvania, Jacob met me at my start point. Jacob had been following my journey and was planning to run the entire day with me. He found out about me and my run through a series of connections that reached back to my ex-girlfriend. Despite the fact that she and I hadn't spoke for over a month, I thought about her every day and missed her dearly. And now a guy was going to run with me the whole day because she had made the connection. Mom and I hoped he could help us navigate all of the back roads and turns we had coming that day.

The maps Carly was looking at on the computer didn't always jive with the actual roads. There were several times where the computer said we were supposed to turn on one road, but the road didn't exist. Or, the road had a different name than what Google Earth or SPOT Tracker indicated. I had to stay on the phone with Carly and she needed to tell me exactly when to turn. It seemed like we were getting lost every couple of hours. I was a frustrated mess. Jacob had a jovial personality and he helped to diffuse my frustrations. He was an ultra-runner and was into trails. He was easy to talk to, and had a gazillion stories to tell. I was really grateful for him that day. He ended up hopping a ride in the van for the last ten miles or so. The slow pace, asphalt and the slope of the road had taken another ultra-runner as a victim. For some reason, I wasn't getting injured like my buddies who met up to run with me. I think these runners were getting a taste of what the break-in period was all about.

The next four days were excruciating. The hills just never stopped. We were constantly going up or down. Mom and I were getting lost. One time, we became separated because she went ahead of me and turned at a second bridge and I turned at a first bridge. When I called Carly, she couldn't zoom in enough to understand how we were separated. I couldn't see Mom and she couldn't see me. It took an hour to get back on course. I was mad and snappy, and so was Mom. We were on the verge of implosion.

Up to that point, every day I'd shared a lesson I had learned or somehow tried to give an encouraging and inspiring message on social media. Whatever was within me that was fueling that positive energy was gone. There was no more positive in Jason. Doubt had placed a marching band on my shoulder and it was screaming *"Quit! Quit! Quit!"* with every step I took.

I stopped posting anything on Facebook for the next four days except for daily mileage. My internal thoughts were, *Nobody cares. I'm all alone. Why am I trying? This isn't fair. Why did I have to be Called to do this? I'm mad, and I don't know why! I'm going to quit. I have to quit. I am dying. I can't do this. I just can't do this."*

I thought I was going crazy. I forced myself to just take one more step. And then when the thoughts came again, I forced myself to take another step. It seemed like I was crying all the time. There were yelling matches taking place in my head.

Quit!

Don't quit!

You're dying out here!

You can make it, Jason—just hold on!

You're going to fail!

You can do it!

I'm not going to stop until you quit!

You are loved!

When I fell back on what I had learned back in Kansas—that I am truly loved and never alone, I was able to stop the negative thoughts. Love was the answer. Love truly never fails. When I reminded myself that I was loved, I regained the strength and power I needed to continue running.

With 230 miles to go, I started the day running into a fog. It was so appropriate for what was taking place in our lives at that moment. I remember thinking:

> *Sometimes you can't see where the path is going to lead you,*
> *but you go anyway.*

By this point in Pennsylvania, I had crossed the Appalachian Trail and run over the Alleghany Mountain Range. We were running out of food and calories on a daily basis. Near the end of the day, I remember Mom saying we were out of food. I knew I needed to eat and I didn't care what I ate. We searched the van for any chips, licorice, or half-drunk sodas. I just needed calories to keep running and I didn't care how it tasted or how long it had been sitting around. Mom was done. She could drive the van and do the most basic things to help me, but she was done. The transcon had finally caught up with her, and me. We were so close. New York seemed like a stone's throw away, and it looked like we weren't going to make it.

With 180 miles to go, angels arrived to save us. My crazy college roommate, Jay Flynn, who had helped crew me many years in the mountains of Leadville and the desert at Badwater, and who had come to Boston to cheer me on at my first Boston Marathon, arrived. Not only did he drive ten hours from Georgia to be there, he dragged along his wife and three kids to be part of the spectacle. Mom loved Jay, and knew what a good friend he was to me. Jay has known me in my highest of highs and my lowest of lows. We were each there for one another in times of need, and he must have known this was a critical moment, because he showed up just in time.

He and his kids took turns running with me. Jay also shared driving duties with Mom so she could just focus on food and drink for me. He also took over navigation duties. Mom and I were giving everything we had, and Jay and his family were picking up everything we were letting fall. Halfway through the day, another one of our college roommates, Greg "Beaver" Weaver, showed up. He had flown in from Austin, Texas and surprised me. We were the three stooges back together again. That alone tapped energy reserves I didn't know existed. We laughed and joked and reminisced, and the miles just seemed to pass. That evening, another reinforcement arrived, Camilo Martinez. I had raced with Camilo in the Florida Keys and at Badwater. He was the real deal, and I knew he could run with me as long as I needed, and he could help crew and drive. By the time Camilo arrived that night, we determined that we had 130 miles to go to reach New York City Hall.

I had to decide whether to take it easy and make it in three days at fifty miles for two days and the third at thirty miles, or, I could try to make it in two days and make my final two days the longest days of VISIONRUNUSA. I talked it over with Mom, Jay, Beav, Camilo, and Carly. I'm not even sure why I asked for input, because I wasn't listening. The run had to be done. It had to be over. I couldn't make it three more days. I wasn't sure if I could make it two more days. In my head, I imagined just making a final 130 mile charge to New York City and not sleeping until I got there. I knew this last strategy was madness given the physical and mental state I was in.

I announced that I was going to finish in two days. The next day would be sixty miles, and the last day would have to be seventy miles. Nobody disputed or questioned me. Our course had been charted and destiny defined. Now all we had to do was fulfill it.

I felt very strong the second to last day. At this point, running felt as natural as breathing. It was effortless and normal. I pondered how I would feel when it was finally over. Then, as soon as the thought entered my mind, I pushed it out. There was no room for the future in my mind or body. I had to remain present and just take one more step. Somehow I was able to run eight- and nine- minute miles for the majority of the day. I even finished sixty miles in the amount of time it usually took me to complete fifty. I knew that, however good I felt, my body didn't have much left.

I went into a gas station bathroom at the end of the day and my nose began bleeding profusely. I came out with a wad of red toilet paper surrounding my nose and tried to make a joke about it, but my mom knew something was wrong. The bleeding wouldn't stop. I just kept changing out the toilet paper as it became drenched and dripped on my shirt. I was literally a bloody mess.

The team had helped me complete sixty miles, and that landed me at the driveway of our motel for the night. I told everybody that I would start running the next morning at 3:00 a.m. We would wake up at 2:00 a.m., meaning that, at best, I would have a few hours of sleep. I was exhausted, but couldn't get to sleep. I tried to close my eyes, but I just kept thinking about how far I'd come. I thought about my kids and I hoped they would be proud of me. I hoped that my dad was following my progress on a minute-by-minute basis, and that wherever he was, he would be proud of me. I hoped my ex-girl-friend was in NYC waiting for me, and that everything could be resolved with a hug and a kiss. Doubt didn't visit me that night. There was no question in my mind about whether I could make it. The only question was how long it would take me. The only thing that would stop me was death, and I had Faith that whatever had protected me for the past several weeks was going to continue to protect me all the way to City Hall in New York City. I turned to Mom and said, "We are going to do it!" I finally dozed off at about 11:00 p.m.

34

The Longest Seventy Miles—
New Jersey and New York

The approach to New York City Hall with Camilo

As I took my first step on May 23, 2016 at 3:00 a.m. EST, I knew my life would never be the same after this day ended. I was alone in my head with my thoughts. I was experiencing all kinds of antagonistic emotions hitting me at the exact same time—joy and misery, elation and depression, confidence and fear, comfort and pain. I was bundled up in running pants and a coat. I had my PrincetonTec headlamp on that I had relied on to illuminate the darkness for me. I pointed it directly at the white line on the road as I shuffled. My right foot was still making a popping noise with every step I took. This had been the case for the last thirty days, but it usually stopped after the first three hours of running. I had grown accustomed to it and didn't feel a sensation any more when the pop happened. It must have been a muscle or tendon or something that was stretching or rolling over a bone in my foot. It really didn't matter—I was still able to make forward progress with the pop.

In front of me was a truck with my college roommates; Beaver piloted and Jay assumed the co-pilot position so he could quickly hop out and give me aid if I needed it. Behind me was the trusty Silver Bullet, piloted by Camilo with Mom as the co-pilot. We had a caravan going, and I was the precious cargo being protected between them. In the back of everybody's mind was the concern that something might happen to me this day—a fall that would cause severe injury, a run-in with a car, or something else that would halt the run and prevent its conclusion at City Hall. Everybody took a lot of extra precautions that I was oblivious to. I just shuffled.

It was pitch-black, but I was told that the part of New Jersey we were in was beautiful. The houses looked like estates with large sprawling yards and typical East Coast architecture. I wondered if people who lived in this area actually commuted to New York City to work on a daily basis. I thought about my kids and what they were doing at that exact time back in Colorado. They were sleeping, as it was 1:00 a.m. back in Denver. There was at least one person, however, who I knew was awake in Denver and paying very close attention to this run at this moment: Carly. In no uncertain terms, I told her that I needed her for the entire day starting at 1:00 a.m. to help me navigate all the way to City Hall. She laughed at first, then, realizing I wasn't kidding, she said, "Sure thing, Jason."

I imagined her staring at the glow of a computer screen in the early morning darkness of her home, and wondered what Mom was thinking as she drank her coffee in the passenger seat, watching me trot along in front of the van. Was she daydreaming about being back at home in her bed, or was she overwhelmed with knowing that her child was going to complete a big challenge, or was she too exhausted to care either way?

Before I knew it, there was a very long hill. I couldn't tell where the top was, and it was too steep to run. I had to walk. First one mile, then two, then three. I was moving too slowly. I wouldn't reach New York in twenty-four hours at this pace. Then, as in life, what goes up, must come down. I began a slow steady descent over the next several miles, winding and turning. Whenever we had to make a turn onto a street, I had the team call Carly and check a map to ensure we didn't get lost. Everybody had the directions on smart phones, and Mom took care to write them out in case we lost cellphone reception. This had been her practice throughout the trip. She always had a Plan B and Plan C, it seemed.

A police officer pulled up beside us as the sun rose and asked what we were doing. Before I could speak, Beaver told him the story of how I began running in California two months earlier, and today I would run all the way to New York City Hall to complete the run. There was no mention of my ailing eyesight. The police officer asked me my name and said, "Good luck, Jason!" with a Jersey accent. We continued moving forward.

As the sun rose, I became sentimental. This would be the last sunrise I would see on this expedition. I had seen so many sunrises in deserts, mountains, city centers, suburbs, and farmlands. Each one was different, special, and beautiful. Each one reminded me that I wasn't totally blind . . . yet. When the sun came up and my eyes were treated to the splendor of light and color, I was always excited to know that I had one more day of light perception. I would be able to see my kids' faces that day. I would be able to see birds and animals scurrying about. I could enjoy funny videos on YouTube. I could even watch a movie and know what was happening without somebody having to explain it to me. When the sun rose, I emerged from the darkness and blindness that sometimes held me hostage in the night.

I asked Mom for my GoPro, as I wanted to capture the moment and my thoughts that final morning. I remember rambling, tearing up, and feeling a burst of adrenaline at that moment. Our progress was slow, but it was steady. I had a goal to finish my first marathon distance by 10:00 a.m., when Jay was going to depart for home in Georgia—a ten-hour drive south. When Jay's wife and children showed up in their minivan to meet our caravan, I was moving pretty good, running eleven-minute miles. This had become an easy shuffle, and I felt like I could run at that pace forever. My breathing was easy, and it didn't even feel like my heart rate was raised the slightest. We pulled over because I knew this meant it was time to bid farewell to Jay and his family. I desperately wanted them to stay to experience the finish with me. They did as well, but, the demands of life, work, and school dictated their departure. I was grateful for the time we were able to share.

I asked Jay why he dragged his entire family all this way and made them follow me at 5 mph. He told me that there are rare times in life when you can really experience something great first-hand, and this was one of those times. Jay wanted his children to see, breathe, and live what I was doing. They had only known me as Uncle Jason—someone who had visited their home from time to time, fell into a pond at their parent's wedding, had shown up at their grandmother's funeral, and was just a normal guy. As Jay drove off with his family, I was sad and wanted to cry. After a couple of hours, Jay called me from a rest stop and told me a story. He told me that when they left me, he and his wife started asking their kids what they had learned from the experience. The two oldest, Fiona and Patrick, shared some pretty deep thoughts about enduring despite adversity. When Jay's youngest daughter Riley responded, she quickly and confidently said, "If you can dream it, you can achieve it."

Wow! I didn't have to preach, tell stories, or convince the kids of anything. They got it. They understood what it had taken me forty-six years to experience, understand, and believe. Jay said he felt compelled to call me and tell me that story. It landed directly on my heart and infused me with strength and energy. They probably never even knew that they were the ones who gave me an extra adrenaline rush to keep pushing onward to City Hall.

I kept telling myself that all I needed to do was to get to the

George Washington (GW) Bridge. The GW Bridge separated Fort Lee, New Jersey from Manhattan, New York. After reaching the bridge, I would have roughly eleven miles to get to City Hall. I knew I would be exhausted, but I could make it on adrenaline alone. I just had to get to that bridge, which was about sixty miles away from my starting point.

The day was heating up, and after thirty miles of running in the Garden State of New Jersey, we transitioned into the congested, high-strung traffic of New Jersey. The closer we got to New York City, the busier things became. We had more turns and chances to go off course. Streets suddenly had dividers and I wasn't able to get to my support vehicle for miles. Everybody was in a rush and honking at me, yelling at me, and telling me to get off the road. We all sensed a lot of nervous energy, and life here was very different from the vast openness of rural farmlands that I had travelled for many weeks. At that point, I wished that I was still a thousand miles away on the calm, tranquil roads of Missouri. The chaos of this part of New Jersey was just another obstacle standing between me and the finish.

By mile forty, my adrenaline rush was wearing thin and my nerves had all but paralyzed me. I needed a break and lay down, telling my crew that I had to rest for thirty minutes. Beaver had stayed as long as he could but needed to make a flight out of Newark and get back home. He, too, had work and family commitments to tend to. I hated to see him go, and sensed he felt the same. Days after he left, Jay told me he received a call from Beaver en route to the Newark airport. Beaver told Jay that I was in bad shape and having to stop all the time. He didn't think I was going to make it to City Hall that day. Jay assured Beaver that I could do it. Jay told stories about how he had been with me when I had finished the Leadville 100 multiple times after vomiting and seemingly being on a trajectory to doom. He told Beaver how I could make a comeback from out of nowhere. It would seem like I was dying, and the next minute I would be flying. This had been my experience in life and in running. As long as I refused to give up, I was always able to keep moving forward and I could always make a comeback.

As I approached a corner in Fort Lee, New Jersey I saw two children and a man holding a sign, yelling, "Jason! It's Darby!" A friend I had made in Puerto Rico eight years prior was standing in front of me with two of his three children. He lived in New Jersey now and had been following my run for the duration. Darby had invited me to stay with his family when we were in town, but our starting and stopping points just didn't enable us to accept his gracious invitation. He had a smile from ear to ear. His voice was energizing and his positive spirit contagious. This was the first time I had met these two children. Darby and his wife had adopted them after leaving Puerto Rico and moving to the tri-state area. Darby's family was wonderful, but after chatting for about fifteen minutes, I had to bid *adieu* and continue marching to City Hall. I was fifty miles into my day and exhausted. It was about 3:00 p.m., and it had been twelve hours since I began that morning.

Only twenty miles more. I did the math and knew I could make it. Even if I walked twenty-minute miles, I could be done in about six and a half hours. That didn't account for taking breaks to be crewed or using the bathroom—those could easily add an extra hour or two to my calculation. It didn't matter; I just had to keep moving forward.

I was talking to Carly at least every hour to make sure we were on course. I was short and curt with her. I felt bad, and I hoped she understood. Mom and Camilo also got a dose of my lack of congeniality many times that day. They forgave me and just encouraged me to keep moving forward. With about fifteen miles to go, Camilo spotted Manhattan. "Look! That's New York!"

I couldn't see what he was seeing. Mom said, "Jay! It's New York!" but I couldn't see what they were seeing.

I started running harder. I ran up hills and down hills, jumping over curbs, and pumping my arms and legs as hard as I could. My movement was no longer a shuffle or a jog—I was actually running. I kept telling myself, *I just have to get to the bridge. I have to get to the bridge.* As I turned a corner, I almost ran directly into two people who were standing on the sidewalk. I tried to move to the side so I wouldn't hit them as I ran. As I passed them, I heard one of them yell my name.

Now, who could this be? My watch told me that I was about five or so miles away from the bridge. The people standing in front of me were Andrea Croak and Kyle Robideaux. They were from the organization in Boston I had originally planned to meet at the original ending point for my run. When I changed the ending point to New York City, they decided to come to me. Andrea and Kyle had rented a car and drove two hundred miles from Boston to New York City to run the last part of my run with me.

Kyle has the same eye condition as I do, and is legally blind as well. When we ran together, Andrea guided Kyle, calling out curbs and obstacles. I tried to help, but couldn't use the energy I had to talk. I felt bad that I was less than cordial and jovial, but I felt like the bottom was about to drop out. I didn't know when I would implode from exhaustion, but I knew it was coming. "I have to get to the bridge!" I muttered with all my strength.

Kyle warned me about upcoming hills, but I asked him not to tell me anything. The hills or anything else just didn't matter. Nothing was going to stop me, and I would just deal with it when I encountered it. Camilo was driving and wasn't stopping every mile to ensure I was consuming calories. Mom was doing her best to tend to my nutrition needs. She and I had a routine, and we weren't following it. I was low on fuel and going into the red zone. After making a left-hand turn, I saw the Silver Bullet parked on the side of the road. I ran up to it and asked what was going on. "There's the bridge!" Camilo said, pointing off into the distance.

It had begun to rain, and it looked like more was coming. I knew Mom couldn't crew us through Manhattan, so our plan was for her to meet me at City Hall—a little over eleven miles away. Camilo and I grabbed food and water. Andrea and Kyle had also caught up to us and were making preparations for our final push to City Hall.

I hugged my mom, kissed her, and I told her I loved her. She said, "Do it, Jay!"

Camilo, Andrea, Kyle and I started trotting toward the bridge. After about twenty minutes, we were actually at the George Washington Bridge on the New Jersey side. The rain began and I donned my waterproof coat. Camilo did the same, but Andrea and Kyle just toughed it out and got wet. While crossing the bridge on the pedestrian walkway, a police escort met us. They knew I was coming. The US Association of Blind Athletes had called ahead and tried to get me an escort through Manhattan. The escort wanted to take me down the West Side which would add an extra few miles to my run. Camilo and I had plans to make a beeline down Broadway and run a more direct route as a crow would fly. I told the police of our plan, and thanked them for their support. They understood and just smiled at me as I ran unshaven with dirty clothes, a big gap between my two front teeth, and the front toes of my shoes cut off. I could only imagine what they were thinking.

On the bridge I was met by Mauricio, a member of the New York Achilles Chapter. As I ran, a lot of people talked to each other and to me. I couldn't handle the noise. It felt like when I was back in Oklahoma and I had to just take off my headphones—I needed silence. I needed to just be. The people I ran with were swarming around me. People were in front of me, on the side, crossing in front of me to take pictures. There were bikes and pedestrians on the bridge as well and the rain made my ability to see very poor. I was getting nervous I would crash into somebody. My anxiety was skyrocketing and it was consuming all of my energy.

When we reached the New York side of the bridge, we ran straight off it and I asked Camilo to lead. He lives in Manhattan and this was his concrete jungle. He knew how to get me to City Hall in the shortest distance possible. From the map, I knew I had eleven miles from the bridge to City Hall. Camilo insisted that all I had was four miles. It was a nice dream, but I knew it was wishful thinking. I had to ask my co-runners to run behind me. For some reason, if they ran by my side or just in front of me, I had the urge to compete. We would continue to accelerate until I imploded.

I felt overwhelming support, but I couldn't thank them. I had lost the ability to function as a human. I felt like a primal animal running to my doom. By the time we reached Harlem, I was done. My ears were ringing, my eyesight was blurring more, and my tunnel was closing into nothingness. I felt like I was going to pass out. I realized I hadn't eaten for the last three hours. I was bonking bad, feeling lightheaded, lethargic, and as if I was about to faint. I told Camilo he had to get me food. I sat down outside a convenience store and wanted to cry. Everybody was standing around me, however, so I didn't let my emotions out. I asked Camilo to get me something with sugar that could get me going again. He came out with a Mountain Dew, a chocolate roll with cream filling, and a small bottle of milk. I guzzled the drinks and scarfed down the chocolate snack. Camilo helped me stand up and we began walking.

After a block, I knew I had to run. I trotted, then jogged, then ran. I was pushing as hard as I could, and my heart felt like it was going to explode right out of my chest. I was dodging pedestrians on the busy sidewalks of Manhattan. With my tunnel vision, I couldn't see people as they crossed in front of me. People didn't seem to care much about some guy running down the sidewalk with a "BLIND" sign on him. Everybody seemed to be in their own little microcosm —me included. My microcosm had laser focus on City Hall.

As it became evening, I realized the sidewalks were going to be too crowded for me to run on. I ran into people as they criss-crossed one another. I knew I couldn't see them and was bumping into them on accident. I wondered if they thought it was intentional.

I jumped off the sidewalks and ran in the street, against traffic. Camilo yelled, "No!" saying I was going to get hit by a car or bus. I told him not to worry—I had squared off with semis, been chased by animals, and hit by a truck. I was confident I wasn't going to die in Manhattan. The entourage following us was a couple of blocks behind. Most of them opted to stay on the sidewalks and dodge people instead of cars.

Why can't I see? I thought something was happening to my eyes. By 7:00 p.m., it was starting to get dark in Manhattan. Although the sun was still up, it was obstructed by the massive skyscrapers. Everything had become shaded.

"Oh no!" I said to Camilo. "I don't have my headlamp!" I felt panicked. I asked Camilo how much farther we had to go. Like clockwork, he was still responding "four miles." I had to run harder than I had run for the past two months. I couldn't let it get dark on me. I increased my pace and Camilo stayed with me. The others dropped back. Soon, I was hitting seven-minute miles, running against traffic down Broadway. At one point, I even dropped a sub-seven-minute mile. I don't know where the energy came from, but I was flying. I had carried an American flag with me in my backpack and took it out when Camilo and I got to Times Square. I draped it over my shoulders and continued sprinting toward City Hall.

I knew friends were waiting for me there. One of my best friends, Todd, and his brother, Greg, had flown in from Denver to see me finish and had been patiently waiting for me at City Hall all day. Members of the Achilles Brooklyn chapter and some other people who were following the run had congregated at City Hall as well. I hoped Mom had found her way there and was waiting for me.

We passed Times Square and I ran as hard as I could. I was in a lot of pain, but all I could think about was that I had to finish before it got dark. I had to get to City Hall before I couldn't see anything. I couldn't let the darkness beat me. Somehow, I had to beat it to City Hall. I was face-to-face with the monster that had stalked and haunted me my entire life. The final showdown was at this moment. I just had to outrun the gloom that was crippling me, sinking its fangs into my heart and spirit, devouring my love and vitality that I was yearning to give to people who were most important to me. I couldn't fail. I thought if I could just outrun the beast to City Hall, everything would be okay.

Soon, I was tripping on curbs and potholes, and clipping side mirrors of parked cars. Finally, Camilo grabbed me and said, "You can't see. Grab my arm." I took his elbow and we slowed way down to a shuffle and hopped back onto the sidewalk. I might as well have had my eyes shut—I couldn't see anything. It was pitch-black, and the darkness had enveloped me once again. I stumbled off curbs and bumped into people and things. I was demoralized, embarrassed and felt defeated.

"There it is!" Camilo said.

"What?" I responded.

"City Hall!" Camilo yelled.

"On the next block?" I asked as I looked at blackness.

"No. We are here! It is here!"

I couldn't see the building. I cried out, "Mom!"

Then, I heard, "Jay!"

I ran toward the voice, not caring if I tripped, yelling "Mom!" all the time.

The voice was getting closer and she was yelling "Jay!" nonstop.

I could sense she was right next to me, and I said, "Where are you?"

"Jason," she said. "I'm right here."

I fell into her arms and cried. She hugged me and said, "I love you. I'm so proud of you."

At the end of my journey, I had to accept that I will never be able to outrun the darkness—I will always need to run directly into it. However, I also discovered that true love will always overcome any and all darkness.

The finish at New York City Hall with my mom

Points to Ponder

The following questions are inspired from Part **III** of my story. There are no wrong answers. There are only your answers, which are right for you.

1. If you were going to die today, who would you need to tell that you loved them? Do it.
2. What do you do when you want to quit?
3. Why do you feel alone at times?
4. When has a stranger helped you?
5. When was the last time you helped a stranger?
6. What will be your legacy?
7. What are you most grateful for?
8. When was the last time you innovated?
9. How will you challenge yourself to change?
10. Do something you love for the next sixty consecutive days.

Afterword

KIDS

After being separated for over two months, my kids and I reunited at my youngest daughter's continuation ceremony. We took a vacation to Cozumel and did nothing but spend time together playing on the beach, eating unlimited ice cream, and swimming in the ocean. Our lives have pretty much returned to our normal routine, although I have become a semi-celebrity with my kids' friends. The best thing that has come out of this for them, from my perspective, has been a mindset to pursue their dreams, regardless of how outlandish those dreams might seem.

MOTIVATIONAL SPEAKING

After the run, I was asked to speak at a celebration party that happened just a week after my return to Denver. I was timid, shy, and not sure what to say. I was still trying to process the run and what had happened. After being asked to speak more and more at events, schools, and service organizations, this storytelling grew into a career, and I now give keynote addresses at conventions, sales meetings, executive retreats, commencement ceremonies, nonprofit galas, and a variety of other venues where people need to be challenged to rise up and exceed their expectations. In order to give back, I regularly speak at youth detention centers, churches, schools, and service organizations *pro bono*.

THE SUCCESS CYCLE

As a result of evaluating the run, my business experience, and life, I developed a theory called "The Success Cycle." I regularly speak about it with business and athletic audiences. The theory incorporates my triple-A strategy which is summed up simply as when there is Adversity, we must Adapt and sometimes fail to Achieve significant success. Incorporated in the Success Cycle are my four tenets of mental toughness that enabled me to cross America on foot.

The first tenet is Hope. We must possess the ability to believe in something for which there can be no evidence. It is the skill of maintaining Hope when the situation looks desperate and bleak, and hanging on to a belief that one's self, one's dreams, and all things are possible.

The second tenet is Patience. In the run, as in life, there are storms, and if we remain calm and have patience, those storms will always pass and things will get better. Regardless of how bad it may seem at any given point in time, if we practice simple patience, our situation will improve and we will be able to run again.

The third is Consistency. We must commit to make relentless forward progress toward our goals on a daily basis. Consistent effort will yield consistent results. The inverse is true as well—inconsistent effort yields inconsistent results.

The final tenet is Forgiveness. We carry around a lot of baggage and anger for no reason. When we are able to truly forgive, we release that weight and burden. We lighten our load, and are able to move more effectively and efficiently in our lives.

MY FATHER

When I was about halfway across the country, I had a telephone conversation with an uncle, my dad's brother. He asked me if I wanted my dad to be at the finish in New York. Apparently, my uncle was going to pay to fly my dad to the finish. I declined the very generous offer, and was still upset with my father for things that had happened over the past forty years. Almost a year after I returned from the run, during the writing of this book, I met with him. I told him how upset I was for all the things he had done to me, and the things he hadn't done for me. I told him that I forgave him and I didn't want to be angry with him anymore. He told me he never wanted to hurt me and he did the best he could.

RUNNING

VISIONRUNUSA was the seventh fastest trancontinental foot crossing of America in history (ranking in the top 3%), and the first ever by a blind person. I ran 3,063 miles in 59.45 days, averaging 51.5 miles per day.

VISIONRUNUSA
ASPIRE • INSPIRE • NEVER THE

MARCH 25 - MAY 23, 2016 • 3,063 MILES • 51.5 MILES/DAY

Since **VISIONRUNUSA** I have continued running. A month

after finishing the run, I ran the Leadville Trail Marathon and attempted Spartathlon a second time just three months after the transcon. I failed at Spartathlon a second consecutive year as I missed the time cut-off at 120 miles. I qualified, applied, and was invited back to attempt Spartathlon a third time and finally completed the race in 2017 in thirty-three hours, fifty minutes. Aside from Spartathlon, in the year since the transcon, I've run Badwater Salton Sea, Bryce Canyon 50, Run Rabbit Run 100, and the Vermont 100 which had the first ever "Athletes with Differences" division for an ultra-marathon. Perhaps I will return to the Badwater 135 and better my time, and hopefully I can get into Western States and HardRock at some point.

I have established and hold thirteen world records in ultra-running for blind and visually impaired runners: 50 kilometer (trail), 50 mile (road), 50 mile (trail), 100 kilometer (road), 100 kilometer (trail), 100 mile (trail), 100 mile (road), 24 hour, 48 hour, 6 day, 10 day, 1,000 mile & USA Transcontinental run. Richard Hunter and Kyle Robideaux, two runners who are legally blind and joined me for different segments of **VISIONRUNUSA** completed their first hundred-mile races since my return.

THE SEA SHELL

The tiny broken sea shell we had carried from the Pacific Ocean to the Atlantic Ocean finally reached its destination on May 24, 2016. I took the seashell to Battery Park in Manhattan, NY, and threw the sea shell into the Atlantic as a sign of final closure. Mom and friends were with me.

THE GIRL

I have always said that every great story has a girl in it. And this story is no different. A few weeks after I finished the run and returned home to Denver, my ex-girlfriend and I agreed to meet to find closure for our relationship. As we talked, I learned why she had let go in the middle of the run. A big misunderstanding, ineffective communication, and a lack of compassion on both our parts all played into the situation. She has described our relationship as one that has "ebbed and flowed" for her. I am still grieving my loss of my eyesight, and at any time, I can find myself in a different part of the grief process—denial, anger, depression, bargaining, or acceptance. I know it has been hard on our relationship and taken a toll. We were able to run the Leadville Trail Marathon together the summer I returned, and it almost felt like we might be able to reconcile.

Regardless of what may happen in our future, I have this woman to thank for at least two very important lessons which have made me a better person. First, she has renewed my tenacity to continue to swing for the fences when it comes to love. We need to take risks in life, and leap into uncertainty. Sometimes you win, and sometimes you lose. When it comes to pursuing love, I challenge us all to never hesitate and risk everything. I never again will turn away from the one I love in a time of hardship. Second, I didn't know how to love correctly, and I didn't love her as I should have. As I talked with people, thought deeply, and researched the issue, I finally discovered how we are supposed to love. My commitment is to learn to love this way going forward, and I have her to thank—so, thank you.

Love

Love is patient, love is kind.
It does not envy, it does not boast, it is not proud.
It does not dishonor others, it is not self-seeking, it is not easily angered,
it keeps no record of wrongs.
Love does not delight in evil but rejoices with the truth.
It always protects, always trusts, always hopes, always perseveres.

Love never fails.

—1 Corinthians 13:4-8

About the Author

Jason is a highly sought-after motivational speaker and the only blind person to run across America. He holds more than ten World Records in Ultra-running, has competed internationally for Team USA at the Paralympic World Marathon Championships, is the subject of a full-length documentary, *Running Vision*, is an author, and is a pioneer for ultra-running for the blind and visually impaired. In addition to being an ultra-endurance athlete, he has been an attorney, and an executive at GE and a nonprofit that helps children with autism. He is on a mission to share what he has learned from his challenges and record-setting run across America.

To learn more about Jason and to contact him for speaking engagements, please visit RelentlessRomero.com.